MotoGP
Season Review 2008

MotoGP
Season Review 2008
Julian Ryder

Published in November 2008

A catalogue record for this book is available from the British Library

ISBN 978 1 84425 567 2

Library of Congress catalog card no 2008926784

Haynes Publishing, Sparkford, Yeovil,
Somerset BA22 7JJ, UK
Tel: +44 (0) 1963 442030
Fax: +44 (0) 1963 440001
E-mail: sales@haynes.co.uk
Website: www.haynes.co.uk

Haynes North America, Inc.,
861 Lawrence Drive, Newbury Park,
California 91320, USA

Printed and bound by J.H.Haynes & Co Ltd,
Sparkford, Yeovil, Somerset BA22 7JJ, UK

This product is officially licensed by Dorna SL,
owners of the MotoGP trademark (© Dorna 2008)

Managing Editor Louise McIntyre
Design Lee Parsons, Richard Parsons
Sub-editor Kay Edge
Special Sales & Advertising Manager
David Dew (david@motocom.co.uk)
Photography Front cover, race action and portraits by
Andrew Northcott/AJRN Sports Photography – except:
Graeme Brown/GeeBee Images 4-5, 10-13, 20-21, 57, 65,
86, 89, 112, 127, 137, 142, 153, 185, 199.
Neil Spalding 22-25, 28-37

Author's acknowledgements

Thanks to:

Toby Moody, Ron Ringguth, Dirk Raudies, Peter Clifford,
Andrew Northcott, Graeme Brown, Neil Spalding,
Andy Ibbott, Mat Oxley, Yoko Togashi, Dr Martin Raines,
Frank Weeink, Dean Adams, Nick Harris

CONTENTS
MotoGP 2008

FOREWORD
CARMELO EZPELETA

There have now been sixty seasons of MotoGP since the very first championship back in 1949, which began on June 17 of that year on the Isle of Man. Much has changed since then in the oldest motorsports world championship, especially in areas such as safety, coverage of the sport and the technology of the bikes themselves.

However, as I had the pleasure of welcoming back past MotoGP World Champions throughout 2008 to give them their own replica versions of the Champions' Tower trophy, it became clear to me that thankfully some things also never change at the top level of this sport.

MotoGP is rightfully proud of its illustrious history, with riders whose exploits have filled many pages of books like this one. From Les Graham to Kenny Roberts, Giacomo Agostini to Wayne Rainey, Mick Doohan to Mike Hailwood, they are heroes who all share a common bond of having been called the greatest motorcycle racers in the world. The link goes beyond that, however, and comparing some of the first World Champions with some of those from today, they all share a unique passion for the sport itself, and enjoy universal respect for their legendary achievements.

Now in their fifth year of the *MotoGP Season Review,* Haynes Publishing has provided us with another set of pages after the 2008 season, with Valentino Rossi reclaiming the title he had missed out on for two years and taking his sixth crown. He didn't get an easy ride though, with four different championship leaders throughout the season – a feat incredibly never matched before in the 60-year history of our sport.

We also saw fabulous performances from the young rookie riders, ten different men standing on the podium, some intriguing head-to-head battles and some old-fashioned dominating wins. MotoGP history was created with the first trip to Indianapolis and its legendary Speedway, where it amazed me to see so many people turn out for a first GP despite the hurricane passing through.

All in all it has been another classic season of action to round off those sixty years, but the championship is in good health and MotoGP is in its prime. Here's to the next sixty.

CARMELO EZPELETA
DORNA SPORTS CEO
OCTOBER 2008

THE SEASON
MAT OXLEY

A YEAR OF BOOM & BUST

A torrid financial year was mirrored by the on-track action in MotoGP, with Casey Stoner, Dani Pedrosa, Jorge Lorenzo and Valentino Rossi all leading the 2008 World Championship chase

It was a strange year. While the global capitalist system shuddered and buckled from its decade-long, credit-fuelled climax, MotoGP went noisily about its business. As stocks and shares crashed, rallied and crashed again, the stock of the different MotoGP machines also rose up and tumbled down. During the early stages of the season you would have wanted your cash stashed on a Yamaha on Michelins. At the next few races you would have been in the money with a Yamaha on Bridgestones, then a Ducati on Bridgestones, before finally the Yamaha/Bridgestone combination was the best bet.

Then, at season's end, as governments bailed out banks in a desperate effort to avoid economic meltdown, so too did MotoGP turn away from the wonders of the free market to instigate a single-tyre rule in a bid to boost the MotoGP spectacle. 'It's a kind of socialism,' muttered some people in pit lane.

In the midst of the global financial turmoil, MotoGP enjoyed its most unpredictable season in almost a decade. Usually the die is cast during the first few races, but not this year. Reigning World Champion Casey Stoner was a runaway winner at the first race, Dani Pedrosa was the victor at round two and Jorge Lorenzo at round three. In all, four different riders led the championship, which isn't normal.

At the first three races Valentino Rossi was under the radar. Beaten into fifth place at Losail by a couple of rookies, among others, he was simply building up to speed, working with his crew to extract the maximum out of his new Bridgestone tyres. Defeated by Stoner in 2007 and by Nicky Hayden in 2006, the former World Champion won rounds four, five and six and suddenly it seemed like the good times were back, like it was 2003

Above It rained a lot in 2008 and hardly a race escaped being affected. This is Casey Stoner during practice for the Czech GP

Below MotoGP attracted the usual quota of celebs – this is Tom Cruise at Laguna Seca

or 2005 all over again. But Ducati were also getting up to speed. Following Stoner's illusive victory in Qatar, the factory had run into trouble with its 2008 engine spec, Stoner for once struggling to control the fiery red V4. 'We couldn't control the way the power came in,' he said. 'It would cut in so hard that the bike was near-on impossible to ride, and when it got too bad you had to close the gas to stop it moving round.' The problem was a major boost in low rpm torque from new variable-length intake trumpets upsetting the rear suspension. Ducati fixed the problem with revised engine mapping at the post-Catalan GP tests, after which it was Stoner's turn to win three on the bounce. He was, it seemed, an unstoppable force once again. And then they went to Laguna Seca...

Rossi's US GP demolition job was the pivotal moment of the season. In fact a whole book could be written about it – Laguna 2008 was MotoGP's rumble in the jungle. The sport hadn't seen anything like it for years. Neither had Stoner. After the race the Aussie raged against Rossi's do-or-die riding tactics. Where the rest of the world had witnessed the most entertaining race in recent years, Stoner could only see a vicious, underhand attempt to snatch away his crown.

Rossi was astonishing at Laguna. His riding was on the outer limits of legitimacy, and of decency, but that's what racers do, they ride the outer limits. As the Italian said following a similar (but less successful) brawl with Loris Capirossi at the 1999 Dutch TT: 'That race wasn't a race, it was a battle. That sometimes happens, you stop with the right lines and just fight, like remove one chip from your brain and put in another.'

The intensity of Rossi's Laguna onslaught was

unforgettable. But the true mark of the man could only be correctly gauged after the race. The BBC's pit-lane reporter had just received a mouthful of what Stoner thought when he turned to ask the winner's opinion. 'About what?' Rossi wondered, all innocence. It was a priceless moment which gave us the real measure of the legend: ineffable cool, just moments after possibly the greatest victory of his career.

Stoner probably seethed all the way home to Sydney, but a few weeks of more peaceful contemplation on the family farm changed his perspective. Perhaps the Aussie media had helped him to see the funny side of things, with the letters pages in one Australian magazine suggesting (in inimitable language) that he should 'harden the fuck up'. Stoner might also try reading some George Orwell: 'Serious sport has nothing to do with fair play. It is bound up with hatred, jealousy, boastfulness, disregard of all rules and sadistic pleasure in witnessing violence. In other words, it is war minus the shooting.'

Laguna was a fatal blow to the 2007 champion. For whatever reason, Stoner's war was over. His attempts to counter-attack at the subsequent Brno and Misano rounds both ended the same way, with front-end, low-side crashes. This is the way his World Championship ended, not with a bang, but with a whimper. Front-end loses always look so humiliating, as Rossi discovered at Valencia in 2006. The uneducated TV fan says: 'Why on earth did he crash?' When it's a highside, there's never any doubt why he crashed.

As his title slipped away, Stoner was impressively dignified in defeat. He kept smiling and was always the first to congratulate Rossi. Perhaps that's one reason

why the fans and the media treated him better than they had in 2007. 'It's nice to have more respect this year for finishing second than what I got last year for winning the thing,' he said. 'Last year everyone said the only reason I won the title was the bike and the tyres. This year I've had more respect from people.'

After Stoner's title hopes turned to dust there were dark whispers in some parts of pit lane that there was some kind of skulduggery afoot. After his Brno off, Stoner complained of strange wear marks on his front Bridgestone; after Misano he again complained of unusual front-tyre behaviour. It was suggested that the Japanese tyre manufacturer had changed course in front-tyre development, veering off in a direction which would please the riding style of the world's favourite racer.

True or not, it seems that the story of the season wasn't the single-tyre rule, though it was the story of a single tyre: Bridgestone's front slick. When Rossi defected from Michelin at the end of 2007, he immediately wanted to know what spec Bridgestone tyres Stoner used. Whatever they were, Rossi knew that he would have to adapt himself and his motorcycle to those same tyres if he were to have a chance of defeating the youngster.

Stoner uses a stiffer front than most Bridgestone riders, a tyre that doesn't necessarily offer a better lap time but does deliver a better race time, because its stiffer, less forgiving construction provides better race-long support/performance. Rossi knew he had to use this front, even if it is as tricky as hell to master. This tyre requires a rare combination of aggression and deft control to work effectively, and also needs a certain

amount of pressure applied during corner entry to make the rubber squirm into the correctly shaped contact patch.

Thus Rossi's crew adapted his M1's set-up to apply the correct load to the front tyre, and then Rossi had to revise his cornering technique to suit the Bridgestones, using smoother, sweeping lines. 'The Bridgestone tyres have a different construction and different character, so I need to ride different lines,' he explained. 'If I use the same line I used with Michelin, I lose time.'

This, perhaps, explains why Bridgestone quickly became dominant when the 800s arrived. While Michelin enjoyed success with the fire-and-brimstone 990s – sideways into the corner, big handfuls of the throttle on the way out – the 800s require a neater, more classical (and less thrilling to watch) arcing line, which perfectly fits the Bridgestones.

'With the 800s, everything becomes more flat,' adds Rossi, explaining that his M1 features less dive into turns and less squat on the way out. 'Now corner speed is the most important issue for the lap time. Before it was more about braking and acceleration, so you had two very different parts to the corner, clearly divided, and you needed to move on the bike in a different way. Now it is corner speed, so the balance of the bike in the corner is very important, so braking and acceleration become a little less important.'

While Rossi adapted to his new tyres and brought some added poise and extra speed to his riding, other Bridgestone riders also tried using the same front in search of better race-long performance. Like most Bridgestone men, Rizla Suzuki's Chris Vermeulen found that he was using up his usual front tyre too quickly

Above left Tyres took up far too much time in '08, but there will only be one brand in '09

Above Rossi broke Ago's record of most wins in the top class – he didn't seem to mind

Below Jorge only got to plant the Lorenzo's Land flag once – still not bad for a rookie!

Above British fans
welcomed their first
125cc winner since
1973 – Scott Redding

Below New 250 Champ
Marco Simoncelli channels
the spirit of Hendrix

was all but decided following the US and Czech GPs.

There was plenty of evidence during 2008 that the same tyres, even the same tyre/bike package, doesn't necessarily mean that everyone is going to ride around in a big gang, slugging it out all the way to the final corner. While Stoner was the fastest rider in the world when things went his way, his fellow Ducati riders had a miserable 2008, mostly wobbling around at the back of the pack. Marlboro team-mate Marco Melandri was humiliated by the GP8 machine, while Alice Duke riders Sylvain Guintoli and Toni Elias mostly fared little better.

Just as Vermeulen couldn't put enough energy into that front tyre, neither could Melandri, Guintoli or Elias energise the GP8. Guintoli explains why: 'With this bike it's like a tyre: if you don't push really hard straight away, the tyre gets cold and then at the next corner you crash. You think "I was slow, so why did I crash?" You crashed because you weren't using it properly. It's the same with the GP8, you can get stuck in the bad zone. Sometimes you go out and ride and you think "Fuck, I don't feel like I can go for it, there's something wrong." So you never get out of that zone and you can actually crash while going slow. But if you manage to get through that zone you've still got a lot to play with before you get to the bike's maximum potential.' The difference between the quick and the slow Duke riders was indeed huge – early in the season Elias's rear tyre usually ran 20 degrees cooler than Stoner's, a night and day difference.

It is difficult to predict what the single-tyre format will do for the racing (Bridgestone says that riders won't have to use identical tyres, because there will be different specs available), but we already know what it means for qualifying: there will be no more qualifying tyres, which means that Saturday afternoon grid shoot-outs will lose some of their intensity. Some people think that's a good thing – it can be just as entertaining to watch riders eke more out of their race tyres on Saturday afternoon and it is certainly more relevant to what happens the following day. Other people will miss the excitement of the super-sticky tyres, Nicky Hayden among them: 'After a run on qualifiers you would sometimes come into the pits shaking because it was that intense.'

Hayden's resurgence towards the end of 2008 was one of the good news stories of the year. Bizarrely, and possibly only by coincidence, the American got stronger once the world knew that he and Honda were going their separate ways. His progress on the challenging Ducati will be watched with great interest. Like Stoner, Hayden learned his riding skills in the loose ways of dirt track, which in theory should suit the Duke. The Kentucky Kid certainly thinks so: 'When I knew there was nothing doing with Honda, I told my manager: go get me a Ducati. I told him I'd ride for free and fly coach.'

Hayden roared back into contention at Indianapolis, the only new race on the calendar and a great success of an event, despite Hurricane Ike's efforts to sink the good ship MotoGP. Some paddock people were concerned that Indy wouldn't know what to do with a motorcycle race, but the Motor Speedway put on a hell of a weekend in the toughest of conditions. The revival of the Indy Mile dirt track was a deciding factor for many fans – here was a chance to watch MotoGP at the world's most historic racetrack (built just a couple of years after the UK's Brooklands circuit) and at the same time witness the breathtaking spectacle of a mile dirt track, the crucible of American road-racing talent and the reason behind the

during races. But when he tried the harder front he couldn't get on with it, because it was too stiff for him, so he couldn't get any feel – and without feel, even the best front tyre in the world is totally useless. Suzuki even built a new frame with revised weight distribution, designed to put more energy into the special front and pressure it into working. John Hopkins and Kawasaki tried to adapt the Ninja to use the same front but were less successful in making the combination work, which might go some way to explaining their dire season.

Eventually even Dani Pedrosa decided he had to use the same front, except that this move to match Rossi's and Stoner's corner-entry performance caused a bit more of a stir. There was talk of Honda's honour and much else besides when the Michelin/Honda contract was binned, but people were forgetting that mid-season defection from one tyre brand to another isn't anything new in premier-class motorcycling. Suzuki's factory squad did just that in 2002, switching from Dunlop to Michelin. Eight years earlier Yamaha had decided that a boot in both camps was the best way forward, swapping its Dunlop front for a Michelin and creating the fabled Michelop brand.

It didn't take Pedrosa long to get up to speed after switching tyres, but he had also been mighty fast earlier in the season, running away with the Jerez and Catalan GPs to lead the World Championship for a time. Michelin's tyres worked brilliantly at some tracks, but the company's woes at Laguna and Brno tested many people's patience beyond breaking point. Honda decided there and then where its future lay in terms of tyre partner, and perhaps the single-tyre rule

nation's amazing run of successes in motorcycling's elite class.

One of dirt track's biggest plus points has always been equality – the equipment barely changes from one decade to the next, let alone from one season to the next, so everyone is on similar tackle, which leaves it down to the rider to make the difference with riding technique. MotoGP finds itself going in that direction with the one-make tyre rule and the new 600 support class, due in 2011. No-one seems fully certain what kind of engines will power the 250 replacements, but most probably it will be 600 supersport motors tuned to a certain degree. Dorna says the emphasis will be on maintaining close competition at a reasonable cost, with a 20,000 euro claiming rule on all engines to discourage excessive tuning. Not everyone is happy about this landmark transformation, KTM team boss Harald Bartol announcing, 'It's like going back to communism.' Sadly, KTM and fellow two-stroke racers Aprilia look unlikely to contest the new class and will probably move out of the MotoGP paddock. Instead, the emphasis might shift back towards smaller 'cottage industry' tuners and chassis builders, perhaps bringing names like Harris and TSR back into the frame. Just like the old days, in fact.

Money is always a concern in racing, but never more so than now. While the new 600s may prove less expensive than 250s, MotoGP costs have escalated dramatically in recent seasons, fast-accelerating technology demanding ever bigger budgets, the 990s more expensive than the 500s and the 800s more expensive than the 990s. And all this just as the world faces its biggest economic recession in six decades, with venerable banks going out of business and some of the

biggest automotive brands already struggling to stay afloat. No doubt about it: hard times are a'comin'. Teams will need all the ingenuity at their disposal to ride out this slump. However, during tough times it is always the best products that survive, and there is no doubt that MotoGP, despite the controversies that have dogged the last two seasons, is still the greatest motorsport show on earth. The racing was better in 2008 than it had been in 2007 and the action should get better still as the 800s go into their third year, just as the racing improved as the 990s matured and more manufacturers got up to speed. Ducati got the jump on everyone during the first year of the 800s, Yamaha caught up last season and in 2009 Honda should be right there too. Money may be too tight to mention, but it's worth remembering that less money doesn't necessarily mean worse racing. There is plenty to look forward to.

Above Ready to rumble under the lights of Losail – MotoGP's first floodlit race

Below Dani Pedrosa's season was blighted by injury and dogged by controversy – the pressure will be on him to deliver in '09

www.dainese.com

ITALIAN LEGENDARY PROTECTION

The champion: Valentino Rossi.
The racing suit: Mission Dainese.

AD: Carmi e Ubertis Milano   Ph: Stefano Cattelan

Mission Dainese Racing suit: recommended by Valentino Rossi.
For its technological innovations in terms of protection, comfort, and ergonomics; for the innovative solutions of fit that
permit the greatest freedom of movement; for the aeration system that ensures the ideal internal microclimate. Because

RIDERS'
RIDER
OF THE
YEAR
2008

VOTED FOR BY Alex de Angelis, Loris Capirossi, Andrea Dovizioso, Colin Edwards, Toni Elias, Sylvain Guintoli, Nicky Hayden, John Hopkins, Jorge Lorenzo, Marco Melandri, Shinya Nakano, Dani Pedrosa, Randy de Puniet, Valentino Rossi, Ben Spies, Casey Stoner, James Toseland, Chris Vermeulen, and Anthony West

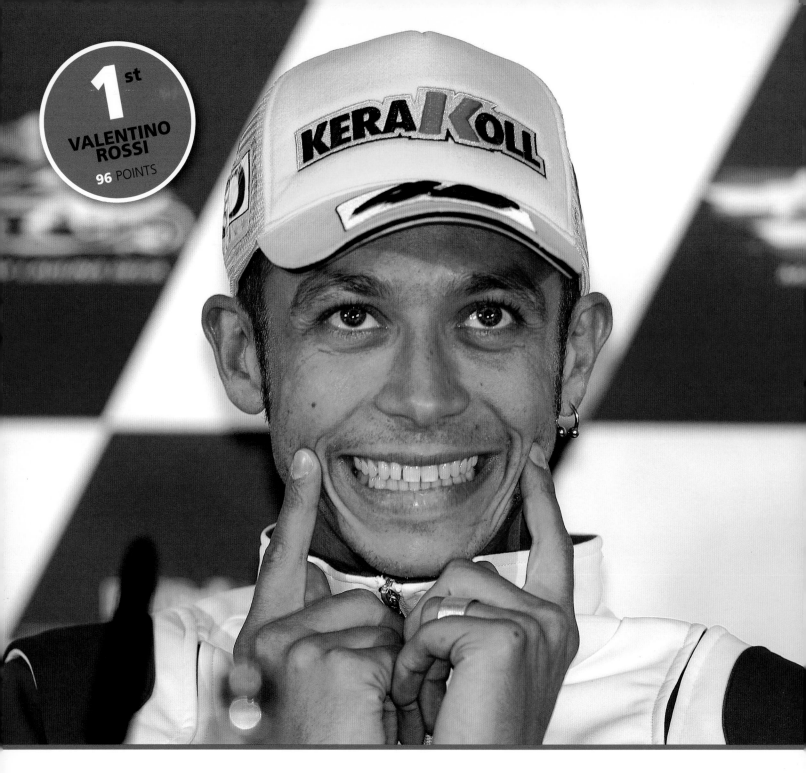

The man who wins the championship isn't always the one his opponents think is the best. To find out who the MotoGP riders think is the fastest of them all, for the fifth year running we polled every rider who has taken part in more than one race. They named their top six men, we counted the votes. Here are the results

The *MotoGP Season Review*'s Riders' Rider of the Year vote has now been running for five years. Every rider who competes in more than one race in the season is entitled to vote. So far, not one has refused.

They're asked to list the top six riders of the year without voting for themselves. The scrutineers then award six points for a first place down to one for sixth. You can see the results on these pages.

To a greater extent than any other year, there was a clear pattern. The top three were well clear of the rest and a significant number of voters listed Rossi, Stoner and Lorenzo, in that order, at the top of their voting papers. The interesting thing here is that Dani Pedrosa, clearly one of the top three riders in the world, not only didn't challenge Lorenzo in our vote, but was in danger from Andrea Dovizioso who finished a close fifth.

Rossi was placed first by 16 of the 17 who voted

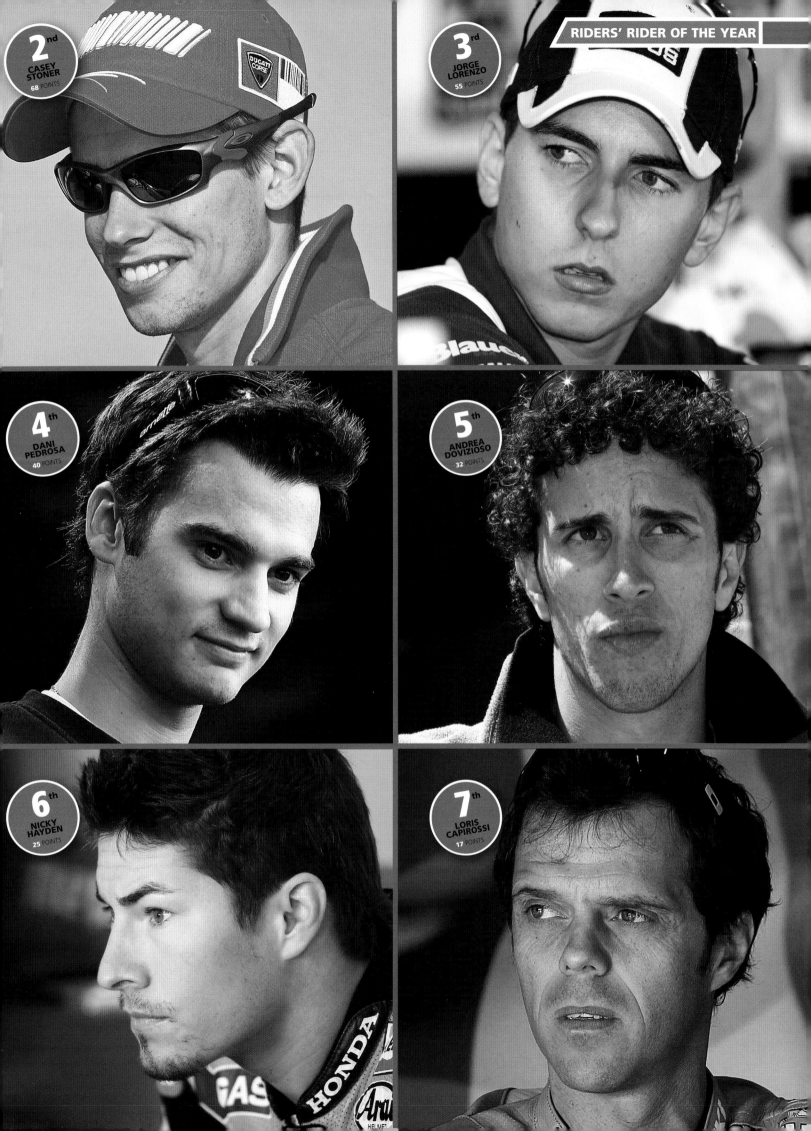

2nd
CASEY STONER
68 POINTS

3rd
JORGE LORENZO
55 POINTS

4th
DANI PEDROSA
40 POINTS

5th
ANDREA DOVIZIOSO
32 POINTS

6th
NICKY HAYDEN
25 POINTS

7th
LORIS CAPIROSSI
17 POINTS

8th JOHN HOPKINS 11 POINTS

9th COLIN EDWARDS 8 POINTS

10th CHRIS VERMEULEN 7 POINTS

for him (he couldn't vote for himself). The other voter put him third. Only one voter put Casey first but 12 put him second. Of the 16 who voted for Lorenzo, ten put him third. It's also worth remembering that only 19 racers were canvassed, and of these 14 voted for Pedrosa, with exactly half of them placing him fifth. Only two fewer, 12, voted for Nicky Hayden and his votes were concentrated in fifth and sixth places.

Below the top six, voting dropped off very quickly with Loris Capirossi next most popular with six votes, two of them for third place. Colin Edwards and John Hopkins only received three votes each but as each one received a first-place nomination that alone was enough to put them into the top ten. Once again Hopper is the man whose position in the poll is most in advance of his finishing position in the championship – eighth versus 16th. Arguably the small number of nominations received by John makes this statement unreliable in strict statistical terms, so maybe it's Loris Capirossi, the only man to win the RROTY poll when not World Champion, who's the one the riders rate higher than the points table would suggest. Loris finished tenth in the World Championship but seventh in the poll.

To make room for rookies Dovizioso and Lorenzo, Marco Melandri and Sylvain Guintoli drop out of the top ten, while Colin Edwards is back in at the expense of Randy de Puniet.

This is, of course, a secret ballot, but we feel it's safe to reveal a few secrets. The top three all voted for each other, and so did Hayden and Pedrosa. Neither of the Repsol Honda riders put each other high on their list though…

RIDERS' RIDER
PREVIOUS RESULTS

	2004	2005	2006	2007
1	Rossi	Rossi	Capirossi	Stoner
2	Gibernau	Capirossi	Rossi	Rossi
3	Biaggi	Melandri	Pedrosa	Pedrosa
4	Edwards	Hayden	Hayden	Hopkins
5	Nakano	Edwards	Melandri	Vermeulen
6	Capirossi	Gibernau	Stoner	Hayden
7	Tamada	Nakano	Roberts	Melandri
8	Hopkins	Hopkins	Hopkins	Guintoli
9	Barros	Biaggi	Checa	Capirossi
10	Hayden	Barros	Vermeulen	De Puniet

TECHNICAL REVIEW

NEIL SPALDING

YAMAHA M1 2008

Mission One is back on target. This is how Yamaha made the M1 the best, and most versatile, bike on the MotoGP grid

Yamaha have come a long way since Valentino Rossi joined them in 2004, with his latest World Championship title providing a further act in the ongoing development of Mission One, Yamaha's designation for their MotoGP project.

The 2008 M1 is the most successful bike in pit lane. All four of its riders have made it onto the front row of the grid at one time or another during the year, and all bar one have been on the podium. With not only the riders' title but also the constructor, rookie and team titles as well, Yamaha cleaned up this year.

However, it took planning, money and the political will to get there – and, more than that, the money had to be spent wisely. Yamaha also had one rider, Rossi, on a different make of tyre from the rest of their riders so, in situations where only one tyre manufacturer got it right, Yamaha had all the bases covered. They had two class rookies among their four riders, but neither was a risky choice, both Lorenzo and Toseland being reigning World Champions.

There was also their new pneumatic valve spring engine, whose development the previous year had been punctuated by several very public blow-ups, but this season they had the technology necessary to keep the engine together.

New throttle control systems were developed, not merely traction control but full-on ride-by-wire technology designed to settle the bike down under all circumstances. Finally, Yamaha reinvented the Tech 3 operation as more of a shadow works team than a satellite squad, with all the Japanese factory support needed to get the very complex bike working well.

Ducati had ambushed all the other manufacturers at

Above Burgess explains the weight change strategy to Davide Brivio

Below Peter Baumgartner, Rossi's Bridgestone technician, discusses progress with Tohru Ubukata, Bridgestone's Manager of Motorcycle Race Tyre Development

new front suspension package. A new chassis was debuted too, after a lot of testing, to ensure no repeats of the chatter problems suffered in 2006.

Yamaha moved from a relatively simple throttle and engine braking control system to one with all the bells and whistles. The most obvious change was a pair of three-axis gyroscopes sitting on top of the air intake at the front of the bike. This took its basic cues from the 2007 Ducati system by using state of the art electronics to predict grip levels at different angles of lean. Yamaha then allowed the throttle to open only to the point where the maximum level of torque that can be used was actually developed, unlike the Ducati system which seemed to need to correct the engine output after excess power has started to spin the tyre. The new Yamaha system never made excess power in the first place and, more crucially in this fuel-restricted class, never used the fuel either. But this system was about more than just corner exit; it also helped calm down corner entry, allowing the Yamahas to be very stable both under braking and into the corners.

Fuel consumption was monitored tightly too, using an active system that initially measures fuel consumption during the first six laps of the race, then uses that data to start to calculate how much the fuel map needs to be leaned out to finish the race. Fuel use is constantly reviewed and fine-tuned all through the race to take into account tyre spin and throttle use.

the start of the 2007 season by using fuel more accurately, and after that it was a question of who could react the quickest. Yamaha started 2007 as second-best bike, and once it became obvious that the championship was lost they concentrated on the 2008 machine. The bike that resulted had more power and used its fuel more carefully than before, but it kept intact all its original strengths.

Suspension and chassis were also uprated with the Ohlins TTX-TR forks being increased to 48mm diameter to help braking stability. Previously only Rossi had used these massive forks and the flexy top triple clamps needed to keep the right feel at full lean.

Revised bodywork also came in, to cover the rider more, helping top-speed aerodynamics and also cooling to offset some of the radiator blocking effect caused by the

ROSSI'S YEAR

Yamaha have raced on Michelins throughout the current MotoGP era – until now, that is. Rossi battled with Stoner as hard as he could in 2007, but he soon realised that whatever he did was going to be undone by the characteristics of the Bridgestone tyres Casey was using. The Bridgestones had been developed for the Ducati's more rearward weight distribution. With a stiffer carcass they could take more power mid-corner, giving Stoner a big advantage in acceleration out onto the straights. To work, this required a front tyre that still gripped even when unloaded by weight transfer under acceleration.

Valentino successfully swapped to Bridgestone at the first test of 2008. He wasn't interested in any old Bridgestone tyre, either (there are several families); he just wanted to get onto the same 'family' of constructions that Casey was using. Testing seemed to go well and the bike arrived in Qatar looking just like it had the year before, but with Bridgestone stickers. However, the race didn't go to plan for Rossi and Yamaha: the set-up wasn't right, the rear tyre started to spin up and Valentino finished a fighting fifth, beaten by Stoner and his own Michelin-shod team-mate, Jorge Lorenzo.

What followed was a change of strategy. Tohru Ubukata, Bridgestone's technical boss, conceded: 'After Qatar we had a BIG meeting.' By the next race, at Jerez, changes were under way. Rossi set his bike up with the rear axle further forward in the swingarm adjusters; the front was different too, with the headstock pushed to the front of its adjustment. Effectively the core weight of the bike, the centre including the engine, had just been moved backwards by about 35mm. This time there was more weight over the rear of the bike so that, as the tyre wore, it had the weight which it needed to keep gripping, and the front didn't let go. And Rossi made it onto the podium.

By the third round, in Portugal, Yamaha had found a way to push the front out further with a degree more rake – that's about 6mm more wheelbase, and 5mm more offset

to quicken up the steering again, which also pushes the front tyre another 5mm further away. At the back the rear axle was as far forward as possible. Again Rossi was on the podium, way in front of the next Bridgestone runner. By China there was a new, shorter, but more flexible swingarm, and at Le Mans a new frame with the headstock pushed even further forward. 'We need to find what works and then push it a bit too far just to make sure,' said Jerry Burgess.

All this created a Yamaha with similar weight distribution to the bike on which the tyres had been developed, Stoner's Ducati. It also meant that Rossi had to change his riding style to accept what must be a very vague front-end feeling and to get on the power earlier and harder, again just like Stoner. With the bike putting its weight where the tyres wanted it, and with the resulting riding style programmed in, Rossi started winning. Yamaha were now getting podium places with two completely different set-ups on one design of motorcycle.

It took Ducati's late resolution of the bugs in their throttle system to catch Valentino but, by then, it was a bare-knuckle fight and the Yamaha was good enough for Rossi to be able to spook Stoner into making mistakes. By Brno the extended front-end chassis had disappeared, and the standard frame stayed.

THREE BIKES ON MICHELIN

Michelin started the year well, with a new tyre more capable of dealing with lower temperatures debuting in the chill of the Qatar night. It achieved wins at Jerez and Portugal in the next few weeks and kept performing well until the summer. In a bid to match the Bridgestones, and get that drive out of the corners, the Michelin side of the Fiat Yamaha garage tried to duplicate some of the rearward weight bias, but the more flexible Michelin rear carcasses couldn't cope. After a few big highsides Jorge Lorenzo had to accept that that particular avenue wasn't open to him.

Both Lorenzo and Colin Edwards tried the short 'flexible' swingarm at several races, but always the wheelbase length would go back up as the practice sessions went on and both riders discovered the limits of the Michelins in terms of early drive. The overall set-up, though, did move weight back, Edwards apparently liking some of the feeling because he holds himself so far forwards on the bike. James Toseland, however, after a superb start to the season with the 'balanced' chassis, struggled to feel happy on the more rearward weight bias that was adopted later on. It was not until the Motegi and Phillip Island races, late in the year, that the right combination was found for him.

Top left Rossi started the year with a 30mm offset top yoke and a normal length chassis

Above left Mid-year the experiment included 35mm offset and an extended headstock chassis. The offset stayed but the chassis didn't

Top right Rossi's Ohlins TTxTR rear shock. The damper rod passes right through the damper and into the area under the top mount

Above right By China Yamaha had built a shorter, more flexible rear swingarm for the 'short rear bike' set-up the good Bridgestones demanded

'WE NEED TO KNOW HOW MUCH WEIGHT ON THE REAR IS TOO MUCH, ONCE WE KNOW IT IS SIMPLE TO BACK IT OFF A BIT'
JERRY BURGESS

IRREGULAR FIRING ORDER

Ever since Rossi got on board the Yamaha it has had a strange, gruff exhaust note and for years no-one really understood why. Now Yamaha have made their reasoning clear.

Five years ago, when the first 990s appeared, it seemed that the V-configuration engines were getting their power to the ground without too much difficulty – it had something to do with the way they delivered their power to the rear tyre, which resulted in better grip.

A classic in-line four-cylinder engine has a crankshaft that provides four firing pulses every four-stroke cycle. That means there is a piston arriving at the top of a stroke every 180 degrees of crank rotation. In these 'normal' in-line four-cylinder engines, crankshafts don't rotate at a constant speed. During each revolution they slow down and speed up a little, depending on where in their stroke the pistons and con-rods are. This is due to the effort taken in moving the weight of each con-rod and piston twice every revolution. At top and bottom dead centre the crank moves the rod and pistons only very slightly, but at mid-stroke the crank decelerates very slightly as it pulls or pushes against the weight and drag of the rod and piston.

Yamaha call this 'inertia torque' and on a 180-degree crank in-line four there are four 'slow-down/speed-up' sessions in every two revolutions. This constant acceleration/deceleration of the crank is normally insignificant, but at small throttle openings and down around 6000rpm it is capable of having a greater effect on tyre speed than each combustion does. It goes without saying that small throttle openings are mostly used while the bike is right over at maximum lean, so the effect is at its worst when the bike's available traction is at its lowest. Just when maximum adhesion is required, the engine introduces a vibration that affects the tyre's grip on the track surface.

At full throttle 'inertia torque' is only greater than 'combustion torque' at engine speeds over about 14,000rpm, but the effect increases exponentially with revs so it is a much more noticeable phenomenon in higher revving MotoGP engines than even with a normal racing superbike.

PNEUMATIC VALVE RECOVERY SYSTEM (PVRS)

On the face of it a PVRS seems, once the basic principles are understood, to be quite simple. Take out steel valve springs and effectively replace each one with a piston in a sealed cylinder containing nitrogen gas pressurised to between 10 and 16 bar. Then bolt on a 200-bar top-up system with enough capacity to replenish leaks for at least an hour – and that's it.

The reason that PVRS technology is suddenly popular in MotoGP is that it allows engine designers and tuners to build more radical engines, that is, engines that rev slightly higher but, more importantly, can have their valves jerked open and closed faster, allowing them to be tuned to use less fuel as well as making more power. This means that the bikes can run at full power for the whole race; the engines don't need to be leaned out for the last few laps in order to eke out what remains of the permitted 21 litres of petrol.

To be competitive in MotoGP today the trick seems to be to do this while duplicating the feel of the older-style valve spring motors; that's part of the strategy that allowed the 2008 Yamaha to work so well. So far MotoGP's 21-litre rule has put a greater restriction on engine performance than the 800cc displacement limit. Yamaha started the year with just Lorenzo and Rossi using pneumatic valve spring cylinder heads, and it took until Estoril for all the bikes to be so equipped.

Below left This is the small nitrogen top-up canister for the pneumatic valve spring system (PVRS) on Jorge Lorenzo's bike. It has to have sufficient capacity to make sure the system is topped up during a race. Normal reservoir pressure is between 140 and 180 bar, and must never drop below 100 bar

Below A Marelli MHP ECU is Yamaha's choice – it has some internal design features specified by Yamaha and all the software is written in-house

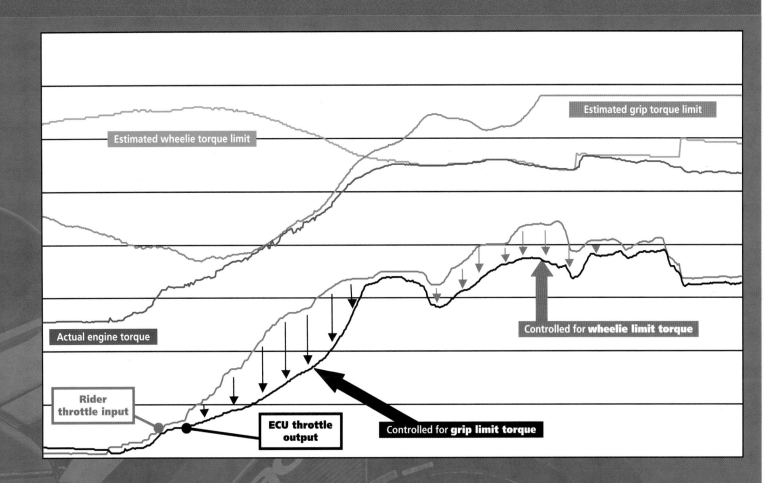

Estimated grip torque limit

Estimated wheelie torque limit

Actual engine torque

Controlled for **wheelie limit torque**

Rider throttle input

ECU throttle output

Controlled for **grip limit torque**

Above These graphs show exactly what fly-by-wire does. The red line shows throttle twistgip opening against time as the rider accelerates out of a corner and the blue line shows the torque being developed as he does so. The ECU compares this actual engine torque with the green and pink graphs, which show torque at the onset of wheelie and excess wheelspin – if the blue graph goes above either of these lines the bike will wheelie or spin the rear tyre excessively. To prevent this happening the ECU opens the throttle by a smaller amount than the rider asks for – that is the black line. Note the area of black arrows: this shows the ECU opening the throttle butterflies by a smaller amount than the rider asks for, thus keeping developed torque (blue line) right on the limit of excess wheelspin (pink line). There is then a short period where the rider gets exactly what he asks for before the blue curve runs up against the green line and the ECU intervenes again to prevent the bike wheelieing – the area of red arrows

RIDE-BY-WIRE THROTTLE

Yamaha fully redesigned their electronic controls for this year. Ducati and Kawasaki still use the Marelli Marvel 4 ECU, but it is apparent the next step in control electronics requires faster processing. Yamaha moved over to the latest Marelli MHP system early in 2007 but are only now making it really work. Two three-axis gyroscopes hidden away under the nose fairing and mounted on the top of the air inlet give the game away. Yamaha have massively uprated their engine-control system. Looking for a much more consistent action than the previous system, this uses state of the art electronics to predict grip levels at different angles of lean and only allows the throttle to open to the point where the maximum level of torque that can be used is developed.

Unlike the Ducati system, which corrects excess power after a tyre has started to spin, this new Yamaha system never makes the power in the first place and, more crucially in this fuel-restricted class, never uses the fuel either. However, this system is about more than just corner exit, because it also helps calm down corner entry, allowing the Yamahas to be very stable under braking and helping achieve the late passes critical to the success of Yamaha's race strategy.

Fuel consumption is monitored tightly, too, with an active system that measures fuel consumption during each six-lap section of the race, then uses that data to calculate how much the fuel map needs to be leaned out in order to finish the race within the 21 litres allowed. Fuel use is constantly reviewed and fine-tuned all through the race to take into account tyre spin and throttle use. At Qatar in 2007 Yamaha could only reduce the rev limit in individual gears to save fuel, really damaging their top-speed potential. Their game has moved on a long way since then.

THE BIKES
2008 MotoGP MACHINERY

YAMAHA
YZR-M1

1 Jorge Lorenzo wanted to try the 'short' swingarm, but to get any balance at all with his Michelins he had to push the axle all the way back in its adjustment. If he had used the standard swingarm it would be in a central position

2 All four Yamahas had the new electronic engine management system using at least two gyroscopes to measure the bike's attitude. Cornering stability – entering, at the apex and exiting – was much better

3 To make sure their tanks could hold exactly the right amount of fuel Yamaha made their tanks slightly too big and then used additional Explosafe sponge to bring the capacity below 21 litres

4 Just to show everything was under control Rossi found time one Friday morning to try a new make of slipper clutch – it was gone in the afternoon

Yamaha came out fighting in 2008. In 2007 they'd had the second-best bike and it was obvious that a small increase in power, and a big increase in corner-exit grip, would get them close enough to Stoner to allow Rossi to fight for the lead.

Achieving that had not been so easy, however, with the first attempts at fitting pneumatic valve spring heads on their bike ending in a smoky mess. First at Misano, then at Motegi in 2007 motors grenaded, either through the effect of the valve spring technology itself or because the rest of the engine was not able to keep up with the new power and higher revs.

Everything changed for 2008: now the pneumatic-valve motor worked, and by round three, in Portugal, all the bikes were equipped with it, and the electronics had gone up a gear or two as well. The electronics were far more sensitive and allowed a very accurate throttle system to deliver more power and more control while all the time using less fuel.

The bike remained very similar in looks to the bike that had been used for the previous four years, but the fine-tuning and honing had worked, while more power, more revs, a better chassis and cleaner aerodynamics all played their part in making a bike which worked well in any conditions and at any circuit.

Yamaha also showed the versatility of their chassis design by winning races with both Michelin and Bridgestone tyres; the best tyres of the two makes have very different requirements on chassis settings. By mid-season the attempts of the Michelin-shod riders to match Rossi's Bridgestones on corner exits started to affect their overall performance, but by the end of the year all the Yamahas were capable of podium finishes.

DUCATI
DESMOSEDICI-RR

1 Ducati introduced a small front fairing at Phillip Island in 2007, then found their riders liked it anywhere where it was twisty

2 This year the Ducati had a proper see-through catch tank for any overflow fuel

3 Nothing was too much trouble for Melandri's crew as they desperately tried to find a way to make him feel comfortable on the bike. Here they tried grippy tape to hold him in place

4 In early 2007 Ducati used a true ride-by-wire system with the potentiometer that read the throttle opening secreted in the twistgrip. For 2008 it was back to cables to a potentiometer on the side of the bike

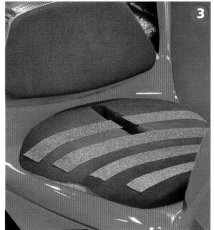

In 2007 the 800cc Desmosedici had been devastatingly efficient, the Ducati machine a quantum leap ahead of its opposition. Using a fuel-conservation strategy totally different from that adopted by the rest of the field, and with a tyre and rider combination seemingly unbeatable on the track, Ducati was expected to rule 2008 as well. Then Valentino Rossi managed to equip himself with Bridgestone tyres and Ducati, in their haste to stay ahead, got a couple of small things wrong.

Marco Melandri replaced Loris Capirossi as team-mate to Casey Stoner. Marco came with good racing credentials. Just a year before he had been the number one candidate for the Ducati seat, but then his Honda team had exercised an option to keep him and Ducati ended up with their third choice, Stoner, on the bike. Melandri was signed up for 2008, but then found he could not deal with the extreme nature of the Ducati throttle system. It's clear that the Ducati electronics are very sophisticated, but to make the system work the rider is required to trust the electronics to deliver the power. That was something that Marco simply could not do. It is now apparent that he needs to find a very delicate connection between power and grip for himself, and then add power.

Stoner, too, was having trouble with some aspects of the throttle system. During the winter Ducati added a variable-length inlet system designed to produce a better spread of power that gave better drive off corners. What it actually did was introduce some sort of pumping action into the suspension, making the bike very difficult to control in corners. It took the team four races to decide further development was needed. They reverted to the 2007 system for two races and then reintroduced a much-improved system in Catalunya.

Externally, the 2008 bike was identical to the 2007 model. Over the course of the year the new short nose fairing (first used at Phillip Island last season) was utilised far more often than expected. In part this was down to the additional manoeuvrability the 'short nose' appears to give the bike, but also because temperatures during this year's racing were much lower than last year's. The short fairing also blanks off some of the cooling area at the front of the bike. The conventional long nose should therefore be considered not just a high-speed fairing but a high cooling-rate fairing as well.

The engine remained externally unchanged – an 800cc 90-degree V4 with desmodromic valve gear revving to over 20,000rpm. Most of the time it was kept under 19,500 rpm to save fuel. The mid-range boosting throttle system made this much easier.

HONDA
RC212V

1 From Misano, Pedrosa had new Showa suspension. It had the preload adjusters in the bottom of the fork leg and compression, rebound and 'pressure balance' adjustment on the top of the fork leg

2 The Pneumatic Valve Recovery System (PVRS or pneumatic valve springs if you prefer) engine had a larger-diameter exhaust with shorter pipes. You would expect an engine with that sort of pipe to have shorter cam duration and higher revs

3 To try and let Nicky experiment with swingarm flexibility without going to the trouble of making new ones, Honda tried bonding carbon on the inner faces

4 The PVRS version of the works Honda engine had two small top-up gas reservoirs for the valve system. These were pressurised to around 20 MPa

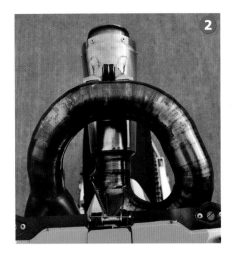

Honda were completely outclassed in 2007. They scored just two wins, one at the Sachsenring where the tight and twisty circuit suited both Pedrosa and his motorcycle, and the other at Valencia where Honda's engine development finally managed to get in front of the Ducati's. The 2008 Repsol bikes were all new, but Honda's customers had to make do with watered-down versions of Pedrosa's '07 Valencia bike, still very sensitive to pitch and still marginally underpowered.

The works bikes, however, had new chassis and engines. The engines were recast to lower the centre of gravity and the new chassis was designed to be easily re-manufactured for various flexibilities. The initial version had engines designed to work with the pneumatic valve system and a throttle system meant to save fuel in the same way as the Ducati. During testing, however, the riders found it was simply too aggressive. Despite being recast the motor could be retro-fitted with the 2007 steel valve spring heads, and this was done late in testing.

Honda managed to get the conventional engine to produce acceptable power but this required very high maintenance levels, with valve springs being changed almost daily. Worse was to come. In testing for Qatar neither Hayden nor Pedrosa could get comfortable in the long sweeping curves that are a characteristic of the circuit. As an emergency measure HRC built four customer-spec bikes for their works riders to use during early practice. Pedrosa soon reverted to the new bike, but Hayden preferred to race the old version.

By the second round, at Jerez, both riders were back on the new bike, but it was obvious that the changes had created a motorcycle more suited to Pedrosa than to Hayden. At certain circuits Pedrosa's low weight and low frontal area allowed him to fight at the front of the field; a demoralised Hayden simply wasn't able to keep up.

The factory was hard at work trying to make the pneumatic valve spring version more user-friendly, and the bike was used at Mugello by Tady Okada, to try to prove it had both good power and reasonable fuel consumption. It was no surprise that Nicky Hayden was the rider who wanted to get hold of the revised motor, which he did for Assen. He ran a good race but it seemed the team's fuel calculations were out by about 100m and he coasted over the line for fourth. This appears to have been a failure of the programming of the throttle system.

Pedrosa switched to Bridgestones after Misano at the end of August and, at the same time, started to use the pneumatic valve spring motor. He set good times but wasn't immediately competitive – the Bridgestones clearly require a very different riding style and, while the chassis seemed able to work with Bridgestone's best tyres, that's not the same as the rider feeling comfortable on them.

SUZUKI
GSV-R

1 Suzuki tested their new bike pre-season but it was downhill all the way. By the time they returned to Jerez to race they had gone back to their 2007 chassis and bodywork to banish the chatter that the new set-up generated

2 The new chassis adopted after Brno raised the front of the motor by about 20mm. As the airbox is directly above the motor it also had to be redesigned

3 The raised engine and redesigned airbox meant that the fuel tank also needed to be changed. The new tank put about three litres more under the rider's seat, effectively moving the weight back

4 After each practice start the clutch is stripped and all the plates checked for wear as 220bhp isn't particularly gentle to clutch plates!

Suzuki started 2008 with new machines: a completely new chassis, tidied-up packaging, new bodywork and upgraded engines. They had one new rider, too, because John Hopkins left and Ducati refugee Loris Capirossi took his seat. Towards the end of testing it became obvious that something wasn't quite right, for the bikes were off the pace both at Phillip Island and at Jerez – and when the garage doors rolled up in Qatar each rider had one each of last year's bikes and a 2008 bike.

Capirossi preferred the older bike for the first meeting, while Vermeulen persevered with the new one. The team was very coy about what had happened, initially explaining they had aerodynamic problems with the new bodywork. In practice it would appear that the new chassis had triggered a bad attack of chatter and the only swift and sure way to cure the problem was to put the new engines into the 2007 chassis. It took four meetings for the chassis numbers to be updated, and the team ran the same equipment until the Misano race.

By early June Suzuki had clearly decided there were benefits to be had from moving the bike's centre of gravity. Vermeulen's machine sported black fork tubes of unknown provenance, but which did appear to be longer than the original gold ones. At the Brno test a new chassis was tried, which lifted the front of the motor by about 15mm. To facilitate this change the airbox was reshaped and some of the fuel-storage capacity moved backwards under the rider's seat. The end result was a higher centre of gravity and a significant rearward weight, at least when the bike was full of fuel. At the same time Suzuki moved across to Bridgestone's RJ family of front tyres, the same ones used by Stoner and Rossi, and immediately saw an improvement in race performance.

Several small experiments were tried with different exhaust systems in an attempt to improve mid-range throttle response. They do not appear to have been successful as the original pipes were refitted.

KAWASAKI
ZX-RR

1 Kawasaki had all sorts of trouble developing a slipper clutch setting that would let their bikes be competitive going into corners

2 Kawasaki started the year with few changes to their 2007 bike, but after it became obvious that the other factories had made big leaps forward in power output changes were needed

3 Kawasaki's interpretation of the in-line four is very conservative. It uses an irregular firing order crankshaft but the crank turns forwards; the engine is also relatively long with the gearbox laid out horizontally

4 John Hopkins received a new higher-fairing cowl at Brno to replace one made from two fairings grafted together that he had used for several earlier races

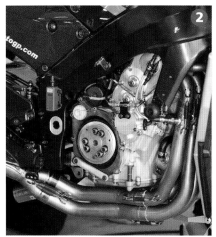

There's no way to hide it: Kawasaki had a horrendous year. Having spent 2007 perfecting a bike that accelerated really well, their stated aim was to build a machine that could go into corners well too. John Hopkins was part of the solution, because the American has the reputation of being very sensitive to set-up changes and also extremely good at corner entry. Development appeared to be split between several different projects, one being to build a screamer version of the 800cc engine. This used a conventional two-up, two-down crankshaft and, as its name implies, had a completely different exhaust note. Factories originally moved away from this style of motor because of major problems with traction; in 2008 Kawasaki's motive was to maximise horsepower while hopefully not losing too much traction. It quickly became apparent that the screamer engines did have a significant disadvantage and, at the same time, it became obvious they were being outclassed by the new Yamaha. All of Kawasaki's engine development was then focused back onto their irregular firing order engine.

To get the bike to work going into corners it was fitted with a longer swingarm to try to stabilise corner-entry behaviour. Unfortunately this seemed to make the bike harder to turn, and also make the front end feel 'loose'. Hopkins did try to push it, as far as was possible, but several crashes led to him missing races in the middle of the year. On his return new swingarms were available which appeared to be shorter and more flexible, and this allowed him to experiment with the best Bridgestone tyres.

By then, however, it was obvious that Kawasaki's very conservative version of the across-the-frame four-cylinder GP bike had taken a wrong turn in its development. A completely new bike is required – one that is shorter, has a higher centre of gravity and is agile enough in the corners to match its opposition.

THE RIDERS
2008

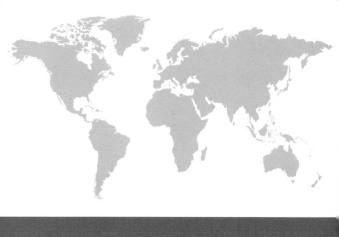

THE SEASON IN FOCUS

Every MotoGP rider's season analysed, from the World Champion to the wild-card entry whose race lasted less than a lap

1	Valentino Rossi	373
2	Casey Stoner	280
3	Dani Pedrosa	249
4	Jorge Lorenzo	190
5	Andrea Dovizioso	174
6	Nicky Hayden	155
7	Colin Edwards	144
8	Chris Vermeulen	128
9	Shinya Nakano	126
10	Loris Capirossi	118
11	James Toseland	105
12	Toni Elias	92
13	Sylvain Guintoli	67
14	Alex de Angelis	63
15	Randy de Puniet	61
16	John Hopkins	57
17	Marco Melandri	51
18	Anthony West	50
19	Ben Spies	20
20	Jamie Hacking	5
21	Tadayuki Okada	2

1 VALENTINO ROSSI
FIAT YAMAHA

The world's supply of superlatives has become exhausted in describing Rossi's season. His year started slowly as he and Jerry Burgess adapted the Yamaha to Bridgestone tyres, but after the first race he was only off the rostrum once and that was due to his single big mistake of the season. Rossi's first-lap crash in the Dutch TT at Assen lost him the championship lead to Dani Pedrosa but he regained the lead at the next round and was never headed again.

The real threat to Valentino came from Casey Stoner and Ducati after the Aussie put together three consecutive wins from pole position in the middle of the season. At this point Valentino announced that he had to improve his qualifying, which had been inconsistent, if he wanted to be able to race Stoner.

For the rest of the season he was off the front row only twice and always finished either first or second.

There's no doubting the crucial race of the season. It was Laguna Seca. Rossi rode as well and as combatively as he's ever done to frustrate Stoner on track and then continue the war on the psychological front off it. Stoner's crashes while leading the next two races seemed almost inevitable.

Valentino's seventh win of the year, Indianapolis, made him the most successful racer ever in the top class in terms of race wins, beating Giacomo Agostini's 32-year-old record. Other records fell to him in the year and you just know there are more to come.

The message Nicky Hayden once had emblazoned on his leathers comes to mind: 'The Numbers Don't Lie'.

NATIONALITY Italian
DATE OF BIRTH 16 February 1979
2008 SEASON 9 wins, 16 rostrums, 2 pole positions, 5 fastest laps
TOTAL POINTS 373

2 CASEY STONER
DUCATI MARLBORO

As you'd expect from an Australian World Champion, Casey Stoner didn't give up the number-one plate without a fight. Without several of them, in fact. Apart from victory in the opening race, the start of the season was a struggle with a Ducati that even he couldn't tame. When the Bologna factory delivered a revised engine-management system after Catalunya, Casey embarked on a rampage that featured six consecutive pole positions (all of them after being fastest in free practice) and five fastest laps. The trio of races in the UK, the Netherlands and Germany were walkovers. Rossi described at as like racing 'a UFO'.

Then came Laguna Seca, the first of an even more significant trio of races. In the USA it took all Rossi's experience and ruthlessness to drag a mistake out of Casey. Then in the Czech Republic and San Marino Casey crashed early, both times while leading and both times with Rossi pressuring him. Brutally honest as ever, Casey later said that it was these mistakes which lost the title.

At Misano he also discovered that a five-year-old scaphoid injury in his left wrist had never healed properly. The staple inserted to hold things together had spread and the bone was in several pieces. Yet he still managed to race and to win. He went into the winter facing a bone-graft operation, a serious procedure that requires lengthy convalescence.

Whatever happens, there will be no reduction in Casey's will to win, and probably his certainty that the world is against him. It isn't, but it could be difficult to convince him otherwise.

NATIONALITY Australian
DATE OF BIRTH 16 October 1985
2008 SEASON 6 wins, 11 rostrums, 9 pole positions, 9 fastest laps
TOTAL POINTS 280

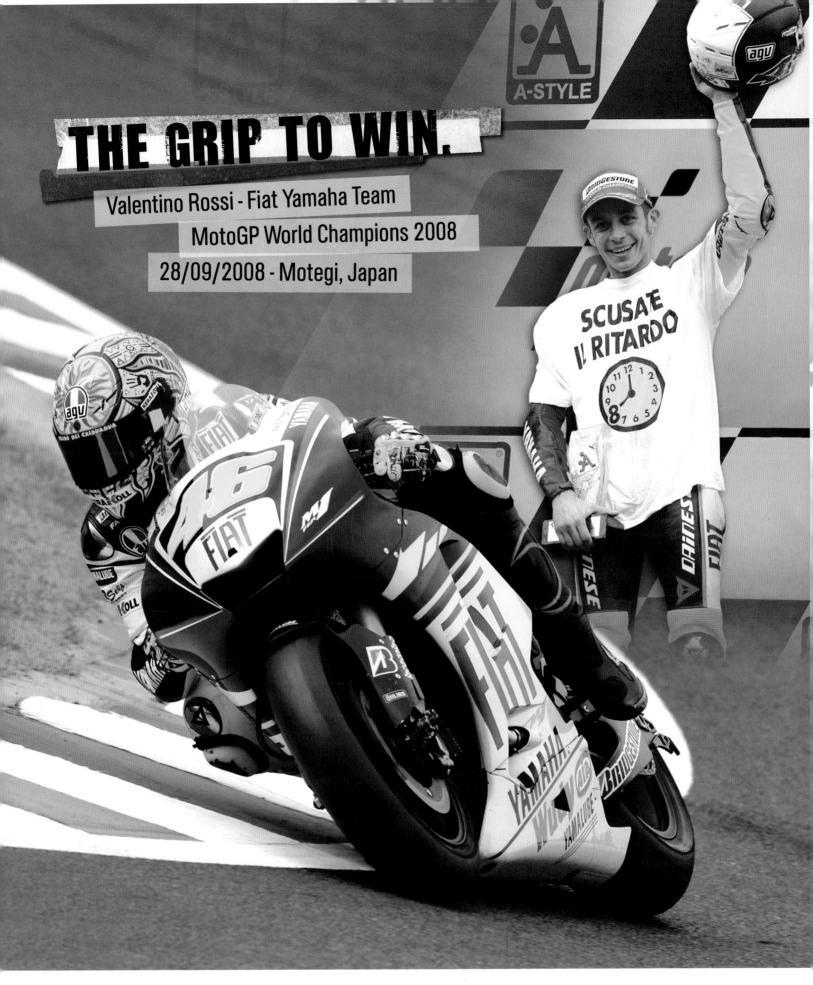

THE GRIP TO WIN.

Valentino Rossi - Fiat Yamaha Team
MotoGP World Champions 2008
28/09/2008 - Motegi, Japan

3 DANI PEDROSA
REPSOL HONDA

NATIONALITY Spanish

DATE OF BIRTH 29 September 1985

2008 SEASON 2 wins,
2 pole positions, 2 fastest laps

TOTAL POINTS 249

It's a great pity that the controversy surrounding Dani Pedrosa's year tends to obscure the fact that at the halfway point of the season he was leading the World Championship having won two races and he had never finished lower than fourth. And on Michelin tyres.

His crash in Germany while seven seconds in the lead was the pivotal moment of Dani's season. He lost the points lead, put himself out of the next race at Laguna Seca, and was barely fit when he returned to competition at Brno. Which is where the real trouble started.

Dani's manager Alberto Puig tried to get all of Michelin's teams to pull out of the race. At the next race in San Marino it was announced that Dani, but not his team-mate Nicky Hayden, would be switching to Bridgestone tyres

immediately. Leaving aside the ethics of tearing up contracts in mid-season, this gave Dani and his crew the task of getting the RC212V to work on a new make of tyres in just five races. It was Pedrosa's misfortune that his first race on Bridgestones was Indianapolis in the wet. He hadn't seen the track or ridden the Japanese company's wet-weather tyres before. However, in the first dry race, Japan, he finished on the rostrum, his first top-three finish for six races.

There's no doubt that Dani is one of the top three racers in the world today but the machinations of his management have embarrassed Honda on more than one occasion. Next year will be Dani's fourth on the factory Honda. Unless he wins the title, as Hayden did in his fourth season, his ride will be in danger.

4 JORGE LORENZO
FIAT YAMAHA

NATIONALITY Spanish

DATE OF BIRTH 4 May 1987

2008 SEASON 1 win, 6 rostrums,
4 pole positions, 1 fastest lap

TOTAL POINTS 190

Fourth is the highest position a rookie has ever finished in MotoGP, and it might have been even higher for the double 250cc champion. He set pole position for the first three races, a unique achievement for the premier class, won the third race and set the fastest lap. At this point he was leading the championship.

From there on it got messy, starting with what everyone thought was the mother of all highsides in practice for China. Amazingly, he raced and finished fourth, then got on the rostrum in France despite more crashes. Then the crashing really started, putting him out of four of the next six GPs. The Laguna Seca highside really was the mother of them all.

Perhaps the scariest aspect of this episode was Jorge's blazingly honest

reaction. He talked of being fit physically but not mentally, of having nightmares, of being scared of the bike. When has anyone heard a racer, let alone a double World Champion, talking like that?

The return to form at Misano was stunning. He kept Rossi honest on his home track, followed it up at Indianapolis with his first ever wet-weather rostrum in any level of racing, and then got back on pole in Japan.

A lot of people were looking forward to disliking Jorge intensely when he came up to MotoGP, but even the most hardened cynics were surprised to find themselves won over by his honesty and charm. Jorge survived his rookie year in a split garage better than seemed possible at mid-season. There's every reason to suppose that he will be even more competitive in 2009.

5 ANDREA DOVIZIOSO

TEAM SCOT MotoGP

If it wasn't for Jorge Lorenzo, the paddock woud have been raving about the performance of another rookie. In one season Andrea Dovizioso did enough on a satellite Honda to earn promotion to the factory team for 2009. A Scot Honda team rider for all of his seven-year GP career, Andrea has been well thought of by HRC since well before his 2004 125cc title. He hung around in the 250 class at the behest of Honda, and was the only man to be able to challenge Lorenzo over a whole season.

That determination transferred to MotoGP and Andrea went about his work inthe same uncomplaining way as he did in the smaller classes. In the three races in which Michelin had their troubles, Andrea was their top finishing rider in each time with fifth, fourth and ninth places. There were three fourth places and four fifth places before he finally got the rostrum he deserved in Malaysia. And all this, remember, was achieved on a satellite team bike that didn't get an upgrade all year and with a crew who were also new to MotoGP.

Before Andrea was confirmed as a Repsol Honda rider for 2009, there was plenty of behind-the-scenes politics to ensure that he would receive equal machinery to Dani Pedrosa. The Italian and the people around him have been getting their retaliation in first. There won't be a wall down the middle of the Repsol Honda pit garage next season, and the interaction between Dovi and his new team-mate will be worth watching. Andrea has already made his position clear: he would prefer a good relationship, but if not that's okay too.

NATIONALITY Italian
DATE OF BIRTH 23 March 1986
2008 SEASON 1 rostrum
TOTAL POINTS 174

6 NICKY HAYDEN

REPSOL HONDA

Nicky Hayden has never got on with Honda's 800cc motor, and for the first half of this season it looked as if he was in for another year of purgatory. Then two things happened: he finally got to use the pneumatic-valve motor, and then he found out that other factories were interested in signing him.

Some of the old confidence returned and he came within 100 yards of getting on the rostrum at Assen. Then came Michelin's tyre troubles and a freak accident practising for the X-Games that broke his right heel. Nicky missed two races and came back for Indianapolis, the closest to his Owensboro, Kentucky, home that he has ever road-raced. He led half the race and got second place, his best-ever result on an 800.

By this time it was known that Nicky was leaving HRC to join Ducati. His position had been made untenable by the machinations not so much of Dani Pedrosa but of the people around his team-mate, specifically Alberto Puig.

Nicky started to take his revenge with some entertaining but barbed remarks in press conferences. The fact that he went so far as to attend an American Ducati dealer convention the day after Indianapolis gives an indication of just how disenchanted he was with some aspects of his job. On the other hand, he got quite emotional discussing his nine years with Honda (he rode for them on dirt and tarmac in AMA racing before coming to GPs) and some of the 'cool bikes' he'd raced for them.

Will he be able to ride the Ducati? 'When I open the throttle I like to go somewhere,' says Nicky. We'll take that as a 'yes'.

NATIONALITY American
DATE OF BIRTH 30 July 1981
2008 SEASON 2 rostrums, 1 fastest lap
TOTAL POINTS 155

7 COLIN EDWARDS
TECH 3 YAMAHA

NATIONALITY
American

DATE OF BIRTH
27 February 1974

2008 SEASON
2 rostrums, 1 pole position

TOTAL POINTS
144

Colin's move from works rider to satellite team seemed to suit all concerned. The Tech 3 squad made him feel at home and Colin was happy to be free of 'that works shit' – and happy enough to improve his championship position by three places. Colin suffered more than most when Michelin hit their problems; if he has no confidence in a front tyre then the results suffer. The highlight of his year was that revengeful third place in Assen but it was followed by a slump in form that saw him out of the top ten for four of the next five races. A solid run of results in the final four races saw him help Tech 3 to fourth in the team table and silence talk of a job swap with Yamaha's new World Superbike Championship rider, Ben Spies.

8 CHRIS VERMEULEN
RIZLA SUZUKI MotoGP

NATIONALITY
Australian

DATE OF BIRTH
19 June 1982

2008 SEASON
2 rostrums

TOTAL POINTS
128

In 2007 Chris became Suzuki's first winner of a MotoGP race, and he's still the only one. He dropped two places in the standings compared to 12 months ago and, to the surprise of many, was outshone by new team-mate Capirossi in the middle of the season. Chris was as far down the points table as 11th after Donington. However, he was back up to sixth place after Indianapolis, only to suffer from a tyre problem in Japan and a first-corner off-track excursion at home in Australia that knocked him back down to eighth. Last year's verdict – that there's more to come from Vermeulen – still applies, but he will need Suzuki to find some horsepower if he's to win again.

200 CONSECUTIVE VICTORIES

9 SHINYA NAKANO
SAN CARLO HONDA GRESINI

NATIONALITY
Japanese

DATE OF BIRTH
10 October 1977

TOTAL POINTS
126

After 133 500cc/MotoGP races, Shinya is off to Superbike in 2009. His final season in GPs only sparked into life after HRC entrusted him with a factory-spec bike for the second half of the year. He immediately finished fourth on it. This bike used a conventional steel valve spring engine and was effectively the machine on which Pedrosa started the year. Team manager Fausto Gresini was heard to growl about Shinya's lack of aggression at times, but three top-five finishes calmed him down. There was talk of him becomng HRC's official tester but Shinya would prefer to keep racing full-time rather than getting one or two wild-card rides a year.

10 LORIS CAPIROSSI
RIZLA SUZUKI MotoGP

NATIONALITY
Italian

DATE OF BIRTH
4 April 1973

2008 SEASON
1 rostrum

TOTAL POINTS
118

There were those who thought that Loris was looking on his move from Ducati to Suzuki as a pension plan. They were proved wrong. But for a nasty hand injury sustained at Barcelona, which put him out of three races and handicapped him for two more, Loris would have been considerably higher up the table. He was sixth when it happened. Typically, when he was fully fit he got on the rostrum in Brno, his 99th rostrum across all classes in GPs. Like his team-mate, Loris's efforts were seriously compromised at some tracks by the Suzuki's lack of top-end. If the factory can give him what he wants, don't bet against the century coming up in '09.

11 JAMES TOSELAND
TECH 3 YAMAHA

NATIONALITY
British

DATE OF BIRTH
5 October 1980

TOTAL POINTS
105

Qualifying on the front two rows six times and achieving six sixth-place finishes in your rookie year has to be counted a success. James's best race was Phillip Island, where he repassed Rossi more than once – very few racers have ever done that. That was on a track where he raced in every year of his World Superbike career – but there were 11 tracks in this year's calendar where he had never raced before. That should mean he starts 2009 much higher up the learning curve. James's points total of 105 was the first time since Niall Mackenzie in 1993 that a British rider has passed the hundred mark in the top category. Tech 3 Yamaha re-signed him very early, so the target for '09 is rostrum finishes.

12 TONI ELIAS
ALICE TEAM

NATIONALITY
Spanish

DATE OF BIRTH
26 March 1983

2008 SEASON
2 rostrums

TOTAL POINTS
92

The satellite Ducati team wasn't a place you wanted to be at the start of the year. Even Casey Stoner couldn't come to terms with the 2009 Desmosedici. Over at the Alice team things were complicated by the departure of team founder Luis d'Antin. The flip side of that disruption was increased support from the Bologna factory, and after Germany a distinct improvement in results. At Laguna Seca Toni was in the top ten, for the first time in the season, and he followed that with back-to-back rostrums. The first one, Brno, was undoubtedly helped by Michelin's tyre troubles. The second, Misano, was achieved on a level playing field. For '09 he returns to the Gresini Honda team for which he rode in '06 and '07.

13 SYLVAIN GUINTOLI
ALICE TEAM

NATIONALITY
French

DATE OF BIRTH
24 June 1982

TOTAL POINTS
67

Two top-ten places in the wet were the highlights of a difficult year. As well as a recalcitrant Ducati, Sylvain also had to deal with injuries, including a dislocated collarbone after a spectacular crash in Phillip Island that saw him surf the bike into the gravel trap at high speed. Nevertheless, he didn't miss a race and scored points in all but one. That was Jerez, where the Bridgestones were at a distinct disadvantage. After two tough years in MotoGP Sylvain heads to BSB to ride for Crescent Suzuki, who also run the MotoGP team – which means the likeable Frenchman will be well-placed to take advantage of any misfortune that may befall the team's regular MotoGP riders.

14 ALEX DE ANGELIS
SAN CARLO HONDA GRESINI

NATIONALITY
San Marinese

DATE OF BIRTH
26 February 1984

TOTAL POINTS
63

Alex equalled de Puniet's tally of seven race crashes – but only remounted once. He got within reach of the rostrum twice, first with a spirited ride from the back of the field at Mugello and then in Germany in totally different conditions. At the Sachsenring he shadowed rainmaster Chris Vermeulen for the second half of the race but couldn't find a way past. That was a considered and mature race which contrasted strongly with some of his crashes. Alex's first-lap get-off in Assen, for instance, didn't amuse team manager Fausto Gresini. However, Alex showed enough promise in his rookie year to be retained by the team for '09. If he can add just a touch of consistency to his speed, he'll be in MotoGP for a while yet.

15 RANDY DE PUNIET
LCR HONDA MotoGP

NATIONALITY
French

DATE OF BIRTH
14 February 1981

TOTAL POINTS
61

For a man who finished in the top ten five times and was never out of the points when he got to the flag, you'd expect the points standing to end up considerably higher than 14th. Randy's problem was that he crashed out of five races, and crashed and remounted in two more! There has never been any doubt about Randy's sheer speed – he qualified outside the top ten only three times all year – but sixth place under stormy conditions at Indianapolis was his best result. He's halfway through a two-year contract with the LCR team so he'll be back in '09. It'll be interesting to see what he can do on the Bridgestone control tyre.

16 JOHN HOPKINS
KAWASAKI RACING

NATIONALITY
American

DATE OF BIRTH
22 May 1983

TOTAL POINTS
57

At the end of the '07 season John was the fourth best rider in the world and a regular rostrum finisher. His big-money move to Kawasaki seemed a good thing for all concerned, but 2008 started badly then got worse. First there was a testing crash that ripped a groin muscle and, it was discovered later, cracked John's pelvis. Then there was the practice crash at Assen that broke his left leg and caused him to miss three races. Worst of all, the Kawasaki simply wasn't competitive. Two top-ten finishes in the first three races flattered to deceive, and the third place on the grid he achieved in the wet at Brno was seven places better than anything else he managed. Kawasaki must give him something better for the '09 season.

17 MARCO MELANDRI
ALICE TEAM

NATIONALITY
Italian

DATE OF BIRTH
7 August 1982

TOTAL POINTS
51

What happened to the man whose championship positions over the past three years have been fifth, fourth and second? Rumour has it that Melandri was the second-best paid rider on the grid in 2008, but unfortunately Ducati's investment didn't pay off. Marco just never got to grips with the bike and his confidence was shot inside three races. Fifth place in China, the fourth race of the year, was a false dawn – he only got into the top ten twice more all season and failed to score in four out of the last five GPs. For 2009, Marco will join John Hopkins at Kawasaki. A return to form for both rider and factory would be more than welcome.

18 ANTHONY WEST
KAWASAKI RACING

NATIONALITY
Australian

DATE OF BIRTH
17 July 1981

TOTAL POINTS
50

Ant expected to finish close behind his team-mate in the points table, but he didn't expect them both to be down near the bottom. Even the prevalence of wet weather didn't help the Aussie as he suffered all season long with the lack of traction that plagued the Kawasakis. The only real bright spot was the Czech Republic where wet qualifying and problems for the Michelin runners helped net Ant a career-best finish of fifth place. His ride is being taken by Marco Melandri for 2009, and Ant will return to the World Supersport Championship riding a Honda CBR600 for his old 250cc GP team-mate Johan Stigefelt.

WILD-CARD & REPLACEMENT RIDERS

If one of a MotoGP team's regular riders is injured, he can be replaced for as many races as necessary. Wild-card entries are also allowed. They're nominated by Dorna (MotoGP commercial rights holders), IRTA (the teams' organisation) and the FIM (the governing body of motorcycle sport worldwide), and take part in one race only

19 BEN SPIES
RIZLA SUZUKI MotoGP

NATIONALITY
American

DATE OF BIRTH
11 July 1984

TOTAL POINTS
20

The triple American Superbike champ replaced Capirossi at Donington and rode as a wild card at the two American races, scoring points all three times. Hot property.

20 JAMIE HACKING
KAWASAKI RACING

NATIONALITY
American

DATE OF BIRTH
30 June 1971

TOTAL POINTS
5

Replaced Hopkins at Laguna Seca where he'd been expecting a wild-card entry. Beat his temporary team-mate and became the oldest rider ever to debut in the 500cc/MotoGP class.

21 TADAYUKI OKADA
REPSOL HONDA

NATIONALITY
Japanese

DATE OF BIRTH
13 February 1967

TOTAL POINTS
2

Honda's veteran test rider debuted the pneumatic valve spring motor at Mugello. Crashed in practice but stalked West all race, passing him just before the flag.

KOUSUKE AKIYOSHI
RIZLA SUZUKI MotoGP

NATIONALITY
Japanese

DATE OF BIRTH
12 January 1975

TOTAL POINTS
0

Had a short race as a wild card at Motegi. Crashed in practice and warm-up, then only lasted three corners in the race. Still, he's won the 8 Hour so no Suzuki person will complain!

NOBUATSU AOKI
RIZLA SUZUKI MotoGP

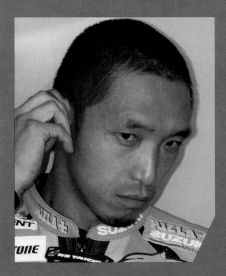

NATIONALITY
Japanese

DATE OF BIRTH
31 August 1971

TOTAL POINTS
0

Suzuki's other test rider rode the Malaysian GP as a wild card. Nobu just missed out on a point on a bike with a very different exhaust system compared to the regular riders' bikes.

MotoGP on DVD

MotoGP Official Review 2008
As the season opened we all wanted to know whether Casey Stoner and his Ducati could be beaten. Fans were treated to unpredictable and fascinating racing - Stoner struggling to stay upright, Valentino Rossi back in winning form, the resurgent Colin Edwards and some stunning 'new boys', including James Toseland, Jorge Lorenzo and Andrea Dovizioso. This review brings you action from every round, including breathtaking on-bike footage, interviews and behind-the-scenes access, making this DVD an absolute must.
£19.99 180mins apx No.1842

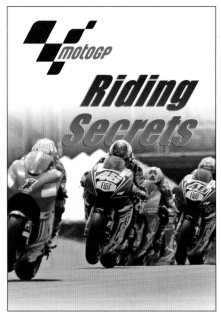

MotoGP Riding Secrets
A fascinating behind-the-scenes look at what it takes to compete in MotoGP. This DVD takes fans through the mental preparation, riding skills, set-up, teamwork and other essential elements of bike racing which heroes like Valentino Rossi must master. It features contributions from every single rider from the 2008 MotoGP field, including Stoner, Lorenzo and Toseland, plus expert insight and advice. This is an exceptional look behind the scenes of the world's leading motorcycle championship.
£16.99 121mins No.1761

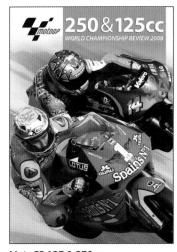

MotoGP 125 & 250cc Official Review 2008
The comprehensive review features awesome action footage, including plenty from on-board the bikes. This is the full story of both the 125cc and 250cc MotoGP title battles, featuring Simoncelli, de Meglio, Talmacsi, Smith and more. As always we bring you coverage of every race, with fast and furious action caught from all the best camera angles.
£19.99 180mins apx No.1843

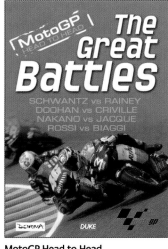

MotoGP Head to Head - The Great Battles
Join the greats for the most intense championship battles. Sparks fly as rivals go elbow-to-elbow at more than 200mph on tracks around the world, and stunning race footage lets you join the drama. Get even closer to the action through fascinating candid interviews. Features Rossi, Biaggi, Doohan, Criville, Schwantz, Rainey and more.
£16.99 60mins No.2135

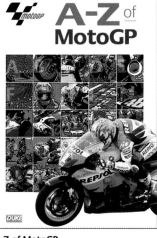

A-Z of MotoGP
The official and definitive guide to the world of MotoGP covers everything, from the names that made the glorious history of the championship to the modern rules and regulations. Experts guide you through the technical aspects of the machines and racing skills, with contributions from Toni Elias, Dr Costa and more. Plus, the champagne celebrations, grid girls and spectacular crashes!
£16.99 71mins No.1744

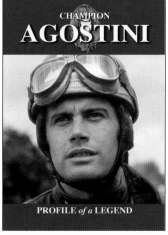

Champion Agostini
Giacomo Agostini is a legend of Grand Prix racing, taking 15 World Championships, 122 Grand Prix wins and victory at the Isle of Man TT. It took three decades for his record of top level wins to be equalled, when Rossi took his 68th Grand Prix victory at Misano in 2008. This DVD captures the essence of the man who combined skill and courage, a man with charm and film star looks, a man who could not stop winning.
£16.99 67mins No.5972

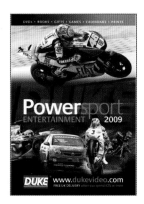

Call now for your FREE Catalogue

Over 8000 products to fuel your passion

01624 640 000 www.dukevideo.com

THE RACES
MotoGP 2008

QATARI GP

LOSAIL INTERNATIONAL RACEWAY

ROUND **1**

March 9

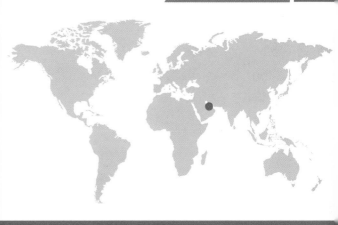

LIGHT FANTASTIC

Ducati and Casey Stoner took up where they left off in 2007, but there was plenty of encouragement for Honda and Yamaha, plus a very fast crop of rookies

Before a wheel was turned the only topic of conversation was the floodlighting, an historic first for motorcycle Grand Prix racing. Just half a dozen laps into the first session, though, the artificial light seemed normal and, apart from a couple of cursory queries to the riders at the end of that day, the subject wasn't mentioned again. Attention quickly reverted to the racing. Despite more winter testing than ever there were still many questions that needed an answer. Was Rossi's switch from Michelin to Bridgestone tyres a mistake? Surely Honda wouldn't repeat the previous season's errors? Would the opposition be able to eat into Ducati's 2007 technical superiority? On the face of it, Casey Stoner doubling his winning margin from the previous season's Losail race would seem to indicate that Ducati's dominance was intact. A closer examination of the evidence undermines that assumption. It is true that Stoner was able to bide his time and watch a frantic fight unfold in front of him before going from fourth to first on the eighth lap. Casey then held off Jorge Lorenzo, the star of a very impressive crop of MotoGP rookies, setting the fastest lap of the race at two-thirds' distance and winning by over five seconds. Still sounds comfortable doesn't it?

The really disquieting aspects of the weekend for Ducati were the alarming underperformance of new works rider Marco Melandri, who finished over 40 seconds adrift of his team-mate, and the failure of the Alice satellite team's new riders, Guintoli and Elias, to trouble the scorers. True, the Ducati was still the fastest thing in a straight line, but the previous year's yawning chasm between the red bikes and the rest was down to just over 4mph over the factory Yamaha. The Suzuki

Above Fast rookie Andrea Dovizioso dives inside Rossi to take fourth place in his first MotoGP race

Opposite Fast rookie James Toseland contemplates turn one from the front row of the grid; he finished a fighting sixth

wasn't far back either, but it was noticeable that of the Honda men only Pedrosa, with the benefit of a tow, could keep up. Without a slipstream he was another 2.5mph behind the Fiat Yamahas. All the Hondas, like the Tech 3 satellite team Yamahas, were still running conventional valve springs as opposed to pneumatic valves. Lorenzo and Rossi demonstrated the difference by blasting past James Toseland down the front straight. The speed disadvantage didn't stop Pedrosa making a remarkable start from the third row and leading the first four laps. Given his almost total lack of winter testing thanks to a hand injury, Dani's performance in the race was stunning – especially as it followed lacklustre practice and qualifying.

HRC took the unexpected step of flying in two 2007 bikes for the Repsol team. Pedrosa took the bike on which he won the final race of 2007 out for a few laps, to rediscover his base line, before parking it and concentrating on the new model. This was an understandable move, but Nicky Hayden's decision to

race the old bike was more doubtful, and the American never got higher than eighth. Valentino Rossi also looked to be suffering from lack of track time – again because of a hand injury. His change to Bridgestone tyres over the winter was a major talking point, and plenty of people were looking for evidence of a major error of judgement by the Doctor. Practice suggested no major difference between Bridgestone and Michelin, but the qualifying hour produced an all-Michelin front row. In fact, only Stoner in fourth and Rossi in seventh stopped every Bridgestone runner qualifying above every Michelin man. In the race Rossi was able to run at the front in the first half but thereafter gave away a second a lap to Stoner, succumbed to Pedrosa eight laps from home and lost fourth place to Dovizioso despite a hectic scuffle over the last two laps. His analysis was simple: he and his team had to throw away all the settings they'd developed with the M1 on Michelins and learn how the bike worked with the new tyres. Valentino had been forced to ride defensively, not his usual race mode.

There was certainly nothing wrong with the Yamaha–Michelin combination. Rookie Lorenzo started from pole – despite nominally being Rossi's team-mate he uses Michelins – with the Tech 3 Yamahas of Toseland, another rookie, and Edwards alongside him. Lorenzo continued his stunning progress in the race by taking Rossi as the Italian started to run into tyre problems, and surviving the fairing bashing of the opening laps, including one eye-watering pass by Toseland, to claim a solid second place. It was the best showing by a rookie since Max Biaggi won from pole at Suzuka in his first race in the top class in 1998. Toseland's front-row start and sixth-place finish were the best showing by a

'THERE WERE GUYS BASHING FAIRINGS AND I JUST TRIED TO STAY OUT OF THE WAY.'
CASEY STONER

British rider on his debut in the premier class since Terry Rymer's ride at the British GP in 1992, and ended a record run of 18 MotoGP races without a Briton scoring a point. Jorge even laughed off that slightly too forceful pass, saying he'd done worse himself and anyway James was a good guy. Toseland was happy to admit he was still learning how to ride a MotoGP bike and how to race with his new opposition. He professed himself delighted with sixth place but couldn't disguise his disappointment at finishing so close behind Rossi and not being able to put a pass on him. James's problem in the closing couple of laps was that Valentino and Andrea Dovizioso were so close together he would have had to try and pass them both in one go. Dovi, yet another impressive rookie, celebrated fourth place, along with his JiR Scot team, as if they'd won. Actually, they were probably celebrating being first Italian home. Being beaten by his fellow-countryman was the only aspect of the weekend that seemed to get to Valentino Rossi.

The first race of 2008 showed that a lot had changed over the close season, notably that Michelin had upped their game considerably and that Yamaha's pneumatic-valve motor was now not just fast but also reliable. Honda's factory and privateer bikes impressed in both race and qualifying while Suzuki and Kawasaki still seemed just off the pace. Jorge Lorenzo also gave warning that he might be even better as a MotoGP rider than he was in the 250 class. However Stoner's victory suggested that, while the opposition had improved, the combination of Ducati, Bridgestone and Casey himself was still the one to beat, even if he was the only man who could make it work.

NIGHT FIGHTERS

It certainly looked good. Whether you were at the track or in front of a TV, the first motorcycle Grand Prix to be run under lights was a thrilling spectacle. Riders and TV viewers alike kept mentioning the similarity to a video game, but any worries about the artificiality of the situation were soon forgotten. When the idea of a Qatari GP was first mooted the plan had been to run it under lights, but it took until this, the fifth year of the event, to make it a reality.

The question 'Why bother?' hung largely unspoken over proceedings. It was suggested that it was for the benefit of European TV audiences, but the time difference is only a couple of hours. The idea of running under floodlights was first made to avoid the 40°C temperatures that MotoGP endured when they went to Losail at the start of October 2004 – and indeed it makes sense if racing in the Middle East at that time of year to do so after dusk. However, when the MotoGP grid formed at 11pm at the start of March, the track temperature was down to the sort of level to be expected on an overcast day at Donington Park: around 12°C.

The riders strongly suggested the date of the race be moved back, maybe by as short a time as three weeks. Whatever the schedule, the Qatari race will be on the calendar until 2016 because the organisers signed a new contract with GP rights-holders Dorna just before the event. No other track has a deal stretching beyond 2011.

There is also the matter of the energy expended in lighting a racetrack. As IRTA President Hervé Poncharal pointed out, compared to the number of football matches played under lights or the carbon cost of keeping ice rinks frozen, this race was insignificant. However, it is the perception of issues like this that matters rather than the bare facts, especially to sponsors. Running under lights in March looks too much like an answer in search of a question. A shift of the date would go a long way towards justifying the energy expended.

Below Rossi led the early laps but couldn't get away from the pack: here he is pursued by Hayden, Lorenzo and Stoner

QATARI GP
LOSAIL INTERNATIONAL RACEWAY

ROUND 1
March 9

RACE RESULTS

CIRCUIT LENGTH 3.343 miles
NO. OF LAPS 22
RACE DISTANCE 73,546 miles
WEATHER Dry, 18°C
TRACK TEMPERATURE 19°C
WINNER Casey Stoner
FASTEST LAP 1m 55.153s, 104.515mph, Casey Stoner (record)
PREVIOUS LAP RECORD 1m 56.528s, 103.282mph, Casey Stoner, 2007

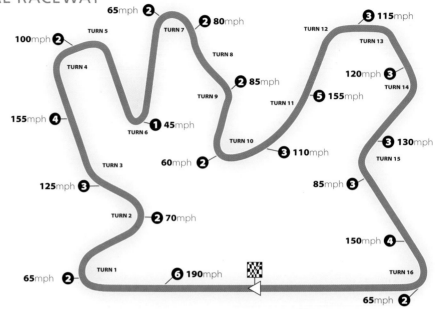

QUALIFYING

	Rider	Nationality	Team	Qualifying	Pole +	Gap
1	Lorenzo	SPA	Fiat Yamaha Team	1m 53.927s		
2	Toseland	GBR	Tech 3 Yamaha	1m 54.182s	0.255s	0.255s
3	Edwards	USA	Tech 3 Yamaha	1m 54.499s	0.572s	0.317s
4	Stoner	AUS	Ducati Marlboro Team	1m 54.733s	0.806s	0.234s
5	De Puniet	FRA	LCR Honda MotoGP	1m 54.818s	0.891s	0.085s
6	Hayden	USA	Repsol Honda Team	1m 54.880s	0.953s	0.062s
7	Rossi	ITA	Fiat Yamaha Team	1m 55.133s	1.206s	0.253s
8	Pedrosa	SPA	Repsol Honda Team	1m 55.170s	1.243s	0.037s
9	Dovizioso	ITA	JiR Team Scot MotoGP	1m 55.185s	1.258s	0.015s
10	Hopkins	USA	Kawasaki Racing Team	1m 55.263s	1.336s	0.078s
11	Vermeulen	AUS	Rizla Suzuki MotoGP	1m 55.540s	1.613s	0.277s
12	De Angelis	RSM	San Carlo Honda Gresini	1m 55.692s	1.765s	0.152s
13	Capirossi	ITA	Rizla Suzuki MotoGP	1m 56.070s	2.143s	0.378s
14	Elias	SPA	Alice Team	1m 56.251s	2.324s	0.181s
15	Nakano	JPN	San Carlo Honda Gresini	1m 56.434s	2.507s	0.183s
16	Melandri	ITA	Ducati Marlboro Team	1m 56.730s	2.803s	0.296s
17	Guintoli	FRA	Alice Team	1m 57.198s	3.271s	0.468s
18	West	AUS	Kawasaki Racing Team	1m 57.445s	3.518s	0.247s

FINISHERS

1 CASEY STONER Not an easy race to start his title defence, but a very effective one. Calm enough to bide his time and wait for the tyres to come good before moving through the leading group and winning by a greater margin than the previous year. Also the highest qualifier on Bridgestone tyres.

2 JORGE LORENZO An astonishing debut, right up there with Biaggi and even Saarinen – the first 500cc/MotoGP rookie to start from pole since Max in 1998. Led an all-Yamaha front row, then diced with the stars at the front, dealing with both team-mate Rossi and sworn enemy Pedrosa without ever looking in difficulty.

3 DANI PEDROSA Still troubled by the hand he broke early in winter testing. Rode last year's bike before deciding on the 2008 machine with a modified chassis. Under these circumstances, plus a crash after tangling with Rossi in practice and then qualifying on the third row, this was a good result.

4 ANDREA DOVIZIOSO The best debut result by an Italian since Biaggi in 1998. Rode superbly all weekend and capped a great race from ninth on the grid by passing Rossi on the last lap to be the first Italian home. His crew welcomed him back to pit lane as if he'd won the race.

5 VALENTINO ROSSI Knew converting a 'Michelin bike' to a 'Bridgestone bike' wouldn't be easy so expected a difficult race. Started losing grip at the rear after half a dozen laps and ended up doing what he described as a 'defensive' race. Only appeared to be upset by losing out to Dovizioso on the last lap.

6 JAMES TOSELAND Another amazing performance by a debutant: second on the grid; bashing fairings with Lorenzo in the opening laps; dropping off the leading group mid-race, then closing right back up to Rossi and Dovizioso in the final laps. As the man himself said: 'Not bad for a Superbike rider.' Best British result since McWilliams at Le Mans in 2003.

7 COLIN EDWARDS Rejuvenated now he has got rid of what he (nearly) called 'that works stuff'. Third in qualifying but

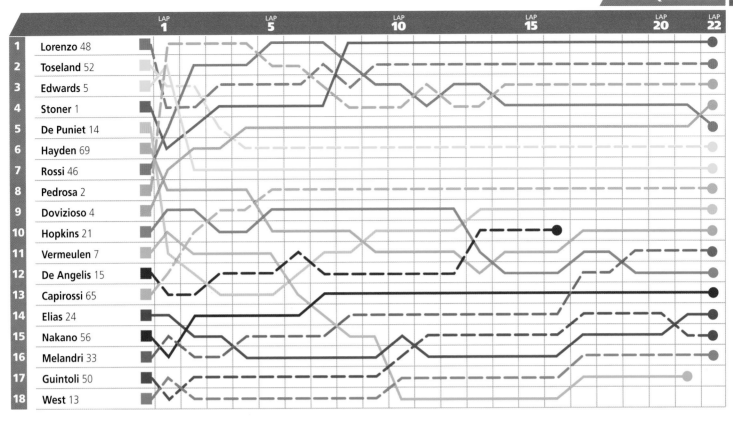

		LAP 1	LAP 5	LAP 10	LAP 15	LAP 20	LAP 22
1	Lorenzo 48						
2	Toseland 52						
3	Edwards 5						
4	Stoner 1						
5	De Puniet 14						
6	Hayden 69						
7	Rossi 46						
8	Pedrosa 2						
9	Dovizioso 4						
10	Hopkins 21						
11	Vermeulen 7						
12	De Angelis 15						
13	Capirossi 65						
14	Elias 24						
15	Nakano 56						
16	Melandri 33						
17	Guintoli 50						
18	West 13						

RACE

	Rider	Motorcycle	Race Time	Time +	Fastest Lap	Average Speed
1	Stoner	Ducati	42m 36.587s		1m 55.153s	103.565mph
2	Lorenzo	Yamaha	42m 41.910s	05.323s	1m 55.528s	103.350mph
3	Pedrosa	Honda	42m 47.187s	10.600s	1m 56.049s	103.138mph
4	Dovizioso	Honda	42m 49.875s	13.288s	1m 55.559s	103.030mph
5	Rossi	Yamaha	42m 49.892s	13.305s	1m 55.693s	103.029mph
6	Toseland	Yamaha	42m 50.627s	14.040s	1m 55.891s	103.000mph
7	Edwards	Yamaha	42m 51.737s	15.150s	1m 55.940s	102.956mph
8	Capirossi	Suzuki	43m 09.092s	32.505s	1m 56.689s	102.265mph
9	De Puniet	Honda	43m 09.590s	33.003s	1m 56.380s	102.245mph
10	Hayden	Honda	43m 14.941s	38.354s	1m 56.954s	102.351mph
11	Melandri	Ducati	43m 20.871s	44.284s	1m 56.972s	101.802mph
12	Hopkins	Kawasaki	43m 26.444s	49.857s	1m 56.491s	101.584mph
13	Nakano	Honda	43m 26.458s	49.871s	1m 57.124s	101.584mph
14	Elias	Ducati	43m 35.119s	58.532s	1m 57.841s	101.247mph
15	Guintoli	Ducati	43m 35.517s	58.930s	1m 57.753s	101.232mph
16	West	Kawasaki	43m 42.230s	1m 05.643s	1m 57.989s	100.973mph
17	Vermeulen	Suzuki	43m 11.483s	1 lap	1m 57.009s	97.526mph
	De Angelis	Honda	31m 26.773s	6 laps	1m 56.501s	102.059mph

CHAMPIONSHIP

	Rider	Team	Points
1	Stoner	Ducati Marlboro Team	25
2	Lorenzo	Fiat Yamaha Team	20
3	Pedrosa	Repsol Honda Team	16
4	Dovizioso	JiR Team Scot MotoGP	13
5	Rossi	Fiat Yamaha Team	11
6	Toseland	Tech 3 Yamaha	10
7	Edwards	Tech 3 Yamaha	9
8	Capirossi	Rizla Suzuki MotoGP	8
9	De Puniet	LCR Honda MotoGP	7
10	Hayden	Repsol Honda Team	6
11	Melandri	Ducati Marlboro Team	5
12	Hopkins	Kawasaki Racing Team	4
13	Nakano	San Carlo Honda Gresini	3
14	Elias	Alice Team	2
15	Guintoli	Alice Team	1

couldn't quite find that pace on race day and lost touch with the group after a couple of big scares going into corners: 'If you paid me a million dollars, I couldn't have gone any faster.'

8 LORIS CAPIROSSI Fully 17 seconds behind Edwards, but winner of his fight with the second group. Suzuki gave him a hybrid machine – the '08 motor with the previous year's chassis and aerodynamics. At least it went better than in pre-season tests, but not the start with a new team he'd hoped for.

9 RANDY DE PUNIET Two big front-end slides in the first two corners persuaded the Frenchman that discretion was the best plan. After half a dozen laps

started to attack and moved up from 13th to harass Capirossi's Suzuki in the final laps. A promising debut on the Honda.

10 NICKY HAYDEN In one of his favoured phrases, 'It wasn't pretty.' Distracted by the arrival of the '07 bikes: despite riding the new bike all winter decided to race last year's model. Hit terminal lack of grip, probably through spinning his rear tyre: 'I really think we just missed the set-up and worked the tyre way too hard.'

11 MARCO MELANDRI If anything could spoil Ducati's day it was the sight of their expensive new signing finishing 44 seconds behind Stoner. The only consolation was that Marco went better in the race than he had in testing, practice or qualifying.

12 JOHN HOPKINS Still nowhere near fit after tearing thigh muscles, Hopper could not use his knee to support the bike when the front tyre started to push. Perhaps more important, missing the bulk of winter testing meant the team was well behind on finding a base set-up.

13 SHINYA NAKANO A slight improvement on practice and qualifying, but not the return to Honda and Bridgestone that Shinya was hoping for. Not a good weekend for the Gresini team.

14 TONI ELIAS A second a lap slower than in warm-up and suffering 'many problems' with the front. Thought he was on for a top-ten finish but the troubles hit after only three laps; only found a good rhythm in the closing stages.

15 SYLVAIN GUINTOLI In contrast to his team-mate, the Frenchman started well but lost his rhythm after the tenth lap. Not helped by a heavy dose of man 'flu.

16 ANTHONY WEST A weekend to forget – went off track several times in practice and qualifying, and the last man on the grid. Things didn't get any better in the race, with the Aussie admitting it was more a matter of his confidence than anything to do with set-up.

17 CHRIS VERMEULEN Started well but pitted after five laps to replace a faulty front tyre. Went out again in case there was a point or two to be had.

NON-FINISHERS

ALEX DE ANGELIS Crashed out on the 17th lap trying too hard to make up for a distinct lack of top end. Never on the pace he set in testing and practice.

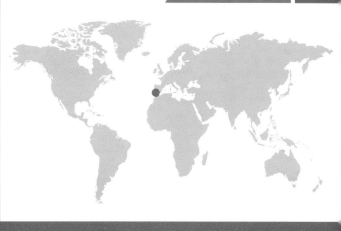

KING FOR A DAY

Pedrosa handed the rest a riding lesson, but the paddock seemed more interested in his feud with Lorenzo. Meanwhile, Rossi achieved his first rostrum with Bridgestone tyres as Stoner and Ducati suffered

It was a great day for Spain. Local heroes Lorenzo and Pedrosa qualified first and second and then both finished on the rostrum, split only by Valentino Rossi. They were presented with their reward by King Juan Carlos, the only man in Spain who could get the two sworn enemies to shake hands.

There are days when Dani Pedrosa looks unbeatable, and this was one of them. The numbers tell the story: in the 27-lap race he did the first 13 flying laps in the 1m 40s bracket and the next 12 in around 1m 41s, before allowing himself a slightly more relaxed final circuit. Those early laps varied by just 0.823 per cent and included a new lap record. The feat is even more remarkable because Dani missed out on the vast majority of winter testing thanks to a hand injury. It also showed that the Honda V4, still without its pneumatic-valve motor, was nevertheless a formidable and convincing machine. Nicky Hayden had a good weekend too, only losing touch with third place when he had a massive front-wheel slide at Turn 1. It was a carbon copy of an incident Colin Edwards had in practice as he, too, saved what looked like a certain crash when his right knee and elbow were on the ground. Pedrosa's race also demonstrated that Michelin had put their problems of the previous year firmly behind them.

Not that Bridgestone had a bad weekend. In the opening race of the year Valentino Rossi had said he'd had to ride defensively. In Jerez he was able to attack in the opening laps, after an average start, disposing of Lorenzo with relative ease to go second on the fourth lap. Thereafter he had to watch Pedrosa's Honda pulling inexorably away, but he could content himself

with his first rostrum finish on the Japanese tyres and the thought that he and the crew were learning very quickly how to set their Yamaha up for the new rubber. He did admit, though, that he might have been a little cautious early on in order to preserve his tyres, and almost handed second to Lorenzo right at the end when he shut off coming over the line to start the last lap – then Valentino saw the look on the face of the mechanic holding his pit board and realised his mistake.

It is a measure of the impact that Jorge Lorenzo had had on MotoGP in just two races that he was palpably disappointed with third place. He was fastest in qualifying again, the first time that a rookie has started from pole in his first two races in the top class, and he set it by the nowadays immense margin of 0.6s. In 2007 the top ten qualifiers had been covered by less than one-third of a second. Like the rest of the top four, Lorenzo had a comparatively uneventful race after the early skirmishes had established the riders in their positions. The same could not be said of the reigning World Champion.

Casey Stoner's problems started with a high-speed crash in practice followed by his worst qualifying since joining Ducati (with the single exception of the Motegi race in '07 when he went on to take the title). The real problem was that neither Casey nor the team could explain why he was suddenly having problems at a track where he had dominated testing effortlessly the previous month. Lack of feel with the front tyre was slowing him going into corners, an area where the

Aussie is usually brutally efficient. After a run-in with Loris Capirossi at the end of qualifying Stoner's race problems started with a second-lap slide which lost him two places, followed a lap later by an excursion into the gravel trap at the end of the back straight that put him at the rear of the field. From there he fought back up to the six-bike battle for fifth place that had been keeping the crowd entertained throughout the race, but an attempt to pass Nakano and Vermeulen in one move resulted in another trip through the same gravel trap he'd visited earlier, consigning Casey to 11th place. This time he blamed the Japanese rider for letting his brakes off and hitting his back wheel.

There wasn't any better news for Ducati elsewhere. Melandri, their other factory rider, was the slowest qualifier, with the two satellite team members, Elias and Guintoli, just in front of him. Only Marco made any progress in the race, and then it was merely to come 12th.

The exciting scrap for fifth was won by Capirossi on the final corner after a hectic set-to with impressive rookies James Toseland and Andrea Dovizioso. Toseland

'THIS IS MY FIRST MOTOGP WIN AT JEREZ, IT COMES AFTER A DIFFICULT TIME'
DANI PEDROSA

Opposite Loris Capirossi in typically aggressive style on the recalcitrant Suzuki

Left Nicky Hayden still didn't find much to like about his conventional valve-spring engine

ruffled a few feathers with passes at the end of the back straight. He'd found a front tyre that enabled him to carry 'unbelievable corner speed' which he then used to compensate for the lack of grunt from his conventional engine (although it was confirmed that the Tech 3 team would get the pneumatic-valve engines at the next round). Chris Vermeulen pointed to the rip in his leathers as evidence that James was too aggressive. The unrepentant Yorkshireman simply said he was paid to overtake people and that was the only way he could do it until he got the new motor. There was hope, too, for Kawasaki, with a nearly fit John Hopkins involved in that fight.

Much post-race attention was focused on whether Pedrosa and Lorenzo would acknowledge each other in any way. Their mutual dislike goes way back to their days in 250 GPs, and was in no way softened by their reunion in MotoGP. The latest chapter in this Spanish soap opera started on the rostrum in Qatar when, according to Lorenzo, Pedrosa refused to shake hands. The Spanish media immediately went into a feeding frenzy, encouraged by a couple of barbed remarks from Lorenzo. After qualifying, as they waited for their TV interviews, Jorge apparently asked Dani why he hadn't shaken hands: 'Why would I want to?' was the reported reply. Then there was Dani's hand gesture as he approached the chequered flag. What exactly did it mean? And if it was what some people said it was, was it aimed at Lorenzo's crew on the pit wall? News of the feud had obviously reached high places. Behind the rostrum, King Juan Carlos, a long-time motorcyclist and racing fan, grabbed both of them by the arm and brought their hands together.

Like all good soap operas, this one will run and run.

Above Dani Pedrosa celebrates the win at his home GP

Below The fight for fifth kept everyone entertained – it was decided on the last corner in favour of Loris Capirossi

Opposite Rossi demonstrating considerable faith in his Bridgestone front tyre

BY ROYAL APPOINTMENT

King Juan Carlos of Spain is no stranger to motorcycles. He doesn't just turn up to present the trophies when a Spanish rider is doing well, he rides on the roads and has a sizeable collection of bikes at his disposal. He lent his MV Agusta F4 to the Art of the Motorcycle exhibition that ran at the Guggenheim Museum in New York and there are stories of bikers encountering him on the road. The best-known concerns a rider who had run out of petrol. A guy on a Honda Dominator stopped and gave him a lift to the nearest fuel station and back. As he left, the Good Samaritan flicked up his visor and the biker realised his rescuer was King Juan Carlos I, Bourbon King of Spain.

Though the story may be apocryphal, it doesn't really matter because Spanish motorcyclists believe it – and one version includes the detail that the Honda rider was wearing a Sito Pons replica helmet. This was before the days of commercially available replica helmets and Spanish motorcycle champions like double 250cc World Champion Pons have been regular visitors to the royal residence on both formal and informal occasions. Sito had presented Juan Carlos with one of his helmets.

As well as Jerez, the King has visited the Catalunya circuit, politically a much more sensitive event. Spanish regional politics are a complex and dangerous business. Suffice to say that the Catalan audience doesn't always greet the Spanish national anthem with universal approval. In Andalucia, however, a region that also has its separatist agenda, the appearance of the monarch and the rendition of the anthem to celebrate Dani Pedrosa's victory were both met with raucous approval.

Above Sito Pons escorts King Juan Carlos on a tour of the Jerez pit lane

SPANISH GP
CIRCUITO DE JEREZ

ROUND 2
March 30

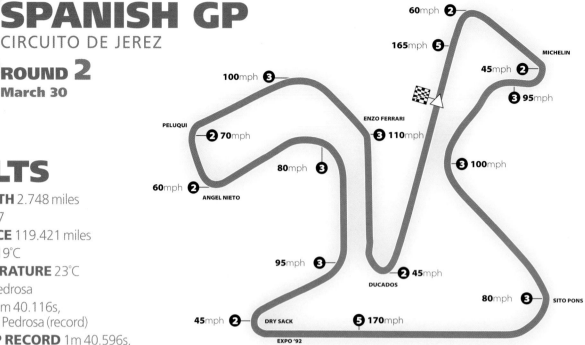

PELUQUI 70mph ②
60mph ② **ANGEL NIETO**
100mph ③
80mph ③
60mph ②
165mph ⑤
45mph ② **MICHELIN**
95mph ③
ENZO FERRARI 110mph ③
100mph ③
95mph ③
45mph ② **DUCADOS**
80mph ③ **SITO PONS**
45mph ② **DRY SACK**
170mph ⑤
EXPO '92

RACE RESULTS

CIRCUIT LENGTH 2.748 miles
NO. OF LAPS 27
RACE DISTANCE 119.421 miles
WEATHER Dry, 19°C
TRACK TEMPERATURE 23°C
WINNER Dani Pedrosa
FASTEST LAP 1m 40.116s, 98.829mph, Dani Pedrosa (record)
PREVIOUS LAP RECORD 1m 40.596s, 98.358mph, Valentino Rossi, 2005

QUALIFYING

	Rider	Nationality	Team	Qualifying	Pole +	Gap
1	Lorenzo	SPA	Fiat Yamaha Team	1m 38.189s		
2	Pedrosa	SPA	Repsol Honda Team	1m 38.789s	0.600s	0.600s
3	Edwards	USA	Tech 3 Yamaha	1m 38.954s	0.765s	0.165s
4	Hayden	USA	Repsol Honda Team	1m 39.061s	0.872s	0.107s
5	Rossi	ITA	Fiat Yamaha Team	1m 39.064s	0.875s	0.003s
6	De Puniet	FRA	LCR Honda MotoGP	1m 39.122s	0.933s	0.058s
7	Stoner	AUS	Ducati Marlboro Team	1m 39.286s	1.097s	0.164s
8	Toseland	GBR	Tech 3 Yamaha	1m 39.334s	1.145s	0.048s
9	Hopkins	USA	Kawasaki Racing Team	1m 39.439s	1.250s	0.105s
10	Capirossi	ITA	Rizla Suzuki MotoGP	1m 39.484s	1.295s	0.045s
11	Nakano	JPN	San Carlo Honda Gresini	1m 39.559s	1.370s	0.075s
12	Vermeulen	AUS	Rizla Suzuki MotoGP	1m 39.704s	1.515s	0.145s
13	Dovizioso	ITA	JiR Team Scot MotoGP	1m 39.767s	1.578s	0.063s
14	De Angelis	RSM	San Carlo Honda Gresini	1m 40.037s	1.848s	0.270s
15	West	AUS	Kawasaki Racing Team	1m 40.088s	1.899s	0.051s
16	Elias	SPA	Alice Team	1m 40.286s	2.097s	0.198s
17	Guintoli	FRA	Alice Team	1m 40.939s	2.750s	0.653s
18	Melandri	ITA	Ducati Marlboro Team	1m 41.027s	2.838s	0.088s

FINISHERS

1 DANI PEDROSA An immaculate start-to-finish victory to put him on top of the world standings for the first time in his MotoGP career. Also beat the lap record, set on a 990, by nearly half a second, the race record by more than eight seconds – and it was the first time he'd scored podium finishes in four successive races.

2 VALENTINO ROSSI First podium on Bridgestone tyres and his 100th in the MotoGP/500cc class, the first rider in the history of the sport to reach that milestone. His and the team's inexperience with the tyres showed in what Vale later admitted was a cautious start.

3 JORGE LORENZO Anyone who thought Qatar was a fluke was quickly disabused of that notion, but Jorge was disappointed with third – in only his second race! The first rider to score poles in his first two rides in the premier class, and the first since Biaggi in 1998 to score podium finishes in them.

4 NICKY HAYDEN Used the new chassis and immediately looked much happier than at Qatar. Ran with the leaders for the first half of the race, then dropped back, only to charge again in the closing stages. Thoughts of the rostrum evaporated when he lost the front big time at Turn 1 and did well to pick it up on his knee.

5 LORIS CAPIROSSI Came out on top in a last-corner fracas with Toseland and Dovizioso, the old Capirossi aggression giving Suzuki its best MotoGP result at Jerez. Didn't qualify particularly well and certainly didn't regard fifth as the limit of his ambitions.

6 JAMES TOSELAND Rattled a few cages with some brutal overtakes at the end of the back straight. Came out of the last-corner melee losing just one place after Dovizioso took him wide and Capirossi got both of them. First British rider since Mackenzie in 1990 to score back-to-back top-six places – doubly impressive as he was suffering from bronchitis.

7 JOHN HOPKINS Just about recovered from his pre-season injury but still ruing the loss of valuable testing time. Got into a good race rhythm after a frenetic opening few laps

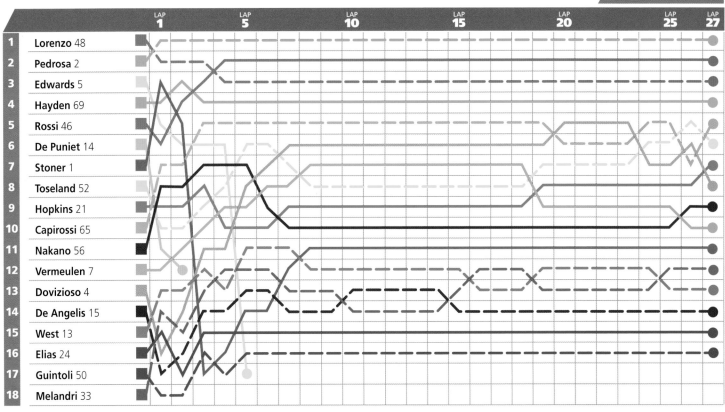

		LAP 1	LAP 5	LAP 10	LAP 15	LAP 20	LAP 25	LAP 27
1	Lorenzo 48							
2	Pedrosa 2							
3	Edwards 5							
4	Hayden 69							
5	Rossi 46							
6	De Puniet 14							
7	Stoner 1							
8	Toseland 52							
9	Hopkins 21							
10	Capirossi 65							
11	Nakano 56							
12	Vermeulen 7							
13	Dovizioso 4							
14	De Angelis 15							
15	West 13							
16	Elias 24							
17	Guintoli 50							
18	Melandri 33							

RACE

	Rider	Motorcycle	Race Time	Time +	Fastest Lap	Average Speed
1	Pedrosa	Honda	45m 35.121s		1m 40.116s	97.673mph
2	Rossi	Yamaha	45m 38.004s	2.883s	1m 40.192s	97.570mph
3	Lorenzo	Yamaha	45m 39.460s	4.339s	1m 40.540s	97.518mph
4	Hayden	Honda	45m 45.263s	10.142s	1m 40.671s	97.312mph
5	Capirossi	Suzuki	46m 02.645s	27.524s	1m 40.402s	96.700mph
6	Toseland	Yamaha	46m 02.929s	27.808s	1m 41.327s	96.690mph
7	Hopkins	Kawasaki	46m 03.417s	28.296s	1m 41.336s	96.673mph
8	Dovizioso	Honda	46m 03.570s	28.449s	1m 40.675s	96.668mph
9	Nakano	Honda	46m 07.690s	32.569s	1m 41.560s	96.523mph
10	Vermeulen	Suzuki	46m 10.212s	35.091s	1m 41.199s	96.436mph
11	Stoner	Ducati	46m 17.344s	42.223s	1m 41.386s	96.188mph
12	Melandri	Ducati	46m 19.619s	44.498s	1m 41.735s	96.110mph
13	West	Kawasaki	46m 20.928s	45.807s	1m 41.767s	96.064mph
14	De Angelis	Honda	46m 20.992s	45.871s	1m 41.982s	96.062mph
15	Elias	Ducati	46m 44.679s	1m 09.558s	1m 42.515s	95.251mph
16	Guintoli	Ducati	46m 49.563s	1m 14.442s	1m 42.880s	95.085mph
	Edwards	Yamaha	9m 10.348s	22 laps	1m 40.700s	89.892mph
	De Puniet	Honda	3m 31.127s	25 laps	1m 41.645s	93.729mph

CHAMPIONSHIP

	Rider	Team	Points
1	Pedrosa	Repsol Honda Team	41
2	Lorenzo	Fiat Yamaha Team	36
3	Rossi	Fiat Yamaha Team	31
4	Stoner	Ducati Marlboro Team	30
5	Dovizioso	JiR Team Scot MotoGP	21
6	Toseland	Tech 3 Yamaha	20
7	Hayden	Repsol Honda Team	19
8	Capirossi	Rizla Suzuki MotoGP	19
9	Hopkins	Kawasaki Racing Team	13
10	Nakano	San Carlo Honda Gresini	10
11	Edwards	Tech 3 Yamaha	9
12	Melandri	Ducati Marlboro Team	9
13	De Puniet	LCR Honda MotoGP	7
14	Vermeulen	Rizla Suzuki MotoGP	6
15	West	Kawasaki Racing Team	3
16	Elias	Alice Team	3
17	De Angelis	San Carlo Honda Gresini	2
18	Guintoli	Alice Team	1

and was in a position to take advantage of Dovizioso's over-enthusiasm at the last corner.

8 ANDREA DOVIZIOSO Another really impressive ride from the rookie that was even better than the result suggests: 16th at the end of the first lap and up to sixth by lap seven. From then on it was a fight with Toseland and Capirossi, going into the last corner in sixth but way wide and losing two places.

9 SHINYA NAKANO A good weekend that saw lap times come down with every session. Made up places off the start, tangled with Stoner towards the end as he was dicing with Vermeulen, and eventually got the better of the Suzuki rider.

10 CHRIS VERMEULEN Picked too soft a compound for his rear tyre so his pace dropped right off in the last couple of laps, although his biggest problem again was qualifying, this time down in 12th.

11 CASEY STONER Jerez was even unkinder than it had been a year ago, with an early off-track excursion and a late-race tangle with Nakano producing his worst result since joining Ducati. Given a clean race he reckoned he should have finished fifth, exactly where he was in 2007.

12 MARCO MELANDRI Came good in the second half of the race, on the brakes and into corners, just like in Qatar, but again complained of lack of grip under acceleration.

13 ANTHONY WEST Another story of lack of traction at the rear. Ant seemed able to deal with Melandri in the early stages but not when the rear tyre started going off badly. Was able to fend off de Angelis in the closing stages.

14 ALEX DE ANGELIS Not happy, and worried that the traction control settings were slowing him down, so much so that he wasn't getting out of corners and was being overtaken on the straights.

15 TONI ELIAS A dismal result at a circuit where he has previously gone well. Never found a direction to go with in set-up: 'This performance hurts.'

16 SYLVAIN GUINTOLI Just as unhappy as team-mate Elias. 'Honestly, I don't

understand why I am so slow.' Turned the bike inside out as regards set-up and trying to change his riding style, but all to no avail.

NON-FINISHERS

COLIN EDWARDS Pushing hard to make up for lack of power (the Tech 3 team would not get the pneumatic-valve Yamaha motor until the next race) and lost the front end. Made the save of the season, picking the bike up off his elbow, when the same thing happened in practice.

RANDY DE PUNIET Lost several positions off the start, having qualified sixth, then crashed when he lost the front on lap three.

PORTUGUESE GP

ESTORIL

ROUND **3**

April 13

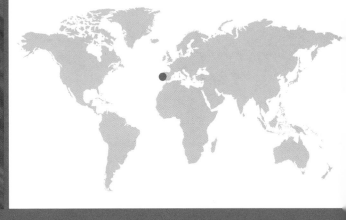

THE EGO HAS LANDED

Three races, three pole positions and now a win – there's never been a rookie quite like Jorge Lorenzo. Who would have thought he'd win a race before his team-mate?

It is almost impossible to overstate Jorge Lorenzo's achievement in winning the Portuguese Grand Prix, his third race in the top class, from pole position, setting the fastest lap and going joint top of the championship. No rookie had ever started from pole position in his first three races – not even Jaarno Saarinen or Max Biaggi, who had both arrived in the old 500 class and immediately challenged the hegemony of great champions Agostini and Doohan. Lorenzo started his premier-class career by overshadowing his team-mate, the seven-times World Champion Valentino Rossi. Actually, calling them team-mates is stretching a point. They both race under the banner of the Fiat Yamaha squad but there is a wall both literal and metaphorical down the middle of the team's pit garage, for Rossi switched to Bridgestone tyres over winter while Lorenzo, along with the Yamaha satellite team riders, uses Michelin. This schism had a lot to do with the outcome of the Portuguese GP, a race that has always been problematical for the Japanese tyre company.

Rossi knew that he would be in tyre trouble for the last ten laps and ran his race accordingly. Starting from his first front-row grid position using Bridgestones, he barged past holeshot man Pedrosa at Turn 3, blocked a charge from Lorenzo at the next corner and set a pace in the low 1m 38s bracket for almost half the race, as the two Spaniards continued their personal battle behind him. 'I tried to ride very smooth to save the tyre,' said Rossi. 'I wait for Lorenzo and Pedrosa.' It looked for a while as if he might be waiting for Andrea Dovizioso, Nicky Hayden and John Hopkins as well. The young Italian made a stunning start from the third row of the grid and clung on to the leading trio for just over half

Above It's a long run down to Estoril's first corner, one of the heaviest braking efforts of the season

Below The rocky outcrops of Portugal's Atlantic coast provide some unusual viewing angles

the race. Hopper, nearly fully fit again, could run the leaders' pace for about the same distance before the onset of front-end chatter saw him more concerned with Casey Stoner closing from behind than what was happening in front of him. Then the two Honda men crashed out within a lap of each other at the same corner, the downhill right before the chicane. Both were unapologetic: Hayden said he was simply not going to finish fourth again, Dovi knew he had to push the front on the way into corners to be able to stay with the factory bikes – and staying with them was the only way he was going to learn. Neither man blamed the sprinkling of rain that blew through just before their crashes; Lorenzo taking the lead a lap earlier and immediately dropping the race pace to 1m 37s was far more relevant.

Jorge made his move on lap 13 of the 28, or more accurately, he made an astonishing double move. The first was to take second off Pedrosa with a regulation outbraking manoeuvre at the first corner, but his pass on Rossi to take the lead was anything but run of

the mill. Estoril's chicane is the slowest corner on the calendar and a place that has caused more than its fair share of crashes. The first part is a better than 90-degree uphill left-hander; Lorenzo went to the inside there and made what looked like a clean pass in the most unlikely of corners, although he later said he should apologise to Rossi for a 'very crazy overtake'. It took two more laps for Pedrosa to take second, by which time Lorenzo already had a lead of over half a second. Three laps later it was a full second. Both men only dropped back into the 1m 38s bracket a couple of times for the rest of the race, leaving Rossi grateful that Dovi and Hayden, who looked likely to challenge him for the final rostrum position, had crashed. Colin Edwards, using the pneumatic-valve Yamaha engine for the first time, ended up fourth but again unhappy with his performance despite it being his best result since July the previous year – he reckoned he should have been on the rostrum.

Stoner had an eventful race, but not in a good way. He again looked out of sorts in practice, running off

'I REMEMBER MAKING MY PASS ON VALENTINO; IT WAS QUITE A RISK, SO I'M SORRY TO HIM'
JORGE LORENZO

Above John Hopkins' fifth place would prove to be a season highlight both for the rider and the Kawasaki team

Below Randy de Puniet tries to distract James Toseland. The Frenchman got back on and salvaged a point

Opposite Stoner's race was ruined by a bizarre problem with a TV control box flapping around on its cable

track several times and crashing once. In the race he suffered from a fault that was not of his or Ducati's making. A control box, part of the on-board TV camera equipment, came loose from its mounting in the fairing's nose and flapped about on its cable. Casey had to take his left hand off the bars on the main straight at around 190mph and stuff the thing back in place, not once but several times. Turbulence would then rip the black box back off its Velcro and it would spend the rest of the lap getting tangled with the handlebar and clutch lever and doing nothing for the Aussie's ability to concentrate on the race. He did consider ripping it off its wire, but as he didn't know what it was he thought that might be a bad idea. Dorna's TV people were quick to apologise after the race. Under the circumstances, and given that Estoril has never been a happy hunting ground for Ducati or Bridgestone, sixth place can probably be considered a decent result.

Portugal brought a few issues into sharp focus. First, Rossi was finding adapting his Yamaha to Bridgestones 'very difficult', yet he had managed to get on the rostrum in two out of the first three races of the year. Second, Ducati's difficulties in Jerez were not an aberration. And third, Jorge Lorenzo was most definitely a very special racer. As he stuck the inevitable 'Lorenzo's Land' flag into the Portuguese gravel trap as a MotoGP winner and joint points leader it was impossible not to wonder how many other territories he was going to annex before the end of the season. There was also the growing suspicion that this rampant rookie, the youngest man on the grid, might just be a genuine championship contender.

TECH 3

In among the general worries about finances and the future, one team could contemplate its prospects with equanimity. Tech 3, the French squad which had only managed to stay in the paddock for the last couple of seasons by being paid to act as Dunlop's development team, had a storming start to 2008. Back on Michelins and benefiting from Yamaha's satellite bikes being very close in specification to the factory team's equipment, both their riders were competitive from the first race. At Estoril team principal Hervé Poncharal secured his operation for the next two years by extending the agreement with Yamaha to the 2010 season and taking up the option he held on James Toseland for 2009. Yamaha also delivered pneumatic-valve engines on schedule, to the delight of both riders.

As in previous seasons, Tech 3 is not cash rich so Edwards's contract is with Yamaha, not the team. The plan was for Colin to leave MotoGP at the end of the season and ride in the 2009 AMA Superbike Championship on the factory's new model R1. Yamaha have spent a lot of money in the American Superbike Championship to no effect, and Edwards has also been expressing a desire to rediscover his homeland and spend more time with his two young children. However, uncertainty over the AMA Championship's regulations and Colin's cracking form – not unconnected with the fantastic working atmosphere within the Tech 3 team – had already given rise to manager and rider intimating that they would be quite happy to maintain the status quo for another season.

PORTUGESE GP

ESTORIL

ROUND 3
April 13

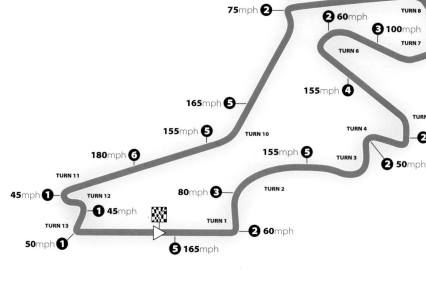

RACE RESULTS

CIRCUIT LENGTH 2.599 miles
NO. OF LAPS 28
RACE DISTANCE 72.772 miles
WEATHER Dry, 18°C
TRACK TEMPERATURE 21°C
WINNER Jorge Lorenzo
FASTEST LAP 1m 37.404s,
96.046mph, Jorge Lorenzo (record)
PREVIOUS LAP RECORD 1m 37.493s,
95.958mph, Nicky Hayden, 2007

QUALIFYING

	Rider	Nationality	Team	Qualifying	Pole +	Gap
1	Lorenzo	SPA	Fiat Yamaha Team	1m 35.715s		
2	Pedrosa	SPA	Repsol Honda Team	1m 35.948s	0.233s	0.233s
3	Rossi	ITA	Fiat Yamaha Team	1m 36.199s	0.484s	0.251s
4	Hayden	USA	Repsol Honda Team	1m 36.266s	0.551s	0.067s
5	Edwards	USA	Tech 3 Yamaha	1m 36.289s	0.574s	0.023s
6	Toseland	GBR	Tech 3 Yamaha	1m 36.790s	1.075s	0.501s
7	Dovizioso	ITA	JiR Team Scot MotoGP	1m 36.998s	1.283s	0.208s
8	De Puniet	FRA	LCR Honda MotoGP	1m 37.223s	1.508s	0.225s
9	Stoner	AUS	Ducati Team Marlboro	1m 37.253s	1.538s	0.030s
10	Hopkins	USA	Kawasaki Racing Team	1m 37.346s	1.631s	0.093s
11	Nakano	JPN	San Carlo Honda Gresini	1m 37.664s	1.949s	0.318s
12	Capirossi	ITA	Rizla Suzuki MotoGP	1m 37.786s	2.071s	0.122s
13	Vermeulen	AUS	Rizla Suzuki MotoGP	1m 37.843s	2.128s	0.057s
14	Elias	SPA	Alice Team	1m 38.561s	2.846s	0.718s
15	West	AUS	Kawasaki Racing Team	1m 38.775s	3.060s	0.214s
16	De Angelis	RSM	San Carlo Honda Gresini	1m 38.823s	3.108s	0.048s
17	Melandri	ITA	Ducati Marlboro Team	1m 39.115s	3.400s	0.292s
18	Guintoli	FRA	Alice Team	1m 39.355s	3.640s	0.240s

FINISHERS

1 JORGE LORENZO Another pole and a storming race, overtaking bitter rival Pedrosa and Rossi on the same lap, then controlling proceedings from the front. Broke all the records for a rookie in his first three races and went joint top of the table. All this and he says he needs an operation to cure arm pump.

2 DANI PEDROSA Watched Rossi and Lorenzo as the trio pulled away from the field, then took Vale as his Bridgestones started to fade but couldn't reel in his fellow-countryman. Delighted to be so competitive after missing most pre-season tests, and if he was annoyed at being beaten by Lorenzo he concealed it well.

3 VALENTINO ROSSI Always knew this would be a difficult track for Bridgestone tyres, especially in the last ten laps, so went to the front to try and control the pace. Couldn't go with Lorenzo and didn't even try to defend when Pedrosa came past. Definitely made the best of the situation.

4 COLIN EDWARDS Best result since Germany '07, achieved with the help of the pneumatic-valve engine the team had been waiting for. Rain early on meant he didn't get heat into the tyre's edge and was lacking edge grip. Was in better shape when it dried, but had the nagging feeling he should've been on the rostrum.

5 JOHN HOPKINS Best-ever result at Estoril for a Kawasaki rider and a career best here for

John. Only qualified in tenth but made up five spots off the start, struggled at mid-distance with front-end chatter, then pressed hard to keep Stoner at a safe distance. Just the sort of encouragement the team needed.

6 CASEY STONER Struggled in practice and qualifying, then had to deal with a TV control box coming off its mountings in the race and flapping about on its cable: he had to stuff it back in the fairing every lap. Was relieved to escape with sixth place under the circumstances. Not happy though, not at all.

7 JAMES TOSELAND Another impressive showing, this time on a track he'd never seen before, putting him fifth in the table, the highest a British rider has been since Mackenzie finished the 1990 season in fourth. Handicapped by losing an hour of

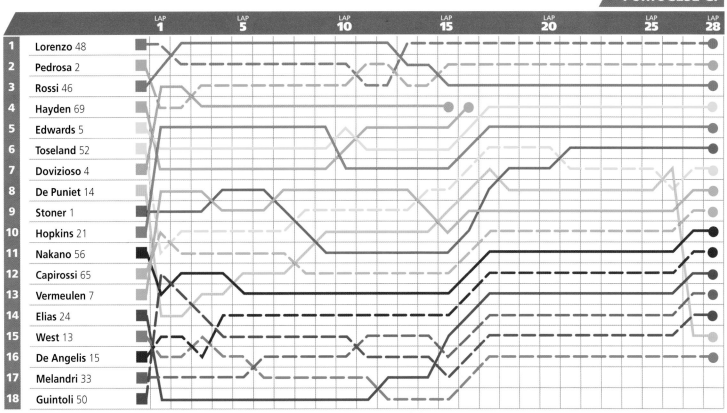

		LAP 1	LAP 5	LAP 10	LAP 15	LAP 20	LAP 25	LAP 28
1	Lorenzo 48							
2	Pedrosa 2							
3	Rossi 46							
4	Hayden 69							
5	Edwards 5							
6	Toseland 52							
7	Dovizioso 4							
8	De Puniet 14							
9	Stoner 1							
10	Hopkins 21							
11	Nakano 56							
12	Capirossi 65							
13	Vermeulen 7							
14	Elias 24							
15	West 13							
16	De Angelis 15							
17	Melandri 33							
18	Guintoli 50							

RACE

	Rider	Motorcycle	Race Time	Time +	Fastest Lap	Average Speed
1	Lorenzo	Yamaha	45m 53.089s		1m 37.404s	95.146mph
2	Pedrosa	Honda	45m 54.906s	1.817s	1m 37.471s	95.084mph
3	Rossi	Yamaha	46m 05.812s	12.723s	1m 37.975s	94.708mph
4	Edwards	Yamaha	46m 10.312s	17.223s	1m 38.083s	94.555mph
5	Hopkins	Kawasaki	46m 16.841s	23.752s	1m 38.228s	94.332mph
6	Stoner	Ducati	46m 19.777s	26.688s	1m 37.972s	94.233mph
7	Toseland	Yamaha	46m 25.720s	32.631s	1m 38.721s	94.032mph
8	Vermeulen	Suzuki	46m 29.471s	36.382s	1m 38.750s	93.905mph
9	Capirossi	Suzuki	46m 31.357s	38.268s	1m 38.773s	93.842mph
10	Nakano	Honda	46m 32.565s	39.476s	1m 38.666s	93.801mph
11	De Angelis	Honda	46m 54.395s	1m 01.306s	1m 39.454s	93.073mph
12	Elias	Ducati	46m 56.956s	1m 03.867s	1m 39.439s	92.989mph
13	Melandri	Ducati	47m 02.614s	1m 09.525s	1m 39.387s	92.802mph
14	Guintoli	Ducati	47m 02.723s	1m 09.634s	1m 39.811s	92.799mph
15	De Puniet	Honda	47m 04.631s	1m 11.542s	1m 38.291s	92.737mph
16	West	Kawasaki	47m 16.718s	1m 23.629s	1m 40.099s	92.341mph
	Hayden	Honda	26m 23.675s	12 laps	1m 37.806s	94.516mph
	Dovizioso	Honda	24m 43.870s	13 laps	1m 37.985s	94.569mph

CHAMPIONSHIP

	Rider	Team	Points
1	Lorenzo	Fiat Yamaha Team	61
2	Pedrosa	Repsol Honda Team	61
3	Rossi	Fiat Yamaha Team	47
4	Stoner	Ducati Marlboro Team	40
5	Toseland	Tech 3 Yamaha	29
6	Capirossi	Rizla Suzuki MotoGP	26
7	Hopkins	Kawasaki Racing Team	24
8	Edwards	Tech 3 Yamaha	22
9	Dovizioso	JiR Team Scot MotoGP	21
10	Hayden	Repsol Honda Team	19
11	Nakano	San Carlo Honda Gresini	16
12	Vermeulen	Rizla Suzuki MotoGP	14
13	Melandri	Ducati Marlboro Team	12
14	De Puniet	LCR Honda MotoGP	8
15	De Angelis	San Carlo Honda Gresini	7
16	Elias	Alice Team	7
17	West	Kawasaki Racing Team	3
18	Guintoli	Alice Team	3

practice to the weather and a tentative start under light rain.

8 CHRIS VERMEULEN Best result of the season so far despite another disappointing qualifying session. Made amends with a first lap that took him from 13th to eighth, then involved in a good group dice with Toseland, de Puniet and Stoner. Had to ease up when the front wheel developed vibration.

9 LORIS CAPIROSSI Disappointed not to be able to run the lap times he had in practice. Thought he'd be competitive on race day, but found he was struggling for grip from the start.

10 SHINYA NAKANO Had trouble finding his rhythm in the first part of the race but just before mid-distance was able to improve his

lap times and catch Capirossi. Closed to within a second and tracked him to the flag but couldn't put a pass on the Suzuki.

11 ALEX DE ANGELIS Improved on his qualifying position despite a nasty bout of 'flu. Found himself alone very early on and had problems keeping his concentration. Not happy with being outside the top eight, a feeling shared by his team-manager who called it 'another unexceptional race'.

12 TONI ELIAS At last some hope for Toni. Despite a bad start, started to pick up the pace after ten laps as the fuel load lightened, passing the Ducatis of Melandri and team-mate Guintoli in one lap for a respectable finish. More significantly, it looked as if the team had found a direction to work in.

13 MARCO MELANDRI Qualifying next to last and being beaten by a satellite team bike shows just how hard he struggled in practice without getting near a usable set-up. All he could do was look forward to China, where the Shanghai track might suit the Ducati better than Estoril.

14 SYLVAIN GUINTOLI Very fast in Sunday morning warm-up on a wet track – unfortunately the track dried for the race. Estoril is his least favoured circuit yet said he'd learned valuable facts about the bike's behaviour in a vital area, the first phase of acceleration coming out of corners. Only a tenth behind Melandri at the flag.

15 RANDY DE PUNIET Another bad start – his third in three races – followed by an impressive fight back to seventh place. Was

lining up Toseland two laps from the flag when he lost the front and slid off, but fortunately able to remount and claim the last point.

16 ANTHONY WEST His season-long struggle with rear traction took another turn for the worse as, for once, he couldn't improve on his practice and qualifying times. The Aussie described his feeling as 'intense frustration' rather than disappointment.

NON-FINISHERS

NICKY HAYDEN Could see the top three and didn't want to finish fourth again, so pressed hard and lost the front at the downhill right-hander on lap 17.

ANDREA DOVIZIOSO Lying fourth for just over half the race, matching the pace of the leading trio and – most impressively – never more than a second behind. Was working the front tyre hard going into corners to make up for a lack of straight-line speed and crashed at exactly the same point as Hayden.

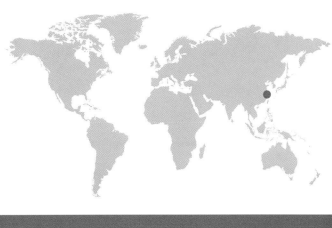

RETURN OF THE KING

Four races, four winners, riding four different bike/tyre combinations – who said the 800s were boring? And who really expected it to take Rossi and his crew just four races to learn how to win on Bridgestone tyres?

By his own standards, this wasn't one of Valentino Rossi's major miracles, yet it was significant in many ways. It was obviously a personal triumph – he stopped on the slow-down lap to embrace his Yamaha and savour the moment – and it had taken him only four races to win on Bridgestone tyres, putting an end to the questions about whether the divorce from Michelin had been a mistake. The Doctor's victory also ended his longest-ever barren streak in the top class, stretching back the best part of eight months to Estoril last season. Even a multiple champion must have been prey to some doubts in that time, surely?

What may well be the last Chinese GP for some time turned into a demonstration of the ultra-professionalism of both Rossi and his pit crew, led by Jerry Burgess. Conditions on race day were so different from anything the riders had seen in practice or qualifying that many, if not most, were caught out in one way or another. During heavy rain which only just stopped in time for the MotoGP race the track temperature dropped a dramatic 25 degrees C from Saturday's reading, and what had been a slight headwind on the back straight swung round to become a gale-force tailwind. Anyone watching the 125 race carefully would have noticed riders sticking their knees out into the slipstream on that straight to prevent their engines over-revving in top gear. Rossi's pit was obviously paying attention.

The second Fiat Yamaha rider was lucky to be able to race at all. Jorge Lorenzo's almost too good to be true start to his rookie season came down to earth literally and figuratively in the first practice session when he highsided, cracking bones in one ankle and damaging ligaments in the other. It wasn't a fast crash – he could

hardly have found a slower corner all year – but he went two metres up in the air, doing a handstand at the apex of his flight path, and slammed down feet first. Not surprisingly he missed the Friday afternoon session, yet on Saturday he qualified fourth. That's not bad for a man with only one fully functioning limb (he had surgery on his right arm to relieve compartment syndrome after the Portuguese race), although he did have to suffer the indignity of remaining seated on his bike when he came into the pit garage and being wheeled about like a child learning to ride a pedal cycle. If there was a major miracle in the race it was probably Lorenzo's ride to fourth place – on his twenty-first birthday.

The surprise of not just the race but of practice as well was Casey Stoner's comparative lack of pace. On the evidence of the previous year Shanghai should have been a track that suited the Ducati; in fact it was easy to make the case that if Ducati couldn't win here then the problems of the previous two races weren't illusory. Stoner finished a puzzled third, unable to work out why he couldn't run the same lap times as he had the previous year. The medium-compound rear tyre got the blame after the race – they should have stayed with the hard rubber Casey usually races on – but that didn't fully explain his third place on the grid. The only session in which he was fastest was the second free practice and he couldn't lap below two minutes in the race, while Rossi did twelve sub-two-minuters and second-placed Dani Pedrosa eight.

Pedrosa, the only man to make Rossi work during the race, found himself under-geared. On the first lap he realised he was over-revving on the long straight but thought it might be because he was catching someone's

slipstream. When he still found himself over-revving while leading he realised he was in trouble, and never tried to exploit the slipstream of Rossi's Yamaha after the Italian took the lead on the fifth lap. Nevertheless, Dani kept the pressure on after Rossi got over his usual average start, pressing the Italian hard until the end of the 19th (of 22) laps. After trading fastest laps, they both set their personal best times on lap 18, by which time Rossi's race lead had crept up to nearly half a second.

The Spanish rider now realised there was going to be no repeat of Portugal, where Valentino's tyres had gone off in the second half of the race, so, fearful for his engine's health, he settled for second place. That was the HRC party line, and indeed the RCV sounded decidedly flat in the closing laps, but that could well have been down to the engine-management system leaning the motor off to save fuel and ensure the bike got to the flag. Honda, of course, denied there was any issue with fuel consumption.

Other potential challengers, like pole-man and early leader Colin Edwards, lost touch when they ran on at the end of the main straight or found they'd made the wrong tyre choice for the conditions. Rookies Dovizioso and Toseland found Shanghai a lot more difficult to come to terms with than they had expected and faded after promising starts. The reverse was true of Lorenzo, who fought back from ninth place, and Marco Melandri,

'I WAS ABLE TO RIDE THE BIKE LIKE I WANT TO THE END'
VALENTINO ROSSI

Opposite Jorge Lorenzo suffered the mother of all highsides during practice; his feet took most of the impact...

Below The twin wings of the Shanghai International Circuit dwarf pole position man Colin Edwards

who at last looked as if he'd worked out how to ride
the Desmosedici. Marco did even more overtaking than
Jorge, fighting back to fifth place after being eleventh
at the end of the first lap. Ducati's hopes were further
buoyed by Toni Elias's eighth place, his best of the
season so far, on the satellite team's Alice Ducati. John
Hopkins – a rostrum finisher a year ago – and the rest
of the Kawasaki team found out the hard way that they
were seriously lacking top-end power. In his 100th GP,
Hopper ran off track more than once trying to make up
for the lack of go.

Everywhere in the paddock teams were worrying
about the implications of their performance in the

Chinese GP, but they were worrying more about the sight
of Valentino Rossi on top of the rostrum again. A look at
the timing sheets only increased the stress: Vale had been
able to up his pace all through the race, so that every
time Pedrosa pushed Rossi was able to respond. 'I was
able to ride the bike like I want to the end.' Burgess and
his rider agreed that there was still more to come from
the Yamaha–Bridgestone combination. And that's exactly
what the rest didn't want to hear.

There was something incongruous about Rossi's
podium appearance however, although it took a while to
realise what it was. He still doesn't look quite right in a
red hat.

ENTER THE DRAGON

There will be a new name on the 125cc GP grid in 2009: Maxtra. The team is to be fronted by the great John Surtees with ex-Suzuki manager Garry Taylor assisting, ex-Aprilia technical guru Jan Witteveen designing the motor and English specialists Harris Performance doing the chassis.

The impetus, though, comes from the giant Chinese Haojue company, the country's largest manufacturer. Haojue is a brand name of the Great River Group (GRG) which made over three million motorcycles in 2007, yet very few people outside China would even know of it. And that, of course, is the point. Anyone who remembers a funny little Japanese company called Honda turning up at the Isle of Man TT in 1959 will now be experiencing a sense of déjà vu. As Surtees himself pointed out, 'The Japanese industry first came to world attention via GP racing. The Maxtra has many echoes of those times.'

Maxtra is intended to be the spearhead of the Chinese industry's breakout from its local markets, and racing is seen not just as a marketing exercise, although GRG chose the name with an eye to future export markets. The intention of team MD Xunmeng 'Simon' Wei is to integrate factory engineers into the squad with a view to building a future full factory racing department along the lines of Honda's HRC.

The reed-valve bike shown at Shanghai was certainly an interesting and innovative design and, even more impressively, it was running in shakedown tests on English tracks before mid-season, turning the sort of lap

times that would have made it competitive in the British Championship.

If GRG's foray onto the world stage is successful, other Chinese companies are bound to follow. How big is the industry? There are ten manufacturers apart from GRG who each make over one million bikes a year.

CHINESE GP
SHANGHAI INTERNATIONAL CIRCUIT

ROUND 4
May 4

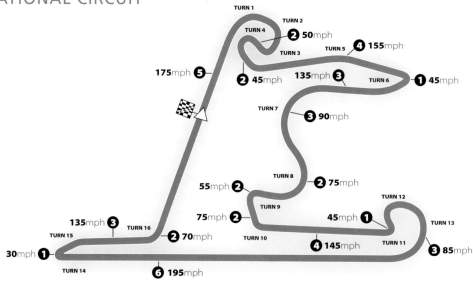

TURN 1
TURN 2
TURN 4 ② 50mph
TURN 3
TURN 5 ④ 155mph
175mph ⑤
② 45mph
135mph ③
TURN 6 ① 45mph
TURN 7 ③ 90mph
TURN 8
② 75mph
55mph ②
TURN 12
TURN 9
45mph ①
TURN 13
75mph ②
135mph ③
TURN 16
② 70mph
TURN 10
TURN 11
④ 145mph
③ 85mph
TURN 15
30mph ①
TURN 14
⑥ 195mph

RACE RESULTS

CIRCUIT LENGTH 3.218 miles
NO. OF LAPS 22
RACE DISTANCE 72.182 miles
WEATHER Wet, 21°C
TRACK TEMPERATURE 21°C
WINNER Valentino Rossi
FASTEST LAP 1m 59.273s, 99.048mph, Valentino Rossi (record)
PREVIOUS LAP RECORD 1m 59.318s, 99.011mph, Dani Pedrosa, 2006

QUALIFYING

	Rider	Nationality	Team	Qualifying	Pole +	Gap
1	Edwards	USA	Tech 3 Yamaha	1m 58.139s		
2	Rossi	ITA	Fiat Yamaha Team	1m 58.494s	0.355s	0.355s
3	Stoner	AUS	Ducati Marlboro Team	1m 58.591s	0.452s	0.097s
4	Lorenzo	SPA	Fiat Yamaha Team	1m 58.711s	0.572s	0.120s
5	Pedrosa	SPA	Repsol Honda Team	1m 58.855s	0.716s	0.144s
6	Capirossi	ITA	Rizla Suzuki MotoGP	1m 58.941s	0.802s	0.086s
7	Toseland	GBR	Tech 3 Yamaha	1m 59.254s	1.115	0.313s
8	Vermeulen	AUS	Rizla Suzuki MotoGP	1m 59.325s	1.186s	0.071s
9	De Puniet	FRA	LCR Honda MotoGP	1m 59.357s	1.218s	0.032s
10	Hayden	USA	Repsol Honda Team	1m 59.507s	1.368s	0.150s
11	Dovizioso	ITA	JiR Team Scot MotoGP	1m 59.559s	1.420s	0.052s
12	Melandri	ITA	Ducati Marlboro Team	1m 59.678s	1.539s	0.119s
13	Nakano	JPN	San Carlo Honda Gresini	1m 59.716s	1.577s	0.038s
14	Hopkins	USA	Kawasaki Racing Team	1m 59.740s	1.601s	0.024s
15	Elias	SPA	Alice Team	1m 59.933s	1.794s	0.193s
16	De Angelis	RSM	San Carlo Honda Gresini	2m 00.316s	2.177s	0.383s
17	Guintoli	FRA	Alice Team	2m 00.760s	2.621s	0.444s
18	West	AUS	Kawasaki Racing Team	2m 00.838s	2.699s	0.078s

FINISHERS

1 VALENTINO ROSSI First win since Portugal '07, seven races ago, and his first on Bridgestone tyres. Able to respond every time Pedrosa put pressure on, setting best lap four laps from the flag, with none of the tyre problems that had dogged him in previous rounds. Out of the 104 races run under MotoGP regulations he has now won 50.

2 DANI PEDROSA Found his bike over-rewving on the long straight from lap one thanks to a strong tailwind, so didn't dare take Rossi's slipstream, but piled the pressure on until four laps from the flag, then started worrying about the gearshift tightening up. May also have been running into fuel consumption problems.

3 CASEY STONER Went for a softer tyre, which turned out to be a mistake. Puzzled as to why he couldn't run the times he'd been doing in practice on a track that should have suited the Ducati. Disappointed not so much with the rostrum finish as with the 15-second gap to the leader.

4 JORGE LORENZO A miraculous result after a massive highside on Friday injured both his ankles, which made everyone forget about his recent arm-pump operation. Started slowly, held eighth place for the middle third of the race, then passed four people in as many laps, but too far behind Stoner to go for a rostrum.

5 MARCO MELANDRI By far his best showing of the year so far, though qualifying was again disappointing. Found a much-improved balance for the bike plus some traction-control settings that allowed him to ride as he wanted, taking a couple of places with aggressive moves in the closing stages. A massive confidence booster.

6 NICKY HAYDEN Like his team-mate ran out of revs in top gear thanks to the tailwind. Handicapped by only qualifying in tenth thanks to a crash but got four places back with a stunning start and brave first corner. Had problems mid-race with his speed in the long corner, but rallied to get the better of Dovizioso and Edwards.

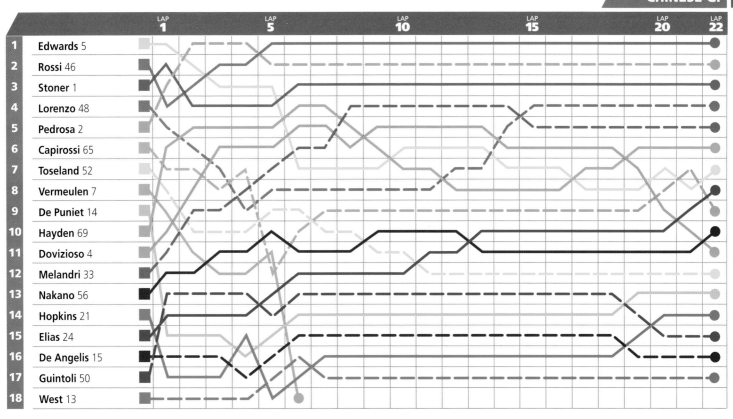

		LAP 1	LAP 5	LAP 10	LAP 15	LAP 20	LAP 22
1	Edwards 5						
2	Rossi 46						
3	Stoner 1						
4	Lorenzo 48						
5	Pedrosa 2						
6	Capirossi 65						
7	Toseland 52						
8	Vermeulen 7						
9	De Puniet 14						
10	Hayden 69						
11	Dovizioso 4						
12	Melandri 33						
13	Nakano 56						
14	Hopkins 21						
15	Elias 24						
16	De Angelis 15						
17	Guintoli 50						
18	West 13						

RACE

	Rider	Motorcycle	Race Time	Time +	Fastest Lap	Average Speed
1	Rossi	Yamaha	44m 08.061s		1m 59.273s	98.148mph
2	Pedrosa	Honda	44m 11.951s	3.890s	1m 59.384s	98.004mph
3	Stoner	Ducati	44m 23.989s	15.928s	2m 00.056s	97.561mph
4	Lorenzo	Yamaha	44m 30.555s	22.494s	2m 00.308s	97.321mph
5	Melandri	Ducati	44m 35.018s	26.957s	2m 00.451s	97.159mph
6	Hayden	Honda	44m 36.430s	28.369s	2m 00.601s	97.108mph
7	Edwards	Yamaha	44m 37.841s	29.780s	2m 00.651s	97.057mph
8	Elias	Ducati	44m 38.286s	30.225s	2m 00.355s	97.040mph
9	Capirossi	Suzuki	44m 39.501s	31.440s	2m 00.435s	96.996mph
10	Nakano	Honda	44m 44.030s	35.969s	2m 01.023s	96.833mph
11	Dovizioso	Honda	44m 44.307s	36.246s	2m 00.619s	96.822mph
12	Toseland	Yamaha	44m 51.252s	43.191s	2m 01.515s	96.573mph
13	De Puniet	Honda	44m 51.503s	43.442s	2m 00.845s	96.564mph
14	Hopkins	Kawasaki	44m 53.916s	45.855s	2m 00.948s	96.477mph
15	Guintoli	Ducati	44m 54.391s	46.330s	2m 01.663s	96.460mph
16	De Angelis	Honda	44m 58.654s	50.593s	2m 01.401s	96.308mph
17	West	Kawasaki	45m 13.654s	1m 05.593s	2m 02.229s	95.775mph
	Vermeulen	Suzuki	12m 37.734s	16 laps	2m 01.742s	93.936mph

CHAMPIONSHIP

	Rider	Team	Points
1	Pedrosa	Repsol Honda Team	81
2	Lorenzo	Fiat Yamaha Team	74
3	Rossi	Fiat Yamaha Team	72
4	Stoner	Ducati Marlboro Team	56
5	Capirossi	Rizla Suzuki MotoGP	33
6	Toseland	Tech 3 Yamaha	33
7	Edwards	Tech 3 Yamaha	31
8	Hayden	Repsol Honda Team	29
9	Dovizioso	JiR Team Scot MotoGP	26
10	Hopkins	Kawasaki Racing Team	26
11	Melandri	Ducati Marlboro Team	23
12	Nakano	San Carlo Honda Gresini	22
13	Elias	Alice Team	15
14	Vermeulen	Rizla Suzuki MotoGP	14
15	De Puniet	LCR Honda MotoGP	11
16	De Angelis	San Carlo Honda Gresini	7
17	Guintoli	Alice Team	4
18	West	Kawasaki Racing Team	3

7 COLIN EDWARDS Started from pole for the third time in his MotoGP career and led the first lap. Was one of many to run on at the end of the back straight, which he did while in third place on lap five – only lost him three seconds but relegated him four places down the order. Frustrated not to take advantage of his pole position.

8 TONI ELIAS Once the first half-dozen laps were over he managed to run at a good pace and put in the fifth-fastest lap of the race. The problems remain, especially with a full fuel load, but at least the result gave him and the team hope.

9 LORIS CAPIROSSI Started from his best grid position of the season so far but another to run on at the end of the back straight and

lose places. Also suffered transmission problems in the closing laps and was lucky just to lose two places. Could easily have suffered the same fate as his team-mate.

10 SHINYA NAKANO Had good pace on race tyres in practice and towards the end of the race – took Dovizioso on the last lap – and finished as the top satellite team Honda.

11 ANDREA DOVIZIOSO Caught out by the changing conditions. Went with a tyre and suspension set-up that was too soft, so very fast for the first half of the race and still in fifth at three-quarter distance but a sitting duck once the tyre went off. Lost six places in the last four laps.

12 JAMES TOSELAND Never got to grips completely with the track and found himself

losing out on corner speed in two vital places. As he said, that's bound to happen some time in a debut season on a track he'd never seen before, especially when weather restricts useful track time.

13 RANDY DE PUNIET Lack of feeling at the front, lack of rear grip, a crash on Saturday and an electrical problem in warm-up were followed by his now traditional bad start and a coming-together with Hopkins at the end of the straight on lap one. At least able to stay upright, get back on track and collect some points.

14 JOHN HOPKINS Not the way he wanted to celebrate becoming the youngest rider to start 100 GPs. Stormed round the outside in Turn 1 but victim of a de Angelis move at the end of the straight

which caused Hopper a punctured knee courtesy of his own footrest. Ran off track more than once as he struggled with rear traction issues.

15 SYLVAIN GUINTOLI Closer to the winner than he has been, but still struggling to adapt his riding style to the Desmosedici.

16 ALEX DE ANGELIS Had a coming-together with Hopkins early in the race, but never got to terms with certain sections of the track. The bike got harder to ride as the race wore on.

17 ANTHONY WEST Not just rear traction problems, like Hopkins, but also lack of grip at the front on the brakes hampered progress. Ran off track more than once, also like his team-mate.

NON-FINISHERS

CHRIS VERMEULEN Suffered mechanical problems from the start. Every time he pressed the chain would jump its sprockets – a problem with something in the transmission, not with the chain itself – and resulted in the clutch basket being sheared off the gearbox shaft.

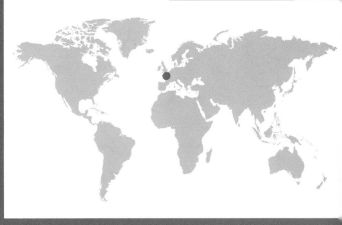

ONE HUNDRED & EIGHTY!

Rossi at his majestic best equalled Angel Nieto's total of 90 Grand Prix wins – and handed his bike over to the great Spaniard for the celebrations. Only Agostini's record remained

Whoever writes Rossi's scripts must have been doing a bit of moonlighting. It wasn't just Valentino who had the sort of race that sends shivers through the opposition, but the whole of the Yamaha operation. Despite Lorenzo's injuries from the previous race, plus two more crashes, one of them a real egg beater, the other Fiat Yamaha rider finished a magnificent second while Colin Edwards was third for the Tech 3 team. That was the first dry-weather rostrum finish by a satellite team rider since Mugello last year, exactly a season's worth of races previously. It was also the first Yamaha clean sweep of a podium in the MotoGP era.

This was the sort of victory in which Rossi and his team of mechanics have always specialised. They went from third in the first free practice session to sixth and nearly three-quarters of a second adrift at the end of Friday. After the last free practice he was second, only 0.34s down on Edwards, before slipping to fourth in qualifying, half a second behind Pedrosa. As usual, the team wasn't distracted by trying to get pole, working on race set-up right until they were putting the sticky qualifying tyres on. That second place at the end of free practice is the most significant statistic, and it was clear Jerry Burgess and the crew would find another improvement in warm-up on Sunday morning.

Just like in China, Rossi didn't panic at the sight of Pedrosa, and this time Stoner too, up at the front. Colin Edwards, who'd got off the line first and then found it was all he could do to hang onto Dani and Casey when they came past, knew he was in trouble when Valentino arrived 'like a cowboy with his guns blazing' and disappeared round the next corner with

nary a movement from the bike or its tyres. That's how it looked from the stands as well. Rossi pulled away inexorably from what turned into an incident-packed fight behind him, because both Pedrosa and Stoner were running into tyre problems – Casey with the right edge of his front tyre, Dani with his front. The Ducati rider was having trouble in the tight right-hander that ends the lap, the Honda man's problems were mainly on the brakes. Pedrosa also had two terrifying moments, the first when he locked the front over the bumps going into Musée, the second a sixth-gear wobble going up to the first corner. They were enough to persuade him that pushing further would be foolhardy.

Just as Stoner was working out what to do about his problem a sprinkling of rain arrived, giving the World Champion hope. That was when his engine decided to shut down. He managed to coax the Ducati round most of the lap, coasting to pit lane from the last corner after the motor finally decided to call it a day. As Race Control had shown the white flag that sanctions bike changes when rain starts, Casey swapped to his wet set-up bike and went out hoping to salvage a point or two. To make the weekend a total disaster for Ducati, Marco Melandri's bike had stalled on the grid and he lost 30 seconds to the leader getting restarted. He went in for his second bike soon after the white flag was displayed and at least had the consolation of getting the final point. Stoner's only solace was maintaining his record of finishing every race he has started for Ducati; this was the first time he had failed to score a point.

Meanwhile Lorenzo was working his way towards the front. This would be remarkable enough if all he was dealing with was the aftermath of his bone-cracking crash in China two weeks previously, but in practice he'd crashed twice more as well as running off track several times. Slow-motion replays of the second crash revealed his right ankle being slapped hard into the gravel trap three times as he tumbled, and he admitted that he was hurting mentally as well as physically before the race. Some people wondered if he really should be out there, but on the grid one of his mechanics reminded Jorge that the guys around him were the same ones he'd beaten in Portugal. He started badly, though, and took until lap eight to find his rhythm. He then overtook three riders in one lap and set about reeling in fifth-placed Chris Vermeulen, who was having his best ride of the season so far. The Spanish youngster was helped a little by the rain – 'for the first time in my life' – and hunted down the trio battling behind Rossi. He passed Edwards and Pedrosa on consecutive laps, taking his old enemy on the same lap that Stoner hit engine problems.

Above Chris Vermeulen's fifth place gave the Rizla Suzuki team some reward for their hard work

Opposite Masao Furusawa joins his riders for a Yamaha party on the rostrum

'TO ARRIVE AT 90 WINS LIKE THIS AND EQUAL ANGEL'S RECORD IS A DREAM FOR ME'
VALENTINO ROSSI

Below Casey Stoner looks back in anger after his Ducati broke its crankshaft

Opposite below Jorge Lorenzo rounds La Chapelle during qualifying under the threatening clouds that seemed to follow MotoGP around all year

When Jorge got on the back of the group, on lap 19, Rossi had a lead of just under four seconds. By the time Lorenzo was second, two laps later, Rossi's lead had somehow more than doubled to 8.25s. A lap later it was ten seconds. It was reminiscent of the soaking race at Donington in 2005 when Rossi magicked a two-second margin out of nowhere. We were all watching him then, but this time everyone was focused on Lorenzo's charge through the field. When they refocused on Rossi he had put in an astonishing three laps in conditions that unnerved the best of the rest. Although the 'nightmare' of the 2006 Le Mans race did cross his mind (his Yamaha broke when he was four seconds in the lead), this time Valentino eased up and took the victory. It was the first time he had taken back-to-back wins since the Italian and Catalan GPs of 2006, and took him to the top of the points table for the first time this season.

That just left some interesting interaction on the rostrum. Lorenzo used crutches to get there and sat on a chair for the formalities. However, when the time came for the group photo, usually taken with all three riders together on the top step of the rostrum, Lorenzo got Rossi to sit on his knee – with a broken ankle! The Doctor fixed Lorenzo with an assessing look before deciding to play along. At the post-race press conference Jorge mentioned that he had taken painkillers but refused injections, simply because he doesn't like them. Rossi was watching him carefully as he made that announcement as well. The development of the relationship between the two team-mates could be one of the season's more interesting sub-plots.

ANGEL NIETO

The man with whom Valentino Rossi drew level on career wins is Spain's greatest-ever racer and a national sporting hero. Angel Nieto became Spain's first World Champion when he won the 50cc class on a Derbi in 1969, and he went on to win twelve more world titles, including the 50/125cc double in 1972. His last race victory was in 1985, in the 80cc class which replaced the 50s, and he also rode for Bultaco, Kreidler, Minarelli and Garelli.

At the height of his fame at home Nieto was as recognisable as the top stars of Real Madrid and Barcelona, and as well paid, something the newly arrived American and Australian stars of the 500cc class always found difficult to comprehend. Although he dominated the smaller capacity classes with a mix of blinding speed and ruthless psychological warfare, Angel's plans to move up to the 250cc class were always thwarted by events outside his control.

In his younger days Nieto had a well-deserved reputation for toughness and a quick temper – machinery that let him down was abandoned without a backward glance as he headed for his Bentley. Nowadays he is a summariser and expert commentator for Spanish television, and anything but an extrovert presence in the paddock. His legendary superstition remains, however: never tell him he won thirteen titles, it has to be twelve plus one, just as the statue to him on the inside of the corner that bears his name at Jerez states.

The idea of Angel riding Valentino's M1 when they drew level on wins was mooted to him by Rossi when the Italian took his 88th victory at Estoril in 2007. With Rossi's win in China, two weeks before the French race, Nieto told him, with the same certainty that marked his own career, that he would join Valentino on the victory lap at Le Mans, the scene of Angel's final triumph in 1985. No pressure then, Vale... Only Giacomo Agostini's mark of 122 career wins remains.

Above Valentino Rossi enjoys the moment with the great Angel Nieto as they share the Fiat Yamaha on the slow-down lap

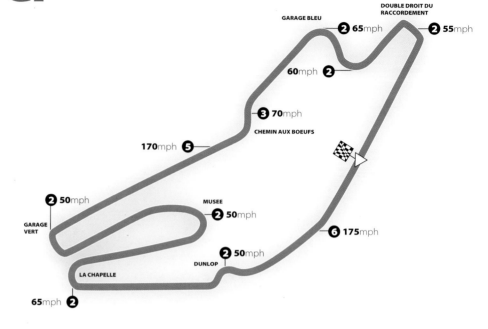

FRENCH GP
LE MANS

ROUND 5
May 18

RACE RESULTS

CIRCUIT LENGTH 2.600 miles
NO. OF LAPS 28
RACE DISTANCE 72.816 miles
WEATHER Dry, 20°C
TRACK TEMPERATURE 26°C
WINNER Valentino Rossi
FASTEST LAP 1m 34.215s, 99,368mph, Valentino Rossi (record)
PREVIOUS LAP RECORD (new circuit)

On the track map: DOUBLE DROIT DU RACCORDEMENT, GARAGE BLEU, 65mph, 55mph, 60mph, 70mph, CHEMIN AUX BOEUFS, 170mph, 175mph, MUSEE, 50mph, GARAGE VERT, 50mph, DUNLOP, 50mph, LA CHAPELLE, 65mph

QUALIFYING

	Rider	Nationality	Team	Qualifying	Pole +	Gap
1	Pedrosa	SPA	Repsol Honda Team	1m 32.647s		
2	Edwards	USA	Tech 3 Yamaha	1m 32.774s	0.127s	0.127s
3	Stoner	AUS	Ducati Marlboro Team	1m 32.994s	0.347s	0.220s
4	Rossi	ITA	Fiat Yamaha Team	1m 33.157s	0.510s	0.163s
5	Lorenzo	SPA	Fiat Yamaha Team	1m 33.269s	0.622s	0.112s
6	Hayden	USA	Repsol Honda Team	1m 33.286s	0.639s	0.017s
7	Toseland	GBR	Tech 3 Yamaha	1m 33.396s	0.749s	0.110s
8	Vermeulen	AUS	Rizla Suzuki MotoGP	1m 33.440s	0.793s	0.044s
9	Hopkins	USA	Kawasaki Racing Team	1m 33.628s	0.981s	0.188s
10	Dovizioso	ITA	JiR Team Scot MotoGP	1m 33.689s	1.042s	0.061s
11	Capirossi	ITA	Rizla Suzuki MotoGP	1m 33.707s	1.060s	0.018s
12	De Puniet	FRA	LCR Honda MotoGP	1m 33.723s	1.076s	0.016s
13	Nakano	JPN	San Carlo Honda Gresini	1m 34.077s	1.430s	0.354s
14	Elias	SPA	Alice Team	1m 34.561s	1.914s	0.484s
15	De Angelis	RSM	San Carlo Honda Gresini	1m 34.670s	2.023s	0.109s
16	Guintoli	FRA	Alice Team	1m 34.747s	2.100s	0.077s
17	Melandri	ITA	Ducati Marlboro Team	1m 35.081s	2.434s	0.334s
18	West	AUS	Kawasaki Racing Team	1m 35.349s	2.702s	0.268s

FINISHERS

1 VALENTINO ROSSI A faultless ride on a bike that looked perfectly prepared for both race and track, giving Rossi back-to-back victories for the first time since 2006. It was also his 90th win in all classes and brought him level with Angel Nieto as the second most successful rider in GP history.

2 JORGE LORENZO Looked lost in practice and qualifying and his injuries from Shanghai weren't helped by two crashes, one big, one small. Not surprisingly started shakily, then carved his way up from 11th, overtaking Stoner and Pedrosa on the same lap to take second.

An astonishing ride that gave him the highest-ever points total for a rookie after five races.

3 COLIN EDWARDS Not as happy as might have been expected. Had no answer to the Fiat Yamaha team riders, so had to be content with third, but did make it the first dry-weather rostrum finish by a satellite team rider since Barros at Mugello a year ago.

4 DANI PEDROSA His and Honda's first pole of the season, but the race saw an end to his run of six consecutive podiums and he also lost the championship lead. Survived two massive moments and had problems with his front tyre that prevented him braking as he wanted to. Not happy

5 CHRIS VERMEULEN By far his best

weekend so far this season and his best finish since Misano '07. Used the hard tyres as usual but lost all feel when the rain shower arrived – ironic since he won this race last year in monsoon conditions.

6 ANDREA DOVIZIOSO After a disappointing couple of races, another average qualifying and just 11th at the end of the first lap, Andrea rode a superb race and the result would have been even better but for the third-lap coming-together with Toseland.

7 LORIS CAPIROSSI Struggled all weekend and never happy with his set-up. Involved in a bunch of riders for the first ten laps but went off track after tangling with Hopkins, then fought hard to recover from tenth place.

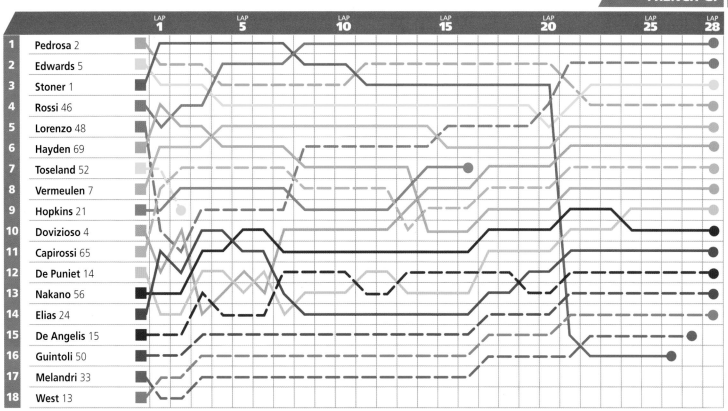

		LAP 1	LAP 5	LAP 10	LAP 15	LAP 20	LAP 25	LAP 28
1	Pedrosa 2							
2	Edwards 5							
3	Stoner 1							
4	Rossi 46							
5	Lorenzo 48							
6	Hayden 69							
7	Toseland 52							
8	Vermeulen 7							
9	Hopkins 21							
10	Dovizioso 4							
11	Capirossi 65							
12	De Puniet 14							
13	Nakano 56							
14	Elias 24							
15	De Angelis 15							
16	Guintoli 50							
17	Melandri 33							
18	West 13							

RACE

	Rider	Motorcycle	Race Time	Time +	Fastest Lap	Average Speed
1	Rossi	Yamaha	44m 30.799s		1m 34.215s	98.148mph
2	Lorenzo	Yamaha	44m 35.796s	4.997s	1m 34.421s	97.965mph
3	Edwards	Yamaha	44m 37.604s	6.805s	1m 34.321s	97.899mph
4	Pedrosa	Honda	44m 40.956s	10.157s	1m 34.469s	97.776mph
5	Vermeulen	Suzuki	44m 52.561s	21.762s	1m 34.585s	97.355mph
6	Dovizioso	Honda	44m 53.194s	22.395s	1m 34.727s	97.332mph
7	Capirossi	Suzuki	45m 58.605s	27.806s	1m 34.992s	97.137mph
8	Hayden	Honda	44m 58.794s	27.995s	1m 35.182s	97.130mph
9	De Puniet	Honda	45m 00.143s	29.344s	1m 35.191s	97.081mph
10	Nakano	Honda	45m 01.621s	30.822s	1m 35.430s	97.029mph
11	Elias	Ducati	45m 05.953s	35.154s	1m 35.422s	96.873mph
12	De Angelis	Honda	45m 07.015s	36.216s	1m 35.327s	96.835mph
13	Guintoli	Ducati	45m 22.837s	52.038s	1m 35.888s	96.272mph
14	West	Kawasaki	46m 00.106s	1m 29.307s	1m 36.550s	94.972mph
15	Melandri	Ducati	46m 10.422s	1 lap	1m 35.922s	91.240mph
16	Stoner	Ducati	44m 47.085s	2 laps	1m 34.561s	90.585mph
	Hopkins	Kawasaki	25m 36.029s	12 laps	1m 34.947s	97.518mph
	Toseland	Yamaha	3m 19.828s	26 laps	1m 36.603s	93.700mph

CHAMPIONSHIP

	Rider	Team	Points
1	Rossi	Fiat Yamaha Team	97
2	Lorenzo	Fiat Yamaha Team	94
3	Pedrosa	Repsol Honda Team	94
4	Stoner	Ducati Marlboro Team	56
5	Edwards	Tech 3 Yamaha	47
6	Capirossi	Rizla Suzuki MotoGP	42
7	Hayden	Repsol Honda Team	37
8	Dovizioso	JiR Team Scot MotoGP	36
9	Toseland	Tech 3 Yamaha	33
10	Nakano	San Carlo Honda Gresini	28
11	Hopkins	Kawasaki Racing Team	26
12	Vermeulen	Rizla Suzuki MotoGP	25
13	Melandri	Ducati Marlboro Team	24
14	Elias	Alice Team	20
15	De Puniet	LCR Honda MotoGP	18
16	De Angelis	San Carlo Honda Gresini	11
17	Guintoli	Alice Team	7
18	West	Kawasaki Racing Team	5

8 NICKY HAYDEN In his own words 'not pretty' on a track that he describes as the 'worst for me on the calendar'. The front end was a problem all weekend. An off-track excursion at half-distance lost him three places, down to tenth, and then his only entertainment was a dice with Capirossi.

9 RANDY DE PUNIET Finally made a good start but was pushed off track at the Dunlop chicane on lap one. Got back in ninth, only to be pushed off track again immediately and relegated to 14th. Changed position 13 times on his way to ninth – impressive, but not what he'd hoped for in front of his home crowd.

10 SHINYA NAKANO Another strangely anonymous weekend. Only got on the pace when it started raining, and didn't impress his team-manager by losing ninth five laps from home when he was outbraked by de Puniet.

11 TONI ELIAS The hope that grew in China didn't survive the first free practice session, and rumours of a deteriorating relationship with his race engineer didn't help either. Things actually looked encouraging at the start, but after a few laps the old problems returned and the rain made things even worse.

12 ALEX DE ANGELIS Happy to run the first half of the race with the group that included other satellite Hondas, but when the rain arrived so did a lot of chatter. Didn't know whether the chatter or the rain caused him to lose all feel from the front tyre.

13 SYLVAIN GUINTOLI Bitterly disappointed with his showing at the race he'd led a year previously, to the delight of the French motards. This time he never got near a useful set-up. Tried to make up for it with bravery early on but ran off track and lost contact with the group.

14 ANTHONY WEST The usual traction problem was exacerbated by a miscalculation on the part of the team, for which they later apologised. The Aussie had 'non-existent' rear grip in the race: 'I don't think I've ever been so happy to see the chequered flag.'

15 MARCO MELANDRI Lost time at the start when his bike stalled on the grid – fortunately he was on the back row, so decided to come in early and change to his wet bike – but the weather didn't co-operate and the gamble failed. Doubly disappointing as he'd gone faster in morning warm-up.

16 CASEY STONER First non-scoring ride for Ducati, but at least preserved his finishing record. Lying third when his motor started to lose power, and two laps later it was really sick: nursed it back to the start of pit lane before it finally stopped with a broken crank. As the race had been declared 'wet' he got on his second bike in the – ultimately vain – hope of salvaging a point.

NON-FINISHERS

JOHN HOPKINS Was lying in a handy seventh place when his chain broke. As it is very rare for a modern chain to fail, there were suspicions this was a symptom of something more fundamental in the engine or transmission.

JAMES TOSELAND Fell on lap three after a coming-together with Dovizioso: the Italian ran a little wide, James tried a move up the inside, their paths intersected and he crashed out unhurt. Called it a 'racing incident', though Dovi had a different opinion.

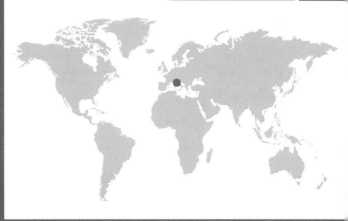

SEVENTH HEAVEN

Valentino Rossi made it three wins in a row and retained his unbeaten MotoGP record at his home race – an achievement unmatched in the entire history of Grand Prix motorcycle racing

It was a very good day for Italy in general and Valentino Rossi in particular. Italians won all three races, Gilera took their first 250cc GP victory, and the Doctor extended his run of wins in the top class at Mugello to seven. The win took him twelve points clear at the top of the table, the biggest lead he'd enjoyed since the end of the 2005 season, and it was the first time he'd strung three consecutive victories together since his last world title-winning season in 2005. He also started from pole for the 50th time in his career, although that wasn't necessarily a good omen as he'd failed to convert his last six poles into wins. The only thing that stopped it from being a perfect race was not setting the fastest lap; second-placed Stoner did that on lap five while chasing Rossi. However, Casey's new mark finally erased Max Biaggi's 2005 time from the record books, so Valentino might have derived some pleasure from it anyway.

There was encouragement, too, for Casey Stoner and Ducati. After a couple of unhappy races he was able to recover from a mistake and repass Pedrosa for second. The Aussie ran wide at the first corner while lying in second, letting the Honda through. It was enough to put Rossi out of reach, although the Ducati's pace in the final laps ensured Valentino couldn't relax. Dani's Honda looked a little bit unstable – it is thought he used the wide front wheel rim which would have traded off a bit of stability in a straight line for the chance to attack Mugello's plethora of ess-bends, especially the downhill ones, with increased certainty. Of the four men who have dominated proceedings so far this year only Lorenzo missed out, losing the front on lap seven. Jorge had a simple explanation: pilot

'FOR ME THE ITALIAN GRAND PRIX HAS ALWAYS BEEN THE MOST IMPORTANT RACE OF THE CHAMPIONSHIP'
VALENTINO ROSSI

Above You really shouldn't use the word 'straight' about the stretch of tarmac between Mugello's last corner and the first

Opposite Alex de Angelis went from last at the end of the first lap to fourth place at the flag

error. There were three other crashers. Randy de Puniet took Melandri with him – when your luck's out, it's really out – and Hopkins.

John's exit was caused by the quickshifter refusing to allow him to change down approaching Turn 1, the quickest section of track of the entire year. Hopper was lucky to walk away from a big crash and made it very clear that he was not amused to be eliminated from consecutive GPs by mechanical failure. Just to add to Kawasaki's gloom, Anthony West was the final finisher, beaten by 41-year-old Honda test rider Tadayuki Okada who was racing as a wild-card entry. Tady got the pneumatic-valve-engined Honda to the flag safely, and collected a couple of points as well.

Nicky Hayden had wanted to use the new motor, but Honda insisted on race-testing it first. This is so far from the normal HRC way of doing things – the only other example anyone can bring to mind is Shinichi Itoh and the allegedly fuel-injected 500 back in 1995 – that it is difficult to understand why Nicky wasn't allowed to race it. He wasn't within a shout of the championship and

was clearly demoralised. For once, HRC could have given him something he wanted. On the other side of the works Honda garage, however, Dani Pedrosa clearly had no interest in changing something that was good enough to win races.

Colin Edwards, in fifth, led team-mate Toseland home to put the Tech 3 squad third in the Team Championship, a remarkable achievement for a satellite outfit. Colin was happier with fifth at Mugello than he'd been with third at Le Mans, where he thought he should have won; previously he's only achieved a best of ninth here. James's ride was impressive for a Mugello debutant, but awarding ride of the day – Rossi excluded – it has to be Alex de Angelis, last coming out of the first corner and fourth at the flag. Until this race Alex had been by far the least impressive of what, it must be said, is a very impressive bunch of rookies, but this was a heroic ride. Toseland was impressed enough to say afterwards that his Yamaha was quicker than the Italian's Honda but he hadn't been able to stay with him. In the closing stages Dani Pedrosa had to stop

worrying about what Stoner was doing in front of him and concentrate on making sure de Angelis didn't get within striking distance.

Valentino was relieved that he'd not let his public down, but more than happy with his Yamaha. Once again the weather had interfered with practice, rain falling in every session except qualifying, so the race showed that the M1's base setting was now very good. Good enough, in fact, to give Bridgestone their first win at Mugello despite the lack of dry track time with race rubber on Friday and Saturday. There was a big hint that the relationship would be extended. Now managing his own business affairs, Rossi said the only question was whether the new contract would be for one or two years. As it's Valentino Rossi we are talking about, there were also two excellent jokes to enjoy. First, there was the deadpan assertion to an Italian newspaper that this was more his home race than any other rider's because he was the only Italian rider in MotoGP who actually lived in Italy. The remark has to be seen in the light of the millions of Euros he paid the local taxman for that privilege in the not too distant past. Then there was the crash helmet design: Valentino always brings out a special paint job for his home race, and this one came about only days before the race when he was discussing a lap of Mugello with Aldo Druidi, designer of all Rossi's colour schemes. He was describing the Casanova-Savelli section when Drudi took the portrait that ended up on top of his helmet. The effect, when Rossi was tucked behind the bubble, heading down to the first corner at over 200mph, can only be described as a work of genius.

Opposite Valentino Rossi celebrates victory in front of the massed ranks of his fan club at Poggio Secco corner

Top Alex de Angelis fights his way past the Tech 3 Yamahas of Colin Edwards and James Toseland

Below Tady Okada gave the pneumatic valve spring Honda RC212V an encouraging debut

AT LAST

Honda's pneumatic-valve engine finally got a public outing in the hands of test rider Tady Okada, although his weekend was severely compromised by the rain. He locked the front and crashed in one session, then had the bike stop on him in the next because of damage from that get-off. Nevertheless, the bike got to the flag. With more set-up time, said Tady, he could have got round the final corner better and been 3mph faster down the straight, which would have put him right up there with the quickest Ducatis. A pneumatic system uses a sealed, flexible chamber to close the valves – think of it as a tennis ball. The advantage is that it works much more quickly than a conventional steel spring.

HRC explained the delay in the new motor's arrival by saying that the conventional engine was performing so well that they'd had to revise their targets upwards. They also revealed that dispensing with conventional steel valve springs had allowed them to raise the V4's rev ceiling by 1000rpm. That would improve acceleration, of course, but give rise to problems with the 21-litre fuel limit, so combustion efficiency would also have to be improved significantly. Doing that while maintaining drivability would necessarily involve some compromises and therein lay the reasons for the delays.

There would also appear to be a significant difference between Honda's approach to pneumatic valves and that of the rest of the manufacturers. HRC seemed to be using them as a route to more power, whereas everyone else adopted them primarily for reasons of fuel economy.

The data from Okada's race was the subject of a lengthy meeting on Sunday night, called to decide whether the new engine would be used by either or both of the Repsol team's riders at Barcelona the following weekend.

ITALIAN GP
MUGELLO

ROUND 6
June 1

RACE RESULTS

CIRCUIT LENGTH 3.259 miles
NO. OF LAPS 23
RACE DISTANCE 74.794 miles
WEATHER Dry, 29°C
TRACK TEMPERATURE 42°C
WINNER Valentino Rossi
FASTEST LAP 1m 50.003s,
106.663mph, Casey Stoner (record)
PREVIOUS LAP RECORD 1m 50.117s,
106.553mph, Max Biaggi, 2005

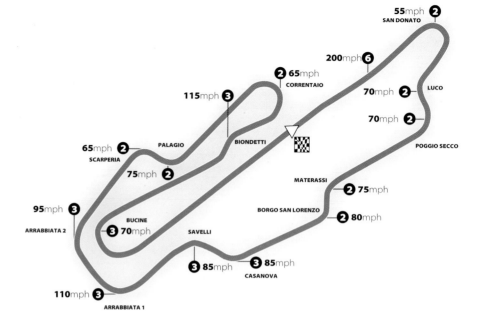

QUALIFYING

	Rider	Nationality	Team	Qualifying	Pole +	Gap
1	Rossi	ITA	Fiat Yamaha Team	1m 48.130s		
2	Pedrosa	SPA	Repsol Honda Team	1m 48.297s	0.167s	0.167s
3	Capirossi	ITA	Rizla Suzuki MotoGP	1m 48.313s	0.183s	0.016s
4	Stoner	AUS	Ducati Marlboro Team	1m 48.375s	0.245s	0.062s
5	Edwards	USA	Tech 3 Yamaha	1m 48.383s	0.253s	0.008s
6	Hayden	USA	Repsol Honda Team	1m 48.666s	0.536s	0.283s
7	Lorenzo	SPA	Fiat Yamaha Team	1m 48.905s	0.775s	0.239s
8	Toseland	GBR	Tech 3 Yamaha	1m 49.025s	0.895s	0.120s
9	Nakano	JPN	San Carlo Honda Gresini	1m 49.095s	0.965s	0.070s
10	De Angelis	RSM	San Carlo Honda Gresini	1m 49.145s	1.015s	0.050s
11	Vermeulen	AUS	Rizla Suzuki MotoGP	1m 49.220s	1.090s	0.075s
12	De Puniet	FRA	LCR Honda MotoGP	1m 49.246s	1.116s	0.026s
13	Dovizioso	ITA	JiR Team Scot MotoGP	1m 49.565s	1.435s	0.319s
14	Hopkins	USA	Kawasaki Racing Team	1m 49.601s	1.471s	0.036s
15	Okada	JPN	Repsol Honda Team	1m 49.829s	1.699s	0.228s
16	Elias	SPA	Alice Team	1m 49.851s	1.721s	0.022s
17	Guintoli	FRA	Alice Team	1m 50.275s	2.145s	0.424s
18	Melandri	ITA	Ducati Marlboro Team	1m 50.465s	2.335s	0.190s
19	West	AUS	Kawasaki Racing Team	1m 50.889s	2.759s	0.424s

FINISHERS

1 VALENTINO ROSSI Three wins in a row for the first time since mid-2005 and seventh consecutive victory at Mugello from his first pole in a season's worth of racing. Took just three laps to move from fourth into the lead. Winning here, he said, was the next best thing to winning the championship.

2 CASEY STONER Lost touch with Rossi when he ran wide at the first corner on lap ten and went back to third behind Pedrosa. It was only a small mistake but he needed four laps to retake second place, and was enough to put the Fiat Yamaha out of range.

3 DANI PEDROSA Got a flying start, as usual, and led the first lap but said it was a tough race. Commented on his Michelin tyres again, specifically a front that was losing performance towards the flag. In the closing stages more concerned with holding off de Angelis than attacking Stoner.

4 ALEX DE ANGELIS Set the best time in morning warm-up but messed his start so comprehensively he was next to last in Turn 1, then rode through the field to fourth after nine laps. Might even have made the rostrum if he'd realised earlier that Pedrosa had problems, but made his team-manager proud.

5 COLIN EDWARDS Best result at Mugello by four whole places. Declared

himself happier with this than his third place in France: 'I'm not a guy that likes fifth but on my biggest bogey track I'll take it.' Made a point of thanking Michelin for their help in selecting the right tyre after it rained for much of practice.

6 JAMES TOSELAND An impressive showing for a Mugello first-timer, especially after two disappointing races. Lost places in Turn 1 when he came together with Nakano, then rediscovered his taste for aggressive overtaking manoeuvres. Followed his team-mate home to take the Tech 3 squad to third in the Team Championship.

7 LORIS CAPIROSSI Suffered lack of grip so couldn't take advantage of his front-row start. High track temperatures on race day meant his tyres lost grip rapidly as he tried to

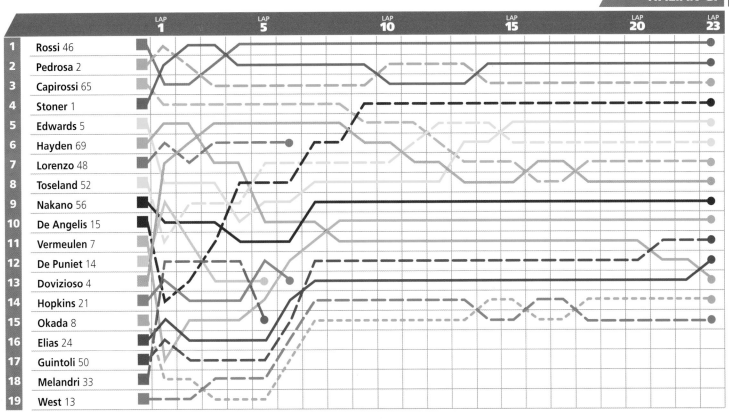

		LAP 1	LAP 5	LAP 10	LAP 15	LAP 20	LAP 23
1	Rossi 46						
2	Pedrosa 2						
3	Capirossi 65						
4	Stoner 1						
5	Edwards 5						
6	Hayden 69						
7	Lorenzo 48						
8	Toseland 52						
9	Nakano 56						
10	De Angelis 15						
11	Vermeulen 7						
12	De Puniet 14						
13	Dovizioso 4						
14	Hopkins 21						
15	Okada 8						
16	Elias 24						
17	Guintoli 50						
18	Melandri 33						
19	West 13						

RACE

	Rider	Motorcycle	Race Time	Time +	Fastest Lap	Average Speed
1	Rossi	Yamaha	42m 31.153s		1m 50.034s	105.781mph
2	Stoner	Ducati	42m 33.354s	2.201s	1m 50.003s	105.690mph
3	Pedrosa	Honda	42m 36.020s	4.867s	1m 50.131s	105.580mph
4	De Angelis	Honda	42m 37.466s	6.313s	1m 50.179s	105.520mph
5	Edwards	Yamaha	42m 43.683s	12.530s	1m 50.502s	105.264mph
6	Toseland	Yamaha	42m 44.959s	13.806s	1m 50.696s	105.211mph
7	Capirossi	Suzuki	42m 45.600s	14.447s	1m 50.523s	105.185mph
8	Dovizioso	Honda	42m 46.472s	15.319s	1m 50.511s	105.150mph
9	Nakano	Honda	42m 46.480s	15.327s	1m 50.886s	105.149mph
10	Vermeulen	Suzuki	43m 01.938s	30.785s	1m 50.916s	104.520mph
11	Guintoli	Ducati	43m 10.774s	39.621s	1m 51.830s	104.163mph
12	Elias	Ducati	43m 21.174s	50.021s	1m 51.793s	103.747mph
13	Hayden	Honda	43m 21.593s	50.440s	1m 50.909s	103.730mph
14	Okada	Honda	43m 30.002s	58.849s	1m 52.445s	103.395mph
15	West	Kawasaki	43m 31.889s	1m 00.736s	1m 52.565s	103.321mph
	Lorenzo	Yamaha	11m 11.489s	17 laps	1m 50.518s	104.840mph
	Hopkins	Kawasaki	11m 17.629s	17 laps	1m 51.215s	103.890mph
	De Puniet	Honda	9m 25.989s	18 laps	1m 51.510s	103.652mph
	Melandri	Ducati	9m 26.358s	18 laps	1m 51.181s	103.584mph

CHAMPIONSHIP

	Rider	Team	Points
1	Rossi	Fiat Yamaha Team	122
2	Pedrosa	Repsol Honda Team	110
3	Lorenzo	Fiat Yamaha Team	94
4	Stoner	Ducati Marlboro Team	76
5	Edwards	Tech 3 Yamaha	58
6	Capirossi	Rizla Suzuki MotoGP	51
7	Dovizioso	JiR Team Scot MotoGP	44
8	Toseland	Tech 3 Yamaha	43
9	Hayden	Repsol Honda Team	40
10	Nakano	San Carlo Honda Gresini	35
11	Vermeulen	Rizla Suzuki MotoGP	31
12	Hopkins	Kawasaki Racing Team	26
13	De Angelis	San Carlo Honda Gresini	24
14	Melandri	Ducati Marlboro Team	24
15	Elias	Alice Team	24
16	De Puniet	LCR Honda MotoGP	18
17	Guintoli	Alice Team	12
18	West	Kawasaki Racing Tea	6
19	Okada	Repsol Honda Team	2

make up in corners what he was losing on the straight. Slipped back from a good start and was almost caught by Dovizioso. Not happy.

8 ANDREA DOVIZIOSO Never found a set-up during the rain-hit free practice and qualified well down. Used a soft tyre to make some rapid progress early in the race but couldn't hold off the Tech 3 duo and Capirossi in the closing stages. Finished only 15 seconds behind the winner.

9 SHINYA NAKANO Victim of a massive crash in wet practice that was reminiscent of his top-speed tyre failure in 2004. Put in a solid race but took too long to get past Hayden to be able to catch the group in front.

10 CHRIS VERMEULEN Boxed out at the first corner and pushed back to 17th. Coming back to take tenth after that, with a bike that didn't have the expected level of grip, has to be counted as a good ride.

11 SYLVAIN GUINTOLI A new Bridgestone front tyre gave the feel and confidence he'd been looking for. Was eighth fastest in final free practice, didn't qualify so well, but made up a lot of places in Turn 1 only to be sideswiped back four places in Turn 2. Beat his team-mate for the first time.

12 TONI ELIAS A really depressing weekend after he seemed to have found something at the race in China: 'I don't have any words today, I have simply never been in the race.'

13 NICKY HAYDEN Qualified better than his form in most free practice suggested, then started even better. However, an unspecified technical ailment, which made its presence felt right from the start, meant he slid down the order with his lap times falling off drastically.

14 TADAYUKI OKADA The first wild-card entry of the year race-tested Honda's pneumatic-valve engine eight years after his last GP. A big crash on Friday led to the bike stopping again on Saturday, so set-up time was severely limited. Spent much of the race stalking West, taking him five laps from home.

15 ANTHONY WEST Once again, rear traction was the problem and this time he was vociferous about it in public as well as in private: 'I'm starting to sound like a stuck record. The bike goes sideways when it's supposed to go forwards.'

NON-FINISHERS

JORGE LORENZO Lost the front trying to repass Dovizioso in a downhill corner. Took all the blame himself and apologised to the team.

JOHN HOPKINS Mechanical failures in two consecutive races. This time the quickshifter decided not to allow him to change down as he came into the first corner: Hopper was lucky to walk away from the inevitable massive crash.

RANDY DE PUNIET Never found a good feeling with the rear so lost places after probably his best start of the season so far. Came together with Melandri at Turn 2 on lap six and crashed – thought he caught his brake lever on the Ducati.

MARCO MELANDRI Like fellow Ducati man Elias, the promise of China was not fulfilled. Run off track by a crashing de Puniet, but at least it put an early end to another weekend of torture.

CATALAN GP

CIRCUIT DE CATALUNYA

ROUND 7

June 8

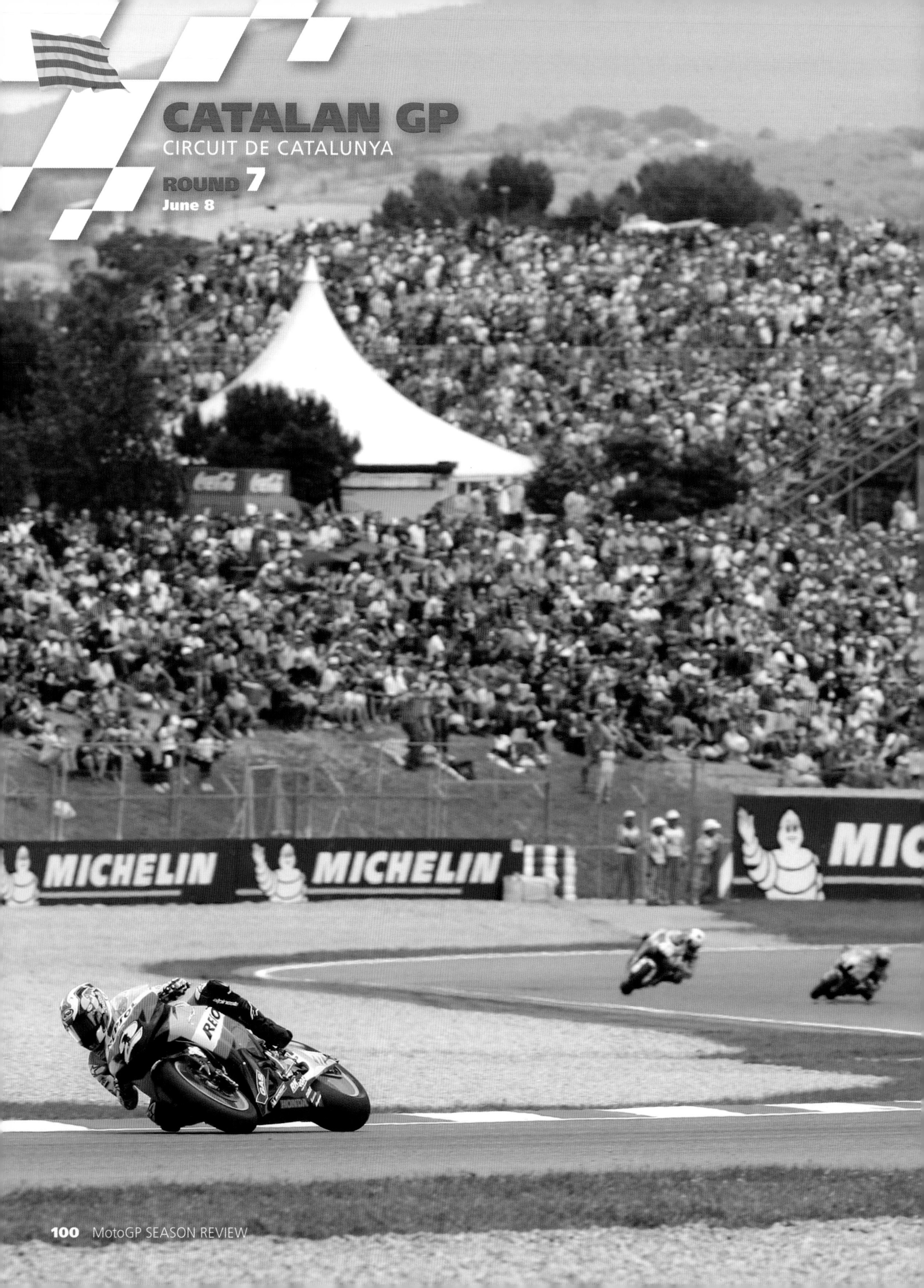

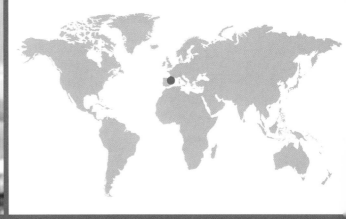

SPANISH HUSTLE

Pneumatic valves? Who needs them? Not Pedrosa, it would seem. HRC decided against putting the new engine on track before tests after the race, but Dani still ran away from the field to win at home

The Pedrosa family is from Sabadell, a Barcelona suburb about three miles from the Circuit de Catalunya, so this really is Dani's home race. He has now won all three GP classes at his local track, and has also taken the most recent victories at the other two Spanish tracks visited by MotoGP, Valencia at the end of 2007 and Jerez in March this year. The win here also underlined Pedrosa's domination of the last ten races, a period during which he has won three races and started from pole four times, scored 189 points (20 more than Valentino Rossi and 27 more than Casey Stoner), and only finished off the rostrum twice – and then he was fourth. The only Honda rider to beat him in this period was Marco Melandri at Sepang in 2007.

It all sounds very easy, and on Sunday afternoon it was. However, despite being fastest on Friday Dani was only eighth after the third free practice session, then used his Michelin qualifiers to good effect to take second on the grid, with only Stoner in front of him. Thirteenth in warm-up on race day didn't inspire confidence in the 113,000 fans who'd braved fuel protesters' blockades to pack the imposing grandstands of the Circuit de Catalunya. What they didn't know was that Dani and his Austrian race engineer, Mike Leitner, had found something in that warm-up session. They weren't about to tell us what, although Pedrosa later dropped a hint about 'the bike's balance'.

Quite frankly, no-one saw which way Dani Pedrosa went once the race started. After one of the rocket starts we now expect, Stoner tried to throw the Ducati under him a couple of times but the gap was half a second by the end of the first lap. The Honda rider extended his lead to over eight seconds without ever

'TODAY WAS VERY IMPORTANT FOR THE CHAMPIONSHIP, I AM FIVE POINTS CLOSER TO THE LEAD'
DANI PEDROSA

Opposite Dani Pedrosa shows the spoils of victory to his fans – his home town is about five kilometres from the track

Below Rossi in replica Italian national soccer kit, complete with football crash helmet, leads Stoner and Dovizioso

conceding time to the chasing group, and he was able to ease up towards the flag. It was an awesome display, but at least Dani looked like he was working hard. How does 1m 42.61s on the first flying lap sound – 0.4s under Nicky Hayden's 2006 lap record, which was set on a 990. Pedrosa was even faster next time round, and again the time after that. He had a lead of 2.8s after four laps, 7s after ten, and by lap 17 of the 25 he was 8s ahead. It was an intense but lonely race, with Dani even admitting to losing concentration while 'all alone' at one point.

There was also the small matter of a new frame. Pedrosa had one to start the weekend and a second arrived and was fitted to his second bike on Friday night. The Michelins did their job, too. Dani had been putting pressure on HRC and his tyre supplier since before Mugello, only too well aware that if he was to beat Rossi he couldn't afford to concede the slightest advantage. Not that Valentino saw much from his third-row start, because it took him nine laps to work his way up from ninth on the grid to second place, and after that he re-enacted the previous year's battle with Casey Stoner,

this time for the runner-up spot rather than the win. It was very noticeable, though, that Rossi and his crew celebrated this hard-fought victory over the Aussie as if they'd won the race itself.

Stoner had tried everything, but the Desmosedici looked as recalcitrant as it ever has, spinning everywhere, snapping sideways, losing the front a couple of times. No doubt about it, the World Champion was having to work hard. The other three Ducatis had the sort of tough weekend they've become accustomed to, with Toni Elias suffering the most after jumping the start and then being black-flagged – at his home race. Andrea Dovizioso was fourth, his best result since the opening race of the year, on what is still a stock Honda. He was looking more and more like a contender for a factory bike next year.

On his victory lap Pedrosa demonstrated that he isn't the corporate robot some mistake him for by carrying a banner protesting against new crash barriers, seen as being dangerous to motorcyclists. How many other MotoGP riders would identify themselves with a local grass-roots motorcyclists' campaign like that?

The only bad news for the Spanish crowd was that they were deprived of a confrontation between Dani Pedrosa and Jorge Lorenzo, who was ruled out of the race after sustaining severe concussion when he lost the front on Friday. When he woke up Jorge told the medics that he had just crashed in practice ... for the Chinese Grand Prix. He also lost some skin off his right hand. An overnight stay in hospital was followed by scans which, thankfully, revealed no bruising or bleeding on the brain. Unluckily, the hand injury would need a skin graft. Unspoken questions concerned the damage to Jorge's

Right James Toseland started well but a forceful move by Rossi meant he spent most of the race dicing with Vermeulen

Below Andrea Dovizioso equalled his best qualifying and race result of the year, while Edwards continued his best ever start to a MotoGP season

confidence and how he would cope with this succession of crashes after that stellar start to his rookie season. John Hopkins's crash in practice was also a bad one, although he was able to race despite being in considerable pain from two cracked vertebrae.

Away from the track, much paddock attention centred on the visiting Sete Gibernau, and specifically whether he would be returning to MotoGP as a replacement for either Marco Melandri or Ant West. Gibernau had only been seen fleetingly at one GP since he retired at the end of 2006, but he looked happy to be back – and very fit. He spent a lot of time in the Kawasaki pit, mainly with his

old race engineer and good friend Juan Martinez, thus fuelling speculation that he might return to the track in green. However, Sete's old employers at Ducati had lined him up to test the Desmosedici, which gave rise to even more conjecture about him replacing the now clearly disaffected Melandri. Gibernau appears to have dealt with his enforced absence from GPs by distancing himself from racing completely and focusing his considerable intellect on building up some business interests. However, would any team-manager be prepared to pay a considerable wages bill for a rider who will be 36 years old before the 2009 season begins?

TV TIMES

One of the real improvements in TV coverage of MotoGP in recent years has been the increased use of on-board cameras to provide both dramatic action shots and unusual angles. The 2008 Catalan GP was the first time that all the bikes on the MotoGP grid carried at least three mini-cameras, and seven of them sported a fourth for special effects. Another eight on-board cameras were used in the 250cc race and even the BMW safety car boasted three.

The three standard mini-cameras on the MotoGP bikes consisted of one in the nose, one on the tailpiece and one facing backwards. The seven fourth cameras were used for more unusual, even experimental angles: at this GP one gave a view of Stoner's front-tyre contact patch, one of Rossi's clutch hand and another of Pedrosa's throttle action. If he had raced, Lorenzo's bike would have had a camera looking at him from the dashboard. Each rider has two bikes and both of them are fully equipped, so that in the event of a bike change in a 'flag-to-flag' race, TV coverage will maintain continuity. The action was, of course, covered by 27 conventional, external cameras: 21 cameras were trackside, and there were four RF cameras in pit lane, one in the helicopter and one paddock camera.

The international TV feed signal that Dorna produces and supplies to all the broadcasters who show MotoGP used a total of 128 cameras at the Circuit de Catalunya, a record for MotoGP and a total with which very few other sporting events can compete.

Above The small fin on the tailpiece of a MotoGP machine holds a forward-facing miniature TV camera

CATALAN GP
CIRCUIT DE CATALUNYA

ROUND 7
June 8

RACE RESULTS

CIRCUIT LENGTH 2.937 miles
NO. OF LAPS 25
RACE DISTANCE 73.425 miles
WEATHER Dry, 27°C
TRACK TEMPERATURE 39°C
WINNER Dani Pedrosa
FASTEST LAP 1m 42.358s,
103.308mph, Dani Pedrosa (record)
PREVIOUS LAP RECORD 1m 43.048,
102.617mph, Nicky Hayden, 2006

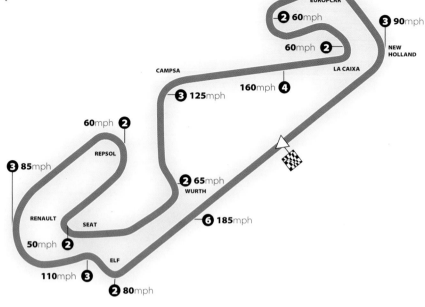

Circuit map with speeds: EUROPCAR 3 90mph, 2 60mph, 3 90mph, 60mph 2, NEW HOLLAND, CAMPSA, LA CAIXA, 3 125mph, 160mph 4, 60mph 2, REPSOL, 3 85mph, 2 65mph, WURTH, 6 185mph, RENAULT, SEAT, 50mph 2, ELF, 110mph 3, 2 80mph

QUALIFYING

	Rider	Nationality	Team	Qualifying	Pole +	Gap
1	Stoner	AUS	Ducati Marlboro Team	1m 41.186s		
2	Pedrosa	SPA	Repsol Honda Team	1m 41.269s	0.083s	0.083s
3	Hayden	USA	Repsol Honda Team	1m 41.437s	0.251s	0.168s
4	De Puniet	FRA	LCR Honda MotoGP	1m 41.571s	0.385s	0.134s
5	Edwards	USA	Tech 3 Yamaha	1m 41.609s	0.423s	0.038s
6	Toseland	GBR	Tech 3 Yamaha	1m 41.820s	0.634s	0.211s
7	Dovizioso	ITA	JiR Team Scot MotoGP	1m 42.053s	0.867s	0.233s
8	Vermeulen	AUS	Rizla Suzuki MotoGP	1m 42.365s	1.179s	0.312s
9	Rossi	ITA	Fiat Yamaha Team	1m 42.427s	1.241s	0.062s
10	De Angelis	RSM	San Carlo Honda Gresini	1m 42.580s	1.394s	0.153s
11	Nakano	JPN	San Carlo Honda Gresini	1m 42.643s	1.457s	0.063s
12	Capirossi	ITA	Rizla Suzuki MotoGP	1m 42.648s	1.462s	0.005s
13	Elias	SPA	Alice Team	1m 42.808s	1.622s	0.160s
14	Hopkins	USA	Kawasaki Racing Team	1m 42.819s	1.633s	0.011s
15	Guintoli	FRA	Alice Team	1m 43.204s	2.018s	0.385s
16	Melandri	ITA	Ducati Marlboro Team	1m 43.719s	2.533s	0.515s
17	West	AUS	Kawasaki Racing Team	1m 44.558s	3.372s	0.839s
	Lorenzo	SPA	Fiat Yamaha Team			

FINISHERS

1 DANI PEDROSA An imperious performance in front of his home-town fans. The rest didn't see which way he went – don't be fooled by the victory margin in the results table – he was over eight seconds in the lead at one point. The lap record went on the first flying lap and he beat the race record by 14 seconds.

2 VALENTINO ROSSI Not bad from ninth on the grid and without the benefit of a good start – he was eighth at the end of the first lap. Cut his way mercilessly through the top ten until he got to Stoner, after which the pair replayed the previous year's battle only with a different result.

3 CASEY STONER Not entirely happy with his riding or set-up, despite starting from pole for the first time this season; also first pole here for Ducati and Bridgestone. Fought to the flag with Rossi, doing two of his best split times on the final lap. His big problem was losing the rear going into corners.

4 ANDREA DOVIZIOSO Equalled both his best qualifying (seventh) and finish of the year. Started brilliantly to go second in the early stages before being passed by Stoner and Rossi – and he re-passed Casey to take back second just before Rossi came through.

5 COLIN EDWARDS Maintained his best-ever start to a MotoGP season and qualified in the top five, as he'd done in every race so far. Rear grip problems very early on meant adjusting his style to cope, but generally happy with his finishing position.

6 JAMES TOSELAND The victim of a forceful Rossi pass on lap two when he dropped to ninth before losing two more places to Vermeulen and de Angelis. Made more overtakes than anyone in the race except Rossi as he fought back to his fourth sixth-placed finish.

7 CHRIS VERMEULEN Again suffered in qualifying, and his chance of a finish that would reflect his pace in free practice was scuppered when hit by de Angelis early in the first lap. Rode a solid race, though, regaining three places on the second lap and spending the rest of the time in combat with Toseland.

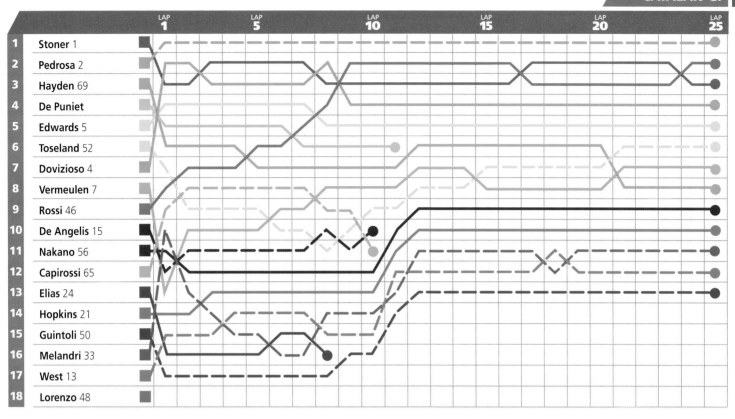

		LAP 1	LAP 5	LAP 10	LAP 15	LAP 20	LAP 25
1	Stoner 1						
2	Pedrosa 2						
3	Hayden 69						
4	De Puniet						
5	Edwards 5						
6	Toseland 52						
7	Dovizioso 4						
8	Vermeulen 7						
9	Rossi 46						
10	De Angelis 15						
11	Nakano 56						
12	Capirossi 65						
13	Elias 24						
14	Hopkins 21						
15	Guintoli 50						
16	Melandri 33						
17	West 13						
18	Lorenzo 48						

RACE

	Rider	Motorcycle	Race Time	Time +	Fastest Lap	Average Speed
1	Pedrosa	Honda	43m 02.175s		1m 42.358s	102.379mph
2	Rossi	Yamaha	43m 04.981s	2.806s	1m 42.555s	102.268mph
3	Stoner	Ducati	43m 05.518s	3.343s	1m 42.831s	102.247mph
4	Dovizioso	Honda	43m 13.068s	10.893s	1m 42.990s	101.949mph
5	Edwards	Yamaha	43m 18.601s	16.426s	1m 42.924s	101.732mph
6	Toseland	Yamaha	43m 23.657s	21.482s	1m 43.323s	101.534mph
7	Vermeulen	Suzuki	43m 23.723s	21.548s	1m 43.165s	101.531mph
8	Hayden	Honda	43m 24.455s	22.280s	1m 43.172s	101.503mph
9	Nakano	Honda	43m 24.550s	22.375s	1m 43.146s	101.500mph
10	Hopkins	Kawasaki	43m 49.010s	46.835s	1m 43.792s	100.555mph
11	Melandri	Ducati	44m 00.166s	57.991s	1m 44.694s	100.130mph
12	West	Kawasaki	44m 01.343s	59.168s	1m 44.413s	100.085mph
13	Guintoli	Ducati	44m 02.954s	1m 00.779s	1m 44.548s	100.024mph
	De Puniet	Honda	19m 01.576s	14 laps	1m 42.935s	101.893mph
	De Angelis	Honda	17m 23.460s	15 laps	1m 43.047s	101.340mph
	Capirossi	Suzuki	17m 23.501s	15 laps	1m 42.871s	101.336mph

CHAMPIONSHIP

	Rider	Team	Points
1	Rossi	Fiat Yamaha Team	142
2	Pedrosa	Repsol Honda Team	135
3	Lorenzo	Fiat Yamaha Team	94
4	Stoner	Ducati Marlboro Team	92
5	Edwards	Tech 3 Yamaha	69
6	Dovizioso	JiR Team Scot MotoGP	57
7	Toseland	Tech 3 Yamaha	53
8	Capirossi	Rizla Suzuki MotoGP	51
9	Hayden	Repsol Honda Team	48
10	Nakano	San Carlo Honda Gresini	42
11	Vermeulen	Rizla Suzuki MotoGP	40
12	Hopkins	Kawasaki Racing Team	32
13	Melandri	Ducati Marlboro Team	29
14	De Angelis	San Carlo Honda Gresini	24
15	Elias	Alice Team	24
16	De Puniet	LCR Honda MotoGP	18
17	Guintoli	Alice Team	15
18	West	Kawasaki Racing Team	10
19	Okada	Repsol Honda Team	2

8 NICKY HAYDEN Frustrated not to be given a chance to try the pneumatic-valve engine in the race; again suffered from lack of tyre life after a promising start.

9 SHINYA NAKANO Not a happy 200th race for Team Gresini: Shinya was off the pace in qualifying and then, according to his team-manager, 'lacking in aggression' in the race. Ominously, Fausto Gresini added: 'This is not the first time we've seen this.'

10 JOHN HOPKINS Suffered a cracked fourth lumbar vertebra when he was slapped into the tarmac at Turn 2 in practice. Not surprisingly, couldn't move about too much on the bike and was in pain at the end, but found early rhythm and spent most of the race on his own, which was probably a good thing.

11 MARCO MELANDRI Another difficult weekend. It was the old story of inability to put the power down, especially in the long corners, making him an easy target. His confidence was dealt another blow in testing after the race, when test rider Nicolas Canepa was faster than him.

12 ANTHONY WEST Spent most of the race dicing with Melandri, frequently passing him into corners only to lose out on the straight. Hadn't got enough tyre left to make a pass on the last lap. Flew to Japan after the race for a private test to try and resolve the traction problems that have bedevilled him all season.

13 SYLVAIN GUINTOLI Ran off track when he caught his team-mate after a bad start, then used up his tyre catching the group in front and had no grip for the last two laps.

NON-FINISHERS

RANDY DE PUNIET Crashed when he lost the front at the first corner for the second time in the weekend (there was also another get-off). Doubly disappointing as he had qualified in his best position of the year at a track where he'd twice won on a 250.

ALEX DE ANGELIS Crashed after tangling with Capirossi – Alex attempted a dive up the inside after the Suzuki rider ran wide, but they came together on the exit. Also had a coming-together with Suzuki's other rider, Vermeulen, on the first lap.

LORIS CAPIROSSI Suffered a broken right hand, specifically a dislocated fracture of the fifth metacarpus, in the crash with de Angelis, plus a nasty gash to, and loss of skin from, the little finger. The injury would definitely keep him out of the next race, at Donington, and probably Assen as well.

EXCLUDED

TONI ELIAS A disastrous home race. Black-flagged after failing to come in for a ride-through penalty for jumping the start – he was so busy dicing with Melandri, Guintoli and West he didn't see the board until it was too late.

NON-STARTER

JORGE LORENZO A big crash on Friday, when he lost the front in the first of the two right-handers that end the lap, resulted in concussion which obviously precluded him from racing. The good news was that he didn't do any further damage to his ankles.

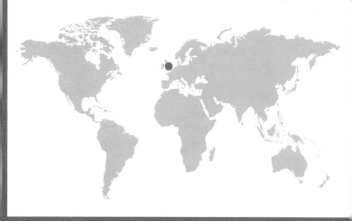

SECOND COMING

Casey Stoner and Ducati turned the clock back twelve months with a dominant win. Rossi and Pedrosa fought their own battle over the lower rostrum positions

It was dry on Friday; Casey Stoner and Ducati were fastest. It was wet on Saturday; Casey Stoner and Ducati were fastest. It was windy on Sunday and – guess what – Stoner started from pole, led into the first corner, headed every lap and won by nearly six seconds. It was just like 2007, although this was only Casey's second win of the season.

The foundations of his victory were laid at the Barcelona tests on the Monday and Tuesday after the Catalan GP, where Stoner tried out a modified engine-management system that smoothed power delivery when he opened the throttle. After the French GP Ducati sent their 2008-specification engine back to Bologna for remedial work and used the '07 model at Mugello and Catalunya. No-one from Ducati was calling it a new system – words like 'modified' and 'evolution' were preferred. Casey was also at pains to point out that the system he'd started the season with had 'made the chassis look bad' when he got on the throttle, and the modifications amounted to a little fine-tuning to the software and nothing else.

Dani Pedrosa also had good reason to remember the Barcelona tests, but not in a good way. He'd spent a night in hospital after a massive highside smacked him into the tarmac, bruising his lower back. One of the first things he did at Donington was highside at Redgate and come down on his backside. Fortunately, he was able to continue, but although Friday was dry, Saturday was forecast to be wet and he knew he had lost valuable set-up time. Valentino Rossi was fast on the first day but not happy with his set-up. Despite finishing second in Saturday's wet qualifying hour he knew he wouldn't be able to go with Stoner. He was also over half a second

slower than the Aussie in the dry Sunday warm-up.

Valentino's suspicions were well founded. Once Casey had taken over half a second out of the field on the first lap there was only going to be one winner. Rossi was second from the off, but from lap eight onwards had to deal with a very determined Pedrosa. 'When I saw his name on my board, from so far back [Dani qualified ninth], I think he must be very strong.' Indeed he was, passing the Yamaha several times, but Rossi always went straight back past and never allowed the Spaniard to lead over the line. Pedrosa was faster in the slow corners that end the lap and was attacking one more time at Foggy's Esses when he made a small mistake. Dani later reported that he'd made a few more mistakes as he tried to get back in touch: 'I lost him.'

Valentino and his crew looked much happier than usual with second place, with Rossi declaring that the points gained on Pedrosa in the championship were more important than the five he'd lost to Stoner, although he was careful not to rule Casey out of the title chase.

In many ways the story of the weekend was really all about Jorge Lorenzo, who'd looked a broken man until the race got going: he came through from 17th on the grid to take an astonishing sixth place. The young Yamaha rider had been impressively open about the difficulties of regaining his confidence after his run of crashes since China, and he seemed genuinely surprised that any fans would still want his autograph.

There was also a lot of attention focused on the MotoGP debut of Ben Spies, replacing the injured Loris Capirossi. Despite thinking that the first half of his race

Above The injured Loris Capirossi gives advice to his temporary replacement, American Superbike Champion Ben Spies

Below Ben Spies in action – you can see why his nickname in the AMA Championship paddock is 'Elbowz'

Opposite The battle for second place between Rossi and Pedrosa provided the best entertainment of the day

'WE'VE TAKEN A BIG STEP FORWARD WITH THE ELECTRONICS SYSTEM'
CASEY STONER

Above Nicky Hayden at last got to race the pneumatic-valve V4 Honda

Below Several riders had to take avoiding action when the crowd invaded

Opposite The Craner Curves are still impressive, even without the Spitfire

was 'garbage', the American Superbike Champion impressed everyone. Judging by his lap times in the second part of the race a top-ten finish would have been a possibility with a dry Saturday. Ben seemed to enjoy his first GP and is obviously anxious to get to MotoGP full time: 'I thought I was young until I saw those kids on the 125s.'

A third effect of the Barcelona test was that Nicky Hayden finally got to race the pneumatic-valve Honda. He out-qualified his team-mate for the first time this season and, not surprisingly, liked the motor: 'I like to go somewhere when I open the throttle.' The old bike? 'I don't care if I never ride it again.' Nicky knew it wasn't going to be a good race day when a warning light came on at the start of the ninth lap, but his old enthusiasm

was back and he fully expected to continue with the new machine for the rest of the year.

If you're looking for the man who really suffered, though, it was Marco Melandri – again. He was pushed into 16th place by Alex de Angelis, who'd fallen at the Melbourne Loop on the second lap but remounted and still beat the Ducati by eight seconds.

Local hero James Toseland was also a contender for unluckiest rider: he fell at the first corner, broke his brake lever, ripped off a footrest and banged himself up. He got back on to finish the race a lap adrift. James's woes had started with a fall in practice and two more at the end of qualifying, which left him down in 16th on the grid. His first-corner crash was a result of Toseland knowing only too well what he had to do off the start to stand a chance of the top-six finish he wanted to give the home fans. There had been much attention on the Tech 3 rider in the run-up to the event and he had a very crowded schedule of promotional engagements. Did he do too much? James himself emphatically denied it. Even the concert on Saturday night? 'Playing with the band is my best way of relaxing.' If he'd thought anything was distracting him he would have refused to do it. None of which made James feel any better about his race, which he described as the worst of his life.

The now seemingly inevitable track invasion plumbed new levels of stupidity, with de Puniet and Vermeulen having to take avoiding action at Craner Curves, and, unfortunately, new levels of abuse for the winner. Casey Stoner later said that Dani Pedrosa had experienced similar treatment when he won: 'They can't be here for the racing, can they?'

AIRBAG LEATHERS

Chris Vermeulen gave the race version of Dainese's D-air airbag system its MotoGP debut at Donington. The airbag itself is packaged under an extra layer of leather held on with sacrificial stitching. The electronic control system lives in the hump of the leathers and consists of three accelerometers, three gyroscopes, GPS, and a digital-control system that fires the high-pressure gas bottle to inflate the bag almost instantaneously. In 40 milliseconds the airbag is inflated to a volume of 37 litres.

The clever bit is to make sure the system only operates when it's needed, when the rider is in the middle of a highside not when his bike suddenly slides or twitches. Collecting the data and programming the electronics to recognise a crash took considerable effort.

Chris went on to wear the system in other races but forunately never tested it. The system is considerably more sophisticated than the one used – and tested! – by 125 and 250cc riders in previous seasons but at the moment it is not used in the wet because bikes tend to move around more on a wet track and the chances of a spurious inflation are too high. Once the system is deployed it can be removed by pulling two toggles, so a racer could get back on his bike without any hindrance.

There are also obvious applications for road riders, although the protection required is not totally analagous to the needs of racers on a closed track, so Dainese run a street D-air project in parallel with the racing system.

Above Simone Grotzky tested the D-air at Valencia '07: the system was triggered by acceleration of 0.45g at a lean angle of 48 degrees and a speed of 69mph. The inset picture of Vermeulen highlights the panel on his leathers that houses the airbag

BRITISH GP
DONINGTON PARK

ROUND 8
June 24

RACE RESULTS

CIRCUIT LENGTH 2.500 miles
NO. OF LAPS 30
RACE DISTANCE 74.993 miles
WEATHER Dry, 20
TRACK TEMPERATURE 26°C
WINNER Casey Stoner
FASTEST LAP 1m 28.773s, 101.378mph, Casey Stoner
PREVIOUS LAP RECORD 1m 28.174s, 101.445mph, Dani Pedrosa, 2006

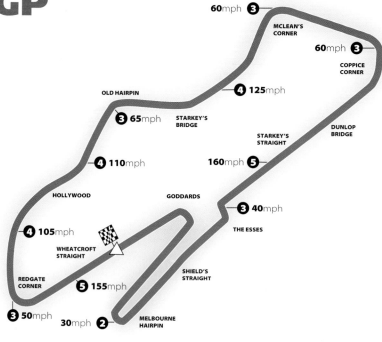

QUALIFYING

	Rider	Nationality	Team	Qualifying	Pole +	Gap
1	Stoner	AUS	Ducati Marlboro Team	1m 38.232s		
2	Rossi	ITA	Fiat Yamaha Team	1m 38.881s	0.649s	0.649s
3	Vermeulen	AUS	Rizla Suzuki MotoGP	1m 39.018s	0.786s	0.137s
4	Hayden	USA	Repsol Honda Team	1m 39.270s	1.038s	0.252s
5	Edwards	USA	Tech 3 Yamaha	1m 39.601s	1.369s	0.331s
6	Dovizioso	ITA	JiR Team Scot MotoGP	1m 39.783s	1.551s	0.182s
7	West	AUS	Kawasaki Racing Team	1m 39.995s	1.763s	0.212s
8	Spies	USA	Rizla Suzuki MotoGP	1m 40.244s	2.012s	0.249s
9	Pedrosa	SPA	Repsol Honda Team	1m 40.350s	2.118s	0.106s
10	Nakano	JPN	San Carlo Honda Gresini	1m 40.417s	2.185s	0.067s
11	Hopkins	USA	Kawasaki Racing Team	1m 40.539s	2.307s	0.122s
12	Guintoli	FRA	Alice Team	1m 40.595s	2.363s	0.056s
13	De Angelis	RSM	San Carlo Honda Gresini	1m 40.667s	2.435s	0.072s
14	De Puniet	FRA	LCR Honda MotoGP	1m 41.110s	2.878s	0.443s
15	Melandri	ITA	Ducati Marlboro Team	1m 41.379s	3.147s	0.269s
16	Toseland	GBR	Tech 3 Yamaha	1m 41.751s	3.519s	0.372s
17	Lorenzo	SPA	Fiat Yamaha Team	1m 41.873s	3.641s	0.122s
18	Elias	SPA	Alice Team	1m 42.933s	4.701s	1.060s

FINISHERS

1 CASEY STONER A half-second faster than anyone in any conditions thanks to the revised '08-spec motor. Won off pole and led every lap without ever looking troubled, but still had a 45-point deficit to championship leader Rossi and refused to talk about the possibility of a title challenge.

2 VALENTINO ROSSI Despite mixed weather rider and team, as usual, made improvements to the bike right up to Sunday morning, but it wasn't enough to let Vale race with Stoner. The good news was his increased lead over Pedrosa at the top of the table after a good fight with the Spaniard.

3 DANI PEDROSA A season's-worst ninth-place qualifying and a good start rather than his customary miracle effort meant it was lap eight before he got behind second-placed Rossi. Made several overtakes but was always repassed immediately, and lost touch when he made a mistake at Foggy's.

4 COLIN EDWARDS Unusually, got thrown by wet practice and annoyed with himself after the race. The short-wheelbase M1 behaves very differently in the wet from the old bike and it took him until part way through the race to realise he had to brake harder and deeper; then ran similar lap times to the top three.

5 ANDREA DOVIZIOSO Again able to run a strong pace in the early laps, and never out of the top five all race long. Took advantage of Hayden's problems to retake fourth just after half-distance. Another impressive race for the rookie on the only track where he won in both smaller classes.

6 JORGE LORENZO By his own admission mentally shattered after a succession of crashes. Qualified on the back row but shoved his way to tenth on the first lap; spent half the race rediscovering his confidence, then overtook four people in the last nine laps to close right up on Dovizioso. A candidate for ride of the day.

7 NICKY HAYDEN Used the pneumatic-valve engine for the first time and had no wish to revert to the old motor. Faster than his team-mate in every session, including qualifying (for the first time this season).

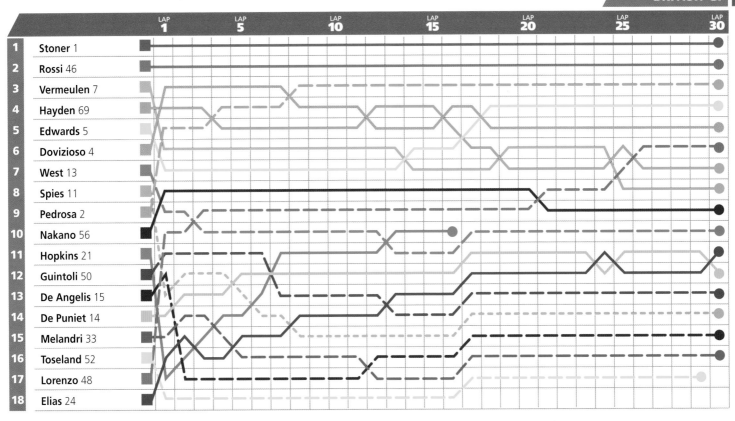

	Rider	LAP 1	LAP 5	LAP 10	LAP 15	LAP 20	LAP 25	LAP 30
1	Stoner 1							
2	Rossi 46							
3	Vermeulen 7							
4	Hayden 69							
5	Edwards 5							
6	Dovizioso 4							
7	West 13							
8	Spies 11							
9	Pedrosa 2							
10	Nakano 56							
11	Hopkins 21							
12	Guintoli 50							
13	De Angelis 15							
14	De Puniet 14							
15	Melandri 33							
16	Toseland 52							
17	Lorenzo 48							
18	Elias 24							

RACE

	Rider	Motorcycle	Race Time	Time +	Fastest Lap	Average Speed
1	Stoner	Ducati	44m 44.982s		1m 28.773s	100.554mph
2	Rossi	Yamaha	44m 50.771s	5.789s	1m 29.080s	100.338mph
3	Pedrosa	Honda	44m 53.329s	8.347s	1m 28.823s	100.243mph
4	Edwards	Yamaha	44m 57.660s	12.678s	1m 29.138s	100.082mph
5	Dovizioso	Honda	44m 59.783s	14.801s	1m 29.053s	100.003mph
6	Lorenzo	Yamaha	45m 00.672s	15.690s	1m 29.275s	99.970mph
7	Hayden	Honda	45m 03.178s	18.196s	1m 29.136s	99.877mph
8	Vermeulen	Suzuki	45m 06.648s	21.666s	1m 29.373s	99.749mph
9	Nakano	Honda	45m 14.336s	29.354s	1m 29.534s	99.467mph
10	West	Kawasaki	45m 26.012s	41.030s	1m 30.024s	99.041mph
11	Elias	Ducati	45m 29.408s	44.426s	1m 29.834s	98.918mph
12	De Puniet	Honda	45m 31.181s	46.199s	1m 30.084s	98.853mph
13	Guintoli	Ducati	45m 33.713s	48.731s	1m 30.441s	98.762mph
14	Spies	Suzuki	45m 34.573s	49.591s	1m 30.106s	98.731mph
15	De Angelis	Honda	46m 07.168s	1m 22.186s	1m 30.059s	97.567mph
16	Melandri	Ducati	46m 15.003s	1m 30.021s	1m 30.750s	97.292mph
17	Toseland	Yamaha	45m 32.234s	1 lap	1m 31.658s	95.521mph
	Hopkins	Kawasaki	24m 18.021s	14 laps	1m 29.827s	98.759mph

CHAMPIONSHIP

	Rider	Team	Points
1	Rossi	Fiat Yamaha Team	162
2	Pedrosa	Repsol Honda Team	151
3	Stoner	Ducati Marlboro Team	117
4	Lorenzo	Fiat Yamaha Team	104
5	Edwards	Tech 3 Yamaha	82
6	Dovizioso	JiR Team Scot MotoGP	68
7	Hayden	Repsol Honda Team	57
8	Toseland	Tech 3 Yamaha	53
9	Capirossi	Rizla Suzuki MotoGP	51
10	Nakano	San Carlo Honda Gresini	49
11	Vermeulen	Rizla Suzuki MotoGP	48
12	Hopkins	Kawasaki Racing Team	32
13	Melandri	Ducati Marlboro Team	29
14	Elias	Alice Team	29
15	De Angelis	San Carlo Honda Gresini	25
16	De Puniet	LCR Honda MotoGP	22
17	Guintoli	Alice Team	18
18	West	Kawasaki Racing Team	16
19	Spies	Rizla Suzuki MotoGP	2
20	Okada	Repsol Honda Team	2

A dash warning light came on at the start of the ninth lap – presumably the motor was using fuel at too high a rate – which took the edge off his confidence and concentration.

8 CHRIS VERMEULEN On the front row for the first time this season thanks to his wet-weather prowess, but unable to convert that into a result. The team had taken a big step forward at the Barcelona test, but he couldn't maintain his pace and lost a couple of places in the last half-dozen laps.

9 SHINYA NAKANO Severe chatter from the front tyre in the second half of the race compromised his promising start and prevented him from attacking Vermeulen in the closing stages as he'd been planning.

10 ANTHONY WEST A test in Japan after the Catalan race boosted Ant's confidence and wet weather helped him achieve Kawasaki's best qualifying performance so far this year – seventh. That performance carried over into the race with a season's best finish so far.

11 TONI ELIAS A gutsy ride after qualifying last, which at least afforded Toni some satisfaction. Rode hard all race and took a place off de Puniet on the last corner.

12 RANDY DE PUNIET A finish at last, after crashes in the two previous races. Sent wide by Toseland's first-bend crash and distracted on the last lap by the track invasion. Not comfortable with his bike going into corners or changing direction.

13 SYLVAIN GUINTOLI Despite the result, there were more hopeful signs for the Frenchman, especially the fifth place he took in wet third free practice and his best qualifying position yet. Used a new front tyre and front-end set-up for the race and maintained an impressive rhythm in the second half.

14 BEN SPIES The double American Superbike Champion made his MotoGP debut as a replacement for the injured Capirossi and impressed everyone, especially with his eighth in qualifying. Didn't make a mistake all weekend and by the second half of the race was running lap times that would have put him in the top ten.

15 ALEX DE ANGELIS Fell at the Melbourne Loop on lap two – like his team-mate he reported serious chatter – but got going 13s behind the pack. Was still able to overhaul poor Melandri inside ten laps and get to the flag for the last point.

16 MARCO MELANDRI Just when you thought his form couldn't get any worse, he had to endure the humiliation of finishing behind rookie de Angelis who had fallen early on and remounted. There was also a telling TV image of team-mate Stoner passing Marco in practice, looking over at him, then giving a slight shake of the head. Ouch.

17 JAMES TOSELAND A traumatic first home GP. Three crashes in practice and qualifying, then another crash at the first corner as he tried to make up for his worst qualifying so far. Banged his head and his hand but picked up the bike and rode to the flag, despite a missing footrest and bent handlebar.

JOHN HOPKINS Seriously hampered by Toseland's crash which put John to the back of the field. Fought back to tenth place before the bike cut out at the Old Hairpin on lap 17.

LORIS CAPIROSSI Ruled out after an operation to repair the hand he broke at Catalunya two weeks earlier. Replaced by Ben Spies.

BACK TO THE FUTURE

Casey Stoner put himself back in championship contention thanks to a second consecutive win and a rare error from Valentino Rossi

Stoner did it again – he was fastest in every session and, once he'd disposed of holeshot man Pedrosa, there was no stopping him. The winning margin was 11 seconds but it could easily have been double that, judging by the relaxed way Casey opened up his lead, from one second at the end of the third lap to five seconds at the end of lap 12. Half of his 26 laps were underneath the existing lap record. At least the World Champion admitted he was apprehensive before the start. He knew Ducati had the package, and the pace, to win whether it was wet or dry 'so the only person who could screw up was me. I was very nervous in the first six or seven laps.' You certainly didn't look it, Casey.

Unlike Valentino Rossi, who had another bad start, then lost the back going too fast into the first left-hander, the remodelled De Strubben, and using too much back brake. The rear slid out and he collected Randy de Puniet. Vale held onto the clutch and, with the help of the marshals, got going 30 seconds behind the field, minus most of his gearchange pedal and with a bent handlebar. Astoundingly, he did the third-fastest lap of the race, 1m 37.173s, changing gear with a bent slice of aluminium, which tends to support his contention that, given the improvements his crew had found, he could actually have given Casey a race. Instead, he said, 'I think I am a dickhead' and decided to finish the race on foot if necessary to get some points. From those 30 seconds back he overhauled Melandri and Elias to finish 11th. Who knows how valuable those five points might be at the end of the year?

There were only thirteen finishers thanks to crashes in the race and in practice. The weekend started with Loris Capirossi taking a high-speed tumble on the fast

session plus qualifying (forecast to be wet) were not sufficient preparation for a Grand Prix, especially with a test session at Indianapolis coming up the following week. Who made the decision? Ben looked unhappy; the team expressed surprise.

John Hopkins was the other serious casualty, sustaining fractures to his left leg and ankle and compression injuries to his knee when he cannoned into an advertising hoarding. Hopper went down very early at the same corner as Capirossi, the Ramshoek, where Elias was injured the previous year and Rossi the season before that. Man and bike skimmed across the tarmac run-off and gravel trap at frightening speed before hitting the hoarding, which was placed in front of the tyre barrier: no air fence. He was lucky, strange as it might seem to use that word about such a collection of injuries, but they would almost certainly keep him out of the German GP and John would find out about his chances of riding at his home race after a trip to Los Angeles to see famed sports surgeon Dr Art Ting.

Behind the runaway winner the Repsol Hondas formed up for what looked like certain second- and third-place finishes. Sure enough, Pedrosa gradually pulled away from team-mate Hayden, who was using the pneumatic-valve motor again; Dani's second place gave him back the lead in the championship. Now Assen is heavy on fuel but it looked as if Nicky was going to take third place and score his first rostrum of the year – right until he came out of the final corner of the final lap and his motor stopped. The bike had been playing up all weekend, running badly when he

Above Nicky Hayden looked more like his old self on the pneumatic-valve Honda

Below Rossi has already clipped de Puniet, putting them both on the floor and forcing Edwards into evasive action

sweepers that end the lap. He might have got away with it, but he tangled with his bike and received a very nasty wound to his right forearm, probably from a footrest. The team was keen to point out that the hand injury the Suzuki rider suffered in Barcelona, and from which he was returning having missed Donington, had no bearing on this crash. It opened the way for Ben Spies, who was at the track in case Loris hadn't been able to start the weekend. However, it was decided that one practice

'WELCOME TO KARMA CORNER!'
COLIN EDWARDS

Above Randy de Puniet went well in qualifying and got his best start of the year only to become a victim of Rossi's mistake

opened the throttle as well as throwing rogue warning lights at him. The problems returned on the warm-up lap and Hayden even considered changing bikes for the race. He reported later that there were no problems in the opening two laps but the trouble returned on the third lap.

Nicky coasted over the line to fourth, just after Colin Edwards had blasted past him to claim third place. No-one needed reminding that this was the corner where Colin crashed two years ago to hand Hayden the win. In the press conference Edwards, grinning from ear to ear, announced: 'There is not one single shred of me that feels sorry for Nicky Hayden!' As Colin had found himself dead last after Rossi's crash this was a more than impressive race to his second rostrum of the year as a satellite team rider. Touchingly, he said how much it meant to have his children there to see their dad up on the rostrum now that they were of an age to understand and remember. He then suggested that the final chicane should be renamed Karma Corner.

Left Edwards signals to Stoner that he'll be seeing him on the rostrum

Below Pedrosa's second place was enough to give him the championship lead

Right Endangered species? A 250cc Aprilia two-stroke V-twin engine

250 FUTURE

The end of the two-stroke 250cc class came a step closer at Assen when the Grand Prix Commission ratified the Motor Sport Manufacturers Association's suggestion for new rules to come into force for the 2011 season.

The MSMA's majority decision – it is difficult to see how Aprilia or KTM would vote for this – was to recommend that the 250cc class switch to 600cc four-stroke engines with a maximum of four cylinders. Presumably the engines would then be bought by teams and built into their own chassis. The GP Commission asked any manufacturer interested in taking part in the new class to notify the FIM and Dorna by the end of July. The announcement was made on June 27. The problem was finding a manufacturer who was willing to declare an interest.

Everyone agreed that the new regulations must produce bikes that would have the characteristics of MotoGP machinery – high corner speeds, high lean angles – at a significantly cheaper price than a factory Aprilia two-stroke. That's if the class is going to continue to be the production line for MotoGP riders. One suggestion, thought to come from IRTA and Dorna, was to use over-the-counter engine components, a control ECU and data logging in order to impose a rev limit, to make an in-line four to build into a team's own engine and chassis. That would avoid the dreaded word 'production' being used, or a control engine. The MSMA doesn't appear to have any such scruples.

One attractive aspect of both suggestions is that it might reopen Grand Prix racing to names like Bimota, Harris, Moriwaki and other specialist chassis designers who were edged out as the top class of racing gradually became restricted to pure factory machinery.

However, the way forward is far from clear.

DUTCH TT
TT CIRCUIT ASSEN
ROUND 9
June 28

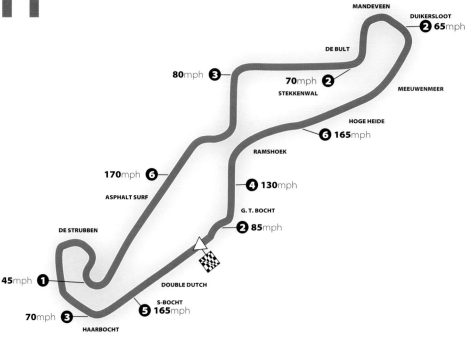

RACE RESULTS

CIRCUIT LENGTH 2.830 miles
NO. OF LAPS 26
RACE DISTANCE 73.592 miles
WEATHER Dry, 20°C
TRACK TEMPERATURE 24°C
WINNER Casey Stoner
FASTEST LAP 1m 36.738s, 105.333mph, Casey Stoner (record)
PREVIOUS LAP RECORD 1m 37.106, 104.934mph, Nicky Hayden, 2006

QUALIFYING

	Rider	Nationality	Team	Qualifying	Pole +	Gap
1	Stoner	AUS	Ducati Marlboro Team	1m 35.520s		
2	Pedrosa	SPA	Repsol Honda Team	1m 35.552s	0.032s	0.032s
3	Rossi	ITA	Fiat Yamaha Team	1m 35.659s	0.139s	0.107s
4	Hayden	USA	Repsol Honda Team	1m 35.975s	0.455s	0.316s
5	De Puniet	FRA	LCR Honda MotoGP	1m 35.895s	0.465s	0.010s
6	Edwards	USA	Tech 3 Yamaha	1m 36.278s	0.758s	0.293s
7	Lorenzo	SPA	Fiat Yamaha Team	1m 36.532s	1.012s	0.254s
8	Vermeulen	AUS	Rizla Suzuki MotoGP	1m 36.768s	1.248s	0.236s
9	Nakano	JPN	San Carlo Honda Gresini	1m 36.804s	1.284s	0.036s
10	Guintoli	FRA	Alice Team	1m 36.823s	1.303s	0.019s
11	Dovizioso	ITA	JiR Team Scot MotoGP	1m 36.899s	1.379s	0.076s
12	De Angelis	RSM	San Carlo Honda Gresini	1m 36.948s	1.428s	0.049s
13	Toseland	GBR	Tech 3 Yamaha	1m 36.978s	1.458s	0.030s
14	Elias	SPA	Alice Team	1m 37.287s	1.767s	0.309s
15	Hopkins	USA	Kawasaki Racing Team	1m 37.643s	2.123s	0.356s
16	West	AUS	Kawasaki Racing Team	1m 37.793s	2.273s	0.150s
17	Melandri	ITA	Ducati Marlboro Team	1m 38.726s	3.206s	0.933s
	Capirossi	ITA	Rizla Suzuki MotoGP			

FINISHERS

1 CASEY STONER From the first moments of free practice there was never any doubt who'd win. Fastest in every session, Casey qualified on pole, was headed for less than a lap, and set new lap and race records. This was also Bridgestone and Ducati's first win at Assen.

2 DANI PEDROSA Qualified on the front row here for the first time. Couldn't match Stoner's pace, but still went back to the top of the table. Used the conventional valve-spring engine again but admitted to being impressed by the performance of the pneumatic-valve motor in the hands of his team-mate.

3 COLIN EDWARDS Dead last after Rossi's crash, he rode through the field to be within three seconds of third-placed Hayden at the end of the penultimate lap. Had settled for fourth when Nicky's machine faltered coming out of the chicane for the last time, so got his revenge for 2006.

4 NICKY HAYDEN Felt a problem on the sighting lap, then a warning light blinked on the grid. The new pneumatic-valve motor hadn't run well all weekend, especially out of the slower corners, and HRC's fuel consumption calculations were out by about 100m; Edwards swept past for the final rostrum spot on the last corner.

5 ANDREA DOVIZIOSO Disappointing qualifying followed by a good race to the position he thought, pre-race, he should be in: 'I believe this is the maximum we could achieve today.' A stunning start from 11th on the grid helped him avoid the first-lap crashes and end the first lap in fifth.

6 JORGE LORENZO Again rode brilliantly in the closing laps after a slightly tentative start and average qualifying. However, it was not the night-and-day Donington performance, hopefully showing that the confidence of the year's first few races is returning.

7 CHRIS VERMEULEN Relieved to salvage a decent finish from a fraught meeting. Effectively lost one free practice session to technical problems and another to rain, then hit the usual mid-race problem

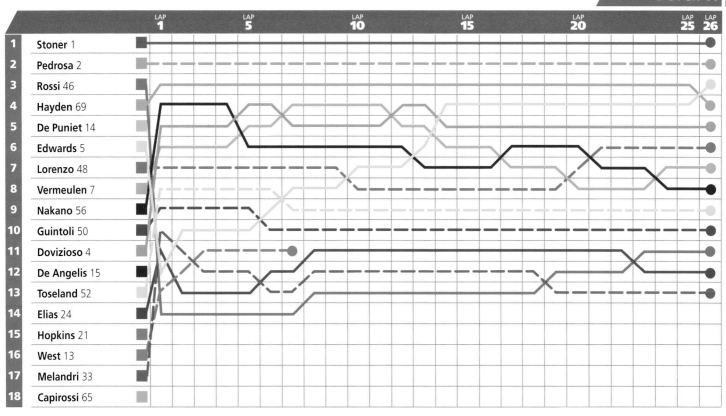

		LAP 1	LAP 5	LAP 10	LAP 15	LAP 20	LAP 25	LAP 26
1	Stoner 1							
2	Pedrosa 2							
3	Rossi 46							
4	Hayden 69							
5	De Puniet 14							
6	Edwards 5							
7	Lorenzo 48							
8	Vermeulen 7							
9	Nakano 56							
10	Guintoli 50							
11	Dovizioso 4							
12	De Angelis 15							
13	Toseland 52							
14	Elias 24							
15	Hopkins 21							
16	West 13							
17	Melandri 33							
18	Capirossi 65							

RACE

	Rider	Motorcycle	Race Time	Time +	Fastest Lap	Average Speed
1	Stoner	Ducati	42m 12.337s		1m 36.738s	104.619mph
2	Pedrosa	Honda	42m 23.647s	11.310s	1m 37.208s	104.154mph
3	Edwards	Yamaha	42m 29.462s	17.125s	1m 37.034s	103.916mph
4	Hayden	Honda	42m 32.814s	20.477s	1m 37.346s	103.780mph
5	Dovizioso	Honda	42m 39.683s	27.346s	1m 37.662s	103.501mph
6	Lorenzo	Yamaha	42m 40.945s	28.608s	1m 37.853s	103.450mph
7	Vermeulen	Suzuki	42m 44.667s	32.330s	1m 37.629s	103.300mph
8	Nakano	Honda	42m 47.229s	34.892s	1m 37.854s	103.197mph
9	Toseland	Yamaha	42m 50.903s	38.566s	1m 37.846s	103.049mph
10	Guintoli	Ducati	42m 51.154s	38.817s	1m 37.982s	103.039mph
11	Rossi	Yamaha	42m 58.362s	46.025s	1m 37.173s	102.752mph
12	Elias	Ducati	43m 00.550s	48.213s	1m 37.705s	102.644mph
13	Melandri	Ducati	43m 11.931s	59.594s	1m 38.676s	102.214mph
	West	Kawasaki	11m 41.383s	19 laps	1m 38.270s	101.695mph
	De Puniet	Honda				
	De Angelis	Honda				

CHAMPIONSHIP

	Rider	Team	Points
1	Pedrosa	Repsol Honda Team	171
2	Rossi	Fiat Yamaha Team	167
3	Stoner	Ducati Marlboro Team	142
4	Lorenzo	Fiat Yamaha Team	114
5	Edwards	Tech 3 Yamaha	98
6	Dovizioso	JiR Team Scot MotoGP	79
7	Hayden	Repsol Honda Team	70
8	Toseland	Tech 3 Yamaha	60
9	Vermeulen	Rizla Suzuki MotoGP	57
10	Nakano	San Carlo Honda Gresini	57
11	Capirossi	Rizla Suzuki MotoGP	51
12	Elias	Alice Team	33
13	Hopkins	Kawasaki Racing Team	32
14	Melandri	Ducati Marlboro Team	32
15	De Angelis	San Carlo Honda Gresini	25
16	Guintoli	Alice Team	24
17	De Puniet	LCR Honda MotoGP	22
18	West	Kawasaki Racing Team	16
19	Spies	Rizla Suzuki MotoGP	2
20	Okada	Repsol Honda Team	2

of running out of grip. Didn't give up, though, and managed to repass Nakano three laps from the flag.

8 SHINYA NAKANO One place higher than his ninth of the previous three races for a season's best so far. His team-manager declared himself satisfied this week – especially with the superb start that saw him up to fourth, where he stayed for the first four laps.

9 JAMES TOSELAND A rebuilding weekend after the disaster of Donington, but setting up severely handicapped by the mixed weather. The short-wheelbase bike is more sensitive than the original, and James and his crew 'have hit a brick wall'. Still, respectably quick in all conditions.

10 SYLVAIN GUINTOLI First top-ten finish of the season after encouraging practice and qualifying. As at Donington was fastest in the final laps, this time while chasing Toseland, and might have finished even higher but for mistakes early on and an off-track excursion as he closed on the Yorkshireman.

11 VALENTINO ROSSI Five valuable points salvaged after he crashed at De Strubben on the first lap, bending a handlebar and breaking the gear lever. His charge back kept the crowd entertained, but he rued a lost opportunity: a change to the front set-up meant he'd had the race pace to go with Stoner. Instead, he lost the championship lead.

12 TONI ELIAS Struggled all through the weekend but at least managed to finish an

Assen race in the top class for the first time. Didn't impress the team by dipping back into the 1m 37s bracket after Rossi came past.

13 MARCO MELANDRI Another horror show despite a promising seventh place in the wet morning warm-up. This time, team-manager Livio Suppo dropped a heavy hint that Marco only had the next two races 'on tracks he likes' to save his job.

NON-FINISHERS

ANTHONY WEST Fought back to 11th after being severely impeded by de Angelis's crash before losing the front himself at Stekkenwal.

RANDY DE PUNIET Often the instigator of crashes, this time the Frenchman was the innocent victim of Rossi's first-lap mistake and was scooped up in the first tight left-hander. Got way with an abraded thigh.

ALEX DE ANGLIS Crashed on lap one in second left-hander, but claimed not to know why. Team-manager Fausto Gresini suggested that after crashing in the previous two races as well, a bit of caution might have been in order.

to his right forearm, probably from a footrest, which put him out of the race.

JOHN HOPKINS Another victim of Ramshoek. Crashed very early in the corner before he'd scrubbed off much speed with the brakes, hammering into the tyre wall feet first at high speed, and breaking his left ankle and tibia. Definitely out of the German GP and probably Laguna Seca too.

NON-STARTERS

LORIS CAPIROSSI Highsided at the very rapid Ramshoek left-hander, probably because the left side of the tyre wasn't up to temperature. Received a nasty puncture wound

GERMAN GP
SACHSENRING CIRCUIT
ROUND 10
July 13

TYRE TROUBLES

Casey Stoner made it three wins in a row to move to within twenty points of the championship leader, as Michelin made a tactical error

Another dominant victory made it three in a row for Casey Stoner, and he gave the rest of the field not a glimmer of hope on Friday or Saturday. The win came from his fourth consecutive pole position, each one being won on the back of being fastest in free practice. He set the fastest race lap for the third time in a row, too.

Yet still the reigning champion sensed there were doubters – journalists pressing him for details of the new electronics package his Ducati might have, or that one of his rivals had told the press he must be using to go so quickly. A Dutch TV man asked Stoner if his form was, perhaps, a function of the hard times he'd had at the beginning of the season. Casey was inclined to agree: 'It was almost necessary to have the bad times ... I looked hard at myself and tried harder, I learned how to push this bike further than it wants.' The Aussie believes he is now reaping the rewards of that effort. He also appears to be drawing strength from what he perceives as the unwillingness of many elements in the media to give him the credit he deserves or, rather, that they are so desperate to find a magic bullet which will explain his speed. 'It amazes me; nobody wants to believe.' This is said with an air of puzzlement. The bike has certainly improved, and so has Stoner, according to Valentino Rossi, who believes both are stronger now than last year. Which is saying something.

For a while it looked as if Dani Pedrosa was going to bury for ever the notion that he can't ride in the rain. In five laps of a streaming wet Sachsenring he opened up a lead of 7.5 seconds before pushing just that fraction too hard and falling at the first corner. He was sliding harmlessly, if rapidly, until he hit the gravel trap, then he

tumbled at high speed into the air fence. There was definite damage to his left hand and wrist plus a suspected broken ankle. Even more serious was the damage to his championship hopes. He lost the points lead to Rossi and went home to Barcelona to see Dr Mir before making a decision about Laguna Seca.

Pedrosa's crash left Stoner, who had been admiring Dani's pace from a distance, out in front. Casey kept an eye on the gap behind him, and set a run of fastest laps around mid-distance to keep his pursuers at bay. The only man who looked as if he might be able to race with him was Valentino Rossi who, for once, should have been grateful that it rained. On a dry track the Yamaha rider was 0.4s off the Ducati's pace and would have been lucky to get on the rostrum. The wet meant Rossi limited the damage. Valentino was fifth when Pedrosa crashed, third by lap eight and second next time round, a position he held until the flag and that put him back on top of the table. As he reminded everyone, not a bad result for his first wet race on Bridgestones at a circuit he doesn't like too much. He made another point very strongly after the race: if he was going to be able to race with Casey, and by implication stave off Stoner's championship challenge, then from now on he was going to have to qualify on the front row. No-one argued with Valentino's assumption that Casey would be a front-row fixture.

The departure of Pedrosa left third place open to someone outside the usual rostrum contenders. Edwards had been there twice this year but he crashed on lap 21, while the top Michelin rider, Dovizioso, ran second early on but couldn't get enough heat in his tyres to stay with the Bridgestone runners. (This was a complete reversal of the tyre situation at the Sachsenring twelve months previously when temperatures had been scorching.) It was down to regular rainmaster Chris Vermeulen to work his way up, along with Ant West, who then crashed out after an uncharacteristic mistake, and surprise package Alex de Angelis. The Gresini Honda man shadowed Chris for the last two-thirds of the race, looking and learning, but couldn't find a way to pass, so Suzuki got their first rostrum of the year. It's worth remembering that this was de Angelis's first wet MotoGP race, and he was fighting for a rostrum with Vermeulen. Chris dislikes the 'rainmaster' tag but there's no denying the fact that when it's wet he figures at the front.

Above Pedrosa slams into the airfence. It was the end of his championship hopes

Opposite Nicky Hayden pitted for a new tyre after just one lap

Below Jorge Lorenzo is helped away after falling, one of three Michelin runners to crash

Above The fight for
third; de Angelis stalked
Vermeulen but never
managed to find a way past

Below Rossi scrapping in
the midfield on the first lap

Opposite Sylvain Guintoli
cheered up the Alice Ducati
team with a remarkable
fifth place – without
traction control

Unfortunately for the Michelin users, the French
company's management insisted that their teams use
hard-compound wet tyres in case the track started
drying. It is true that in comparison with the Bridgestone
opposition wet Michelins destroy themselves remarkably
quickly if a dry line appears. However, Michelin's
management must have been the only people in the
whole of Germany who were under the impression that
the weather was going to change for the better.
Edwards, Lorenzo and Pedrosa all fell, while Nicky
Hayden had to come in at the end of the first lap to
change his rear tyre, which made the increasingly
impressive Andrea Dovizioso's fifth place all the more
praiseworthy. However, he was 42 seconds behind
the winner.

Both first- and second-place men had the added
satisfaction of setting new records. Casey Stoner took the
100th victory by an Australian in the top class, while
Valentino Rossi started his 202nd consecutive Grand Prix.
He hasn't missed a race since he started his GP career, and
to make it even sweeter the man he took the record off is
none other than his old enemy, Max Biaggi.

CHANGE OF OWNER

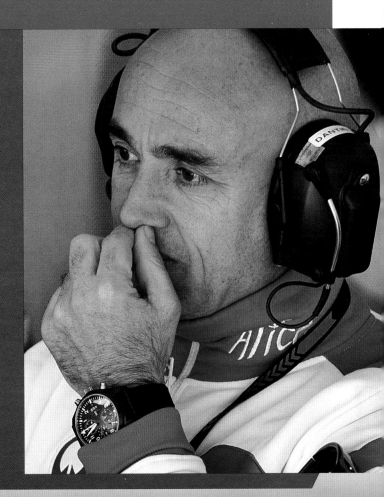

Luis d'Antin, ex-racer and founder of the Pramac d'Antin Alice-sponsored Ducati satellite team, was conspicuous by his absence from the Sachsenring. His MotoGP pass was pulled by Dorna after the Dutch TT following meetings between Dorna, d'Antin and Paolo Campinoti, co-owner of the team as well as boss of naming sponsor Pramac. The team had underperformed all season and there were rumours of unpaid hotel bills and of mechanics wages arriving late or not at all. The riders had not fared much better. Alex Barros even reported that the team hadn't bothered to employ a suspension technician when he was riding for them.

Campinoti took over the entire assets of the team at no cost prior to d'Antin's departure.

D'Antin was one of the five team owners who were signatories to Dorna's franchise contracts. The teams of Sito Pons, Kenny Roberts and Peter Clifford/Bob McLean had all folded over recent seasons, leaving only the Tech 3 team of Hervé Poncharal surviving from the original five.

Campinoti's immediate task was to reassure Alice, the team's sponsor, that things would improve and improve quickly. There were also signs that Ducati's Bologna headquarters were going to take a much closer interest in their satellite squad. Updated electronics with variable-length inlet tracts were the first evidence of this more hands-on approach. There was also talk of the team being linked more directly with the factory, perhaps as a junior or academy team. Whatever the future holds, Sylvain Guintoli cheered the team up with a season's best sixth place. What's more, he did it after switching off his malfunctioning traction control, thus gladdening the hearts of traditionalists everywhere.

GERMAN GP
SACHSENRING CIRCUIT
ROUND 10
July 13

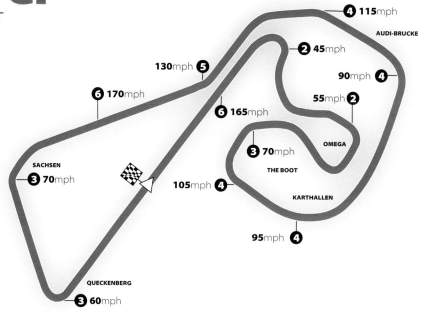

4 115mph
AUDI-BRUCKE
2 45mph
130mph 5
90mph 4
6 170mph
55mph 2
6 165mph
OMEGA
3 70mph
THE BOOT
SACHSEN
3 70mph
105mph 4
KARTHALLEN
95mph 4
QUECKENBERG
3 60mph

RACE RESULTS

CIRCUIT LENGTH 2.281 miles
NO. OF LAPS 30
RACE DISTANCE 68.43 miles
WEATHER Wet, 14°C
TRACK TEMPERATURE 17°C
WINNER Casey Stoner
FASTEST LAP 1m 32.749, 88.541mph, Casey Stoner
PREVIOUS LAP RECORD 1m 23.082, 98.844mph, Dani Pedrosa, 2007

QUALIFYING

	Rider	Nationality	Team	Qualifying	Pole +	Gap
1	Stoner	AUS	Ducati Marlboro Team	1m 21.067s		
2	Pedrosa	SPA	Repsol Honda Team	1m 21.420s	0.353s	0.353s
3	Edwards	USA	Tech 3 Yamaha	1m 21.519s	0.452s	0.099s
4	Dovizioso	ITA	JiR Team Scot MotoGP	1m 21.656s	0.589s	0.137s
5	Lorenzo	SPA	Fiat Yamaha Team	1m 21.795s	0.728s	0.139s
6	De Puniet	FRA	LCR Honda MotoGP	1m 21.821s	0.754s	0.026s
7	Rossi	ITA	Fiat Yamaha Team	1m 21.845s	0.778s	0.024s
8	Hayden	USA	Repsol Honda Team	1m 21.876s	0.809s	0.031s
9	Nakano	JPN	San Carlo Honda Gresini	1m 21.920s	0.853s	0.044s
10	De Angelis	RSM	San Carlo Honda Gresini	1m 21.977s	0.910s	0.057s
11	Toseland	GBR	Tech 3 Yamaha	1m 22.126s	1.059s	0.149s
12	Elias	SPA	Alice Team	1m 22.256s	1.189s	0.130s
13	Capirossi	ITA	Rizla Suzuki MotoGP	1m 22.542s	1.475s	0.286s
14	Vermeulen	AUS	Rizla Suzuki MotoGP	1m 22.601s	1.534s	0.059s
15	Guintoli	FRA	Alice Team	1m 22.938s	1.871s	0.337s
16	Melandri	ITA	Ducati Marlboro Team	1m 23.131s	2.064s	0.193s
17	West	AUS	Kawasaki Racing Team	1m 23.158s	2.091s	0.027s

FINISHERS

1 CASEY STONER Four poles and three victories in consecutive races. Casey dominated all weekend and gave Ducati and Bridgestone their first wins at the Sachsenring. It was also the 100th victory by an Australian in the top class. Dedicated the win to his team as a thank you for their hard work.

2 VALENTINO ROSSI Happy to be back on top of the championship and to have set a new record for consecutive GP starts – 202 of them – but never got near Stoner in the race. Made the point that if he wants to beat the reigning champion he will need to start from the front row.

3 CHRIS VERMEULEN First rostrum of the season for Suzuki, and a great ride from 14th on the grid, taking just ten laps to get up to third. May say he doesn't enjoy riding in the rain, but it's doubtful he'd have figured anywhere near the rostrum without it. Relieved he took Bridgestone's advice to use a hard tyre.

4 ALEX DE ANGELIS A stunning result in his first wet MotoGP race, doubly so as he started from tenth on the grid. Pressed Vermeulen hard from half-distance, never more than 0.75s behind the Aussie and a lot closer in the closing stages. Probably deprived of the chance of a last-lap attack by backmarker Elias.

5 ANDREA DOVIZIOSO Started from fourth, his best grid position in MotoGP, and finished first Michelin runner on a track he professes to dislike in his first wet-weather ride on the RCV. Ran second for the first eight laps before being passed by Vermeulen, de Angelis and Edwards – couldn't go with them because his rear tyre was too hard.

6 SYLVAIN GUINTOLI Easily his best result of the season so far, despite a massive crash on Saturday morning that saw him qualify 15th. A great start set him up for a good race that might've turned bad when his traction control started playing up – so he switched it off. Used variable-length inlet tracts for the first time.

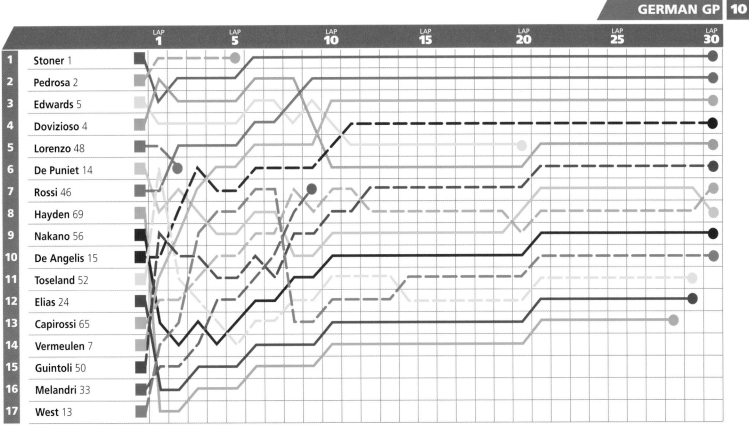

		LAP 1	LAP 5	LAP 10	LAP 15	LAP 20	LAP 25	LAP 30
1	Stoner 1							
2	Pedrosa 2							
3	Edwards 5							
4	Dovizioso 4							
5	Lorenzo 48							
6	De Puniet 14							
7	Rossi 46							
8	Hayden 69							
9	Nakano 56							
10	De Angelis 15							
11	Toseland 52							
12	Elias 24							
13	Capirossi 65							
14	Vermeulen 7							
15	Guintoli 50							
16	Melandri 33							
17	West 13							

RACE

	Rider	Motorcycle	Race Time	Time +	Fastest Lap	Average Speed
1	Stoner	Ducati	47m 30.057s		1m 32.749s	86.441mph
2	Rossi	Yamaha	47m 33.765s	3.708s	1m 33.041s	86.329mph
3	Vermeulen	Suzuki	47m 44.059s	14.002s	1m 33.446s	86.019mph
4	De Angelis	Honda	47m 44.181s	14.124s	1m 33.405s	86.015mph
5	Dovizioso	Honda	48m 12.079s	42.022s	1m 33.923s	85.185mph
6	Guintoli	Ducati	48m 16.705s	46.648s	1m 34.316s	85.049mph
7	Capirossi	Suzuki	48m 34.540s	1m 04.483s	1m 35.274s	84.529mph
8	De Puniet	Honda	48m 34.645s	1m 04.588s	1m 35.343s	84.526mph
9	Nakano	Honda	48m 46.830s	1m 16.773s	1m 35.710s	84.174mph
10	West	Kawasaki	48m 59.332s	1m 29.275s	1m 35.191s	83.816mph
11	Toseland	Yamaha	47m 41.757s	1 lap	1m 36.239s	83.219mph
12	Elias	Ducati	47m 43.954s	1 lap	1m 35.631s	83.155mph
13	Hayden	Honda	48m 13.749s	2 laps	1m 36.789s	79.460mph
	Edwards	Yamaha	32m 10.373s	10 laps	1m 34.066s	85.083mph
	Melandri	Ducati	14m 50.161s	21 laps	1m 35.750s	83.028mph
	Pedrosa	Honda	8m 05.615s	25 laps	1m 35.954s	84.553mph
	Lorenzo	Yamaha	3m 23.795s	28 laps	1m 40.562s	86.806mph

CHAMPIONSHIP

	Rider	Team	Points
1	Rossi	Fiat Yamaha Team	187
2	Pedrosa	Repsol Honda Team	171
3	Stoner	Ducati Marlboro Team	167
4	Lorenzo	Fiat Yamaha Team	114
5	Edwards	Tech 3 Yamaha	98
6	Dovizioso	JiR Team Scot MotoGP	90
7	Vermeulen	Rizla Suzuki MotoGP	73
8	Hayden	Repsol Honda Team	73
9	Toseland	Tech 3 Yamaha	65
10	Nakano	San Carlo Honda Gresini	64
11	Capirossi	Rizla Suzuki MotoGP	60
12	De Angelis	San Carlo Honda Gresini	38
13	Elias	Alice Team	37
14	Guintoli	Alice Team	34
15	Hopkins	Kawasaki Racing Team	32
16	Melandri	Ducati Marlboro Team	32
17	De Puniet	LCR Honda MotoGP	30
18	West	Kawasaki Racing Team	22
19	Spies	Rizla Suzuki MotoGP	2
20	Okada	Repsol Honda Team	2

7 LORIS CAPIROSSI Suffering much more than he expected from the Assen arm injury, so grateful for Sunday's wet weather which made changes of direction less painful. Had every excuse for taking it easy but fought all the way and overtook de Puniet on the very last corner.

8 RANDY DE PUNIET Blamed his hard tyres for a lack of grip on the right side throughout the race: 'I was riding on eggs.' Nevertheless, second Michelin user home despite going straight on at the first corner on lap eight.

9 SHINYA NAKANO Another less than impressive showing, especially for a rider on Bridgestone tyres. Lost the front a couple of times early on and never got a good feeling from his front tyre.

10 ANTHONY WEST Two big crashes in practice left Ant with cracked vertebrae, but the weather on race day should have helped him. Got up to seventh behind de Angelis and Vermeulen before making an uncharacteristic mistake on lap eight. Remounted and made two passes before the flag.

11 JAMES TOSELAND Not an easy wet-weather MotoGP debut. A great start turned into an average race, continuing James's run of disappointing results. Lack of grip at the rear was the main problem.

12 TONI ELIAS Said it was probably the worst wet race he'd ever run. Reported feeling 'a lot of weight on the front' and consequently he 'couldn't handle the rear'.

13 NICKY HAYDEN Stopped at the end of the first lap to change his rear tyre, only to hit serious electrical problems. A weekend Nicky himself described as 'a bit of a disaster'.

NON-FINISHERS

COLIN EDWARDS Started from the front row and got up to third early on but suffered from lack of rear grip. Realised a rostrum was out of the question so tried to keep Dovizioso behind him, to be first Michelin runner

home, then crashed in the downhill left, giving his neck a severe jolt.

MARCO MELANDRI Just when it all looked to be going well – he was up to seventh, having passed seven riders and had just set fastest lap – Marco crashed on lap ten. There were signs of improvement in the dry as well as the wet, so team and rider both hoped they'd reached a turning point.

DANI PEDROSA For five laps it looked as if he was going to win by a record margin. Had a lead of more than 7s over Stoner when he went down hard on the first corner of the sixth lap and hit the air fence. Broke bones in his left hand, potentially compromising his US GP outing in a week's time.

JORGE LORENZO Another victim of lack of rear-tyre grip. Was trying to regain two places lost a couple of corners earlier when he spun the rear coming out of Turn 4 and crashed, fortunately without injury.

NON-STARTER

JOHN HOPKINS Back in the US and recovering from an operation to repair the damage suffered to his left leg at Assen. Kawasaki did not put another rider on his bike for the German GP, but announced that Jamie Hacking would ride it at Laguna Seca the following weekend.

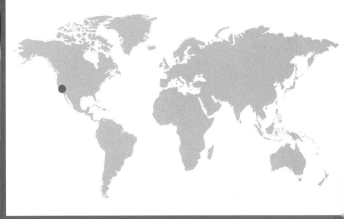

MASTER CLASS

Valentino Rossi won the best race of the 800cc era and then dealt a few psychological blows to Casey Stoner. Vermeulen made it consecutive rostrums for Suzuki

With hindsight it is possible to work out what got to Casey Stoner. After losing the hardest fought race of the 800cc formula (between the two best riders of the moment) Stoner permitted himself a minor grumble about Rossi's riding and then somehow escalated his complaints into accusations of favouritism and talk of losing respect. Finally he allowed questioners to lead him into all but accusing Valentino of deliberately brake-testing him. It is true that Rossi put a couple of hard passes on him while riding the perfect defensive line for a tight and twisty track, repassing the Ducati immediately any time Casey managed to get in front. The pass at the top of the Corkscrew on lap four, for instance, where Valentino ran off track after diving up the inside, was definitely close to the edge. On lap 23 after yet another exchange of the lead Rossi's sweep round the outside of Stoner at Turn 4 was truly awe inspiring, and led to the pivotal moment of the race (and the championship?). Rossi never let the Ducati have a clear run down the front straight – Casey always had to try and go the long way round the Yamaha – so Valentino was gaining an instant couple of bike lengths' advantage out of the final turn. The one time the Aussie did get past over the flat-out hump of Turn 1, Rossi pulled that move at the Corkscrew later the same lap.

Now Casey came up through dirt track before tackling the 125 and 250cc classes, so he can't be afraid of a bit of elbow bashing – although it should be noted that the bikes never touched. What must have rattled him was the sudden disappearance on race day of the massive advantage he'd had all through practice

Above On his second
MotoGP ride, Ben Spies
again impressed

Below AMA Superbike
veteran Jamie Hacking
replaced John Hopkins and
beat his temporary team-
mate Ant West

and qualifying – 0.7s and 0.4s, respectively, on a lap of
just over 1m 20s. It was his fifth successive pole, too,
and although no rider, least of all the driven man that
is Casey Stoner, would ever admit to complacency,
surely there must have been just a hint of satisfaction
with a job that seemed well done?

What happened was that Rossi put into effect the
lessons he'd learnt in Germany, namely that he had to
start from the front row and he had start well. A
minor glitch with the M1's clutch took some of the

blame, although it must be said Valentino has never
been one for rocket starts followed by a rapid
disappearing act. That bad habit was well and truly
cured. He was aided yet again by a couple of tenths of
a second that Jerry Burgess and the crew magicked up
on Sunday morning, the time probably coming from
front-end tweaks that fine-tuned the Yamaha's already
exemplary stability on the brakes, which enabled
Valentino to get in and out of the nasty, better than a
right-angle left-hander that ends the lap significantly
faster than the Ducati. (The watching Randy Mamola
pinpointed this as the vital area of the lap.) Because
Rossi gained ground coming out of the corner Stoner
didn't have enough time to wind the Ducati up and
power past over Turn 1 and then have enough of an
advantage to keep the Yamaha behind him when they
hit the brakes for Turn 2. He knew it; Valentino knew
it. So Casey was over-riding into that final corner, on
more than one occasion kicking the Ducati's back
wheel in the air and having to move wide and off-line
as Rossi hugged the efficient inside line.

The mistake that decided the race came here, on
lap 24 of 32, when Stoner again pushed too hard in
the final corner and ran on into the gravel trap. What
he didn't know was that the gravel started as just a
shallow layer on tarmac but suddenly got much
deeper. When he hit that area he tumbled at low
speed. Such was the advantage the two leaders had
pulled on the field that Casey was able to remount
without forfeiting second place. He lost nearly 14
seconds to Rossi but kept an advantage of 9s over
third-placed Chris Vermeulen.

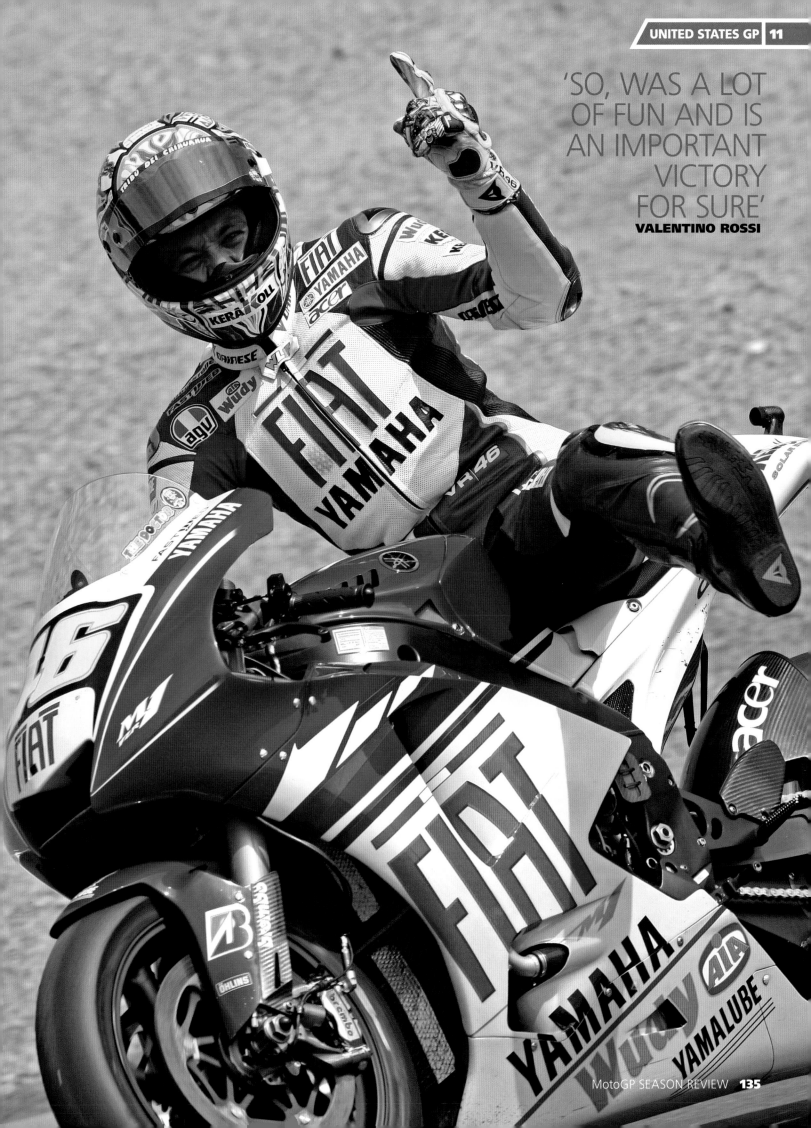

'SO, WAS A LOT OF FUN AND IS AN IMPORTANT VICTORY FOR SURE'

VALENTINO ROSSI

from. The upshot was that most Michelin users ended up with just two suitable tyres: one was obviously saved for race day, the other was used on Saturday afternoon. The situation was so bad that we were treated to the sight of riders using intermediates for morning sessions.

Come race day, the Hondas on Michelins took a few laps to get some heat into their tyres but Dovizioso, Hayden and de Puniet were then able to get up to speed and finish fourth, fifth and sixth, respectively. Edwards and Toseland on the Tech 3 Yamahas, however, never had their tyres within 15° of their working temperature; Colin, always a front-end rider, just never got going while James lost all traction in the closing laps. The Michelin man who suffered most, though, was Jorge Lorenzo who endured an even bigger highside than he had in Shanghai, on the second corner of the first lap – a classic cold-tyre crash.

Having found Stoner's vulnerable point on the track, Rossi kept it going after the flag. He waited in parc fermé until Casey was talking to the BBC's interviewer, then came across to offer his hand and say 'Great race'. The Aussie did not agree, said so, and refused to shake hands. Valentino came back with 'That's racing, Casey' and got 'We'll see' in response. Things were more cordial on the rostrum, but when the press started probing Casey's complaints he became more vocal. According to noises emanating from the Fiat Yamaha camp, this had the sole effect of making Valentino Rossi a very angry man.

Above Rossi gives thanks for his first Laguna Seca win

Below Chris Vermeulen got on the rostrum for the second race running

Opposite Stoner picks the Desmosedici out of the Turn 11 gravel trap. The pivotal moment of the season?

The intensity of their fight for the win and, one felt, for psychological dominance, overshadowed everything else. The battle behind Rossi and Stoner was, for the second race running, determined largely by which tyres were being used. And Michelin got it wrong for the second race running, bringing harder tyres than their riders wanted. This wasn't a failure of the product but, as at Sachsenring, a mistake by management. The front tyre that Colin Edwards habitually uses and in which he has total confidence, for example, wasn't even in the selection he could pick

ROSSI VERSUS THE REST

In his 500cc/MotoGP career, Valentino Rossi has had three great rivals: Max Biaggi, Sete Gibernau and, now, Casey Stoner. Being beaten by a rider who is not a long-term threat for the title doesn't bother him – he joins in the back-slapping and doesn't waste ammunition. Tiger Woods is exactly the same when a one-hit wonder wins a tournament, but not when the world number two triumphs. Rossi's attitude to and analysis of his three challengers is illuminating.

Max he characterises as strong on a two-stroke but 'not a lot of problem' on a four-stroke. However, Biaggi had 'strong media power' and in the beginning that caused a few problems with the Italian press.

Gibernau, says Vale, was 'faster than Max and good on a four-stroke'. Sete's problem was that he got too wound up before a race and arrived with 'too much emotion and aggression, so he make mistakes'. And Gibernau as a person? 'At the start I think I like him, then I get to know him and decide I don't like him. But, you put Max's head on Sete...'

Which brings us to Stoner. 'He is very, very fast, especially at the limit. He knows it and uses it – you need a great feeling for that.' What about Casey's ability to ride the Ducati that no-one else can master? Valentino spreads the fingers on both hands, then brings them together so they interlock: 'Perfect fit.'

'However, he knows he is the best and therefore does not respect his rivals; I have to give him a problem.'

It is safe to say that Valentino had done just that.

UNITED STATES GP
LAGUNA SECA

ROUND 11
July 20

OFFICIAL TIMEKEEPER

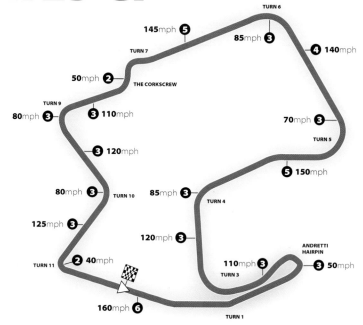

RACE RESULTS

CIRCUIT LENGTH 2.243 miles
NO. OF LAPS 32
RACE DISTANCE 71.776 miles
WEATHER Dry, 21°C
TRACK TEMPERATURE 34°C
WINNER Valentino Rossi
FASTEST LAP 1m 21.488s,
99.103mph, Casey Stoner (record)
PREVIOUS LAP RECORD 1m 22.542s,
97.838mph, Casey Stoner, 2007

QUALIFYING

	Rider	Nationality	Team	Qualifying	Pole +	Gap
1	Stoner	AUS	Ducati Team	1m 20.700s		
2	Rossi	ITA	Fiat Yamaha Team	1m 21.147s	0.447s	0.447s
3	Hayden	USA	Repsol Honda Team	1m 21.430s	0.730s	0.283s
4	Lorenzo	SPA	Fiat Yamaha Team	1m 21.636s	0.936s	0.206s
5	Toseland	GBR	Tech 3 Yamaha	1m 21.848s	1.148s	0.212s
6	De Puniet	FRA	LCR Honda MotoGP	1m 21.921s	1.221s	0.073s
7	Edwards	USA	Tech 3 Yamaha	1m 21.947s	1.247s	0.026s
8	Vermeulen	AUS	Rizla Suzuki MotoGP	1m 21.971s	1.271s	0.024s
9	Dovizioso	ITA	JiR Team Scot MotoGP	1m 21.974s	1.274s	0.003s
10	Elias	SPA	Alice Team	1m 21.999s	1.299s	0.025s
11	Capirossi	ITA	Rizla Suzuki MotoGP	1m 22.039s	1.339s	0.040s
12	Nakano	JPN	San Carlo Honda Gresini	1m 22.092s	1.392s	0.053s
13	Spies	USA	Rizla Suzuki MotoGP	1m 22.127s	1.427s	0.035s
14	Guintoli	FRA	Alice Team	1m 22.719s	2.019s	0.592s
15	Melandri	ITA	Ducati Team	1m 22.957s	2.257s	0.238s
16	De Angelis	RSM	San Carlo Honda Gresini	1m 23.035s	2.335s	0.078s
17	Hacking	USA	Kawasaki Racing Team	1m 23.309s	2.609s	0.274s
18	West	AUS	Kawasaki Racing Team	1m 24.525s	3.825s	1.216s
	Pedrosa	SPA	Repsol Honda Team			

FINISHERS

1 VALENTINO ROSSI First win in the USA. Rode the perfect defensive race on a tight track and was able to repass Stoner whenever he found a way to the front. An excellent win, but credit must go to his pit crew, too: they found Vale the extra couple of tenths after warm-up that enabled him to race Casey and the Ducati.

2 CASEY STONER Lost his chance of the win by running straight on at the last corner on lap 24, forfeiting 14s but keeping second place. Not happy with a couple of Rossi's moves, but arguably even less happy not winning after being so much faster than everyone in practice, and setting pole and fastest lap again.

3 CHRIS VERMEULEN Two podiums in a row for the first time, and two in a row at Laguna as well. His eighth-place qualifying time came on race tyres and he had to fight with Hayden and Dovizioso before taking third at quarter-distance, after which he had a lonely race.

4 ANDREA DOVIZIOSO His third fourth place of the season and fifth successive top-five finish – all the more remarkable as the MotoGP rookie and Laguna Seca debutant was first Honda and first Michelin user home, getting the better of Hayden and de Puniet on similar equipment.

5 NICKY HAYDEN Set his bike up using a tyre that had done 35 laps by the end of practice so the grip of a new race tyre changed its balance significantly, and he found the front pushing a lot in the race. Couldn't hold off Vermeulen or Dovizioso, but did keep de Puniet behind him.

6 RANDY DE PUNIET The LCR team's best weekend of the year so far. Qualified sixth after a terrible Friday and despite the usual Michelin rear-grip issues and his traditional iffy start got back up to sixth for his best finish in the first part of the season.

7 TONI ELIAS Best finish of the season so far despite the fact he yo-yo'd up and down the standings in the early laps after a superb start. In the last three laps he took Spies, Toseland and Nakano. This was more like the Toni Elias we've been used to seeing.

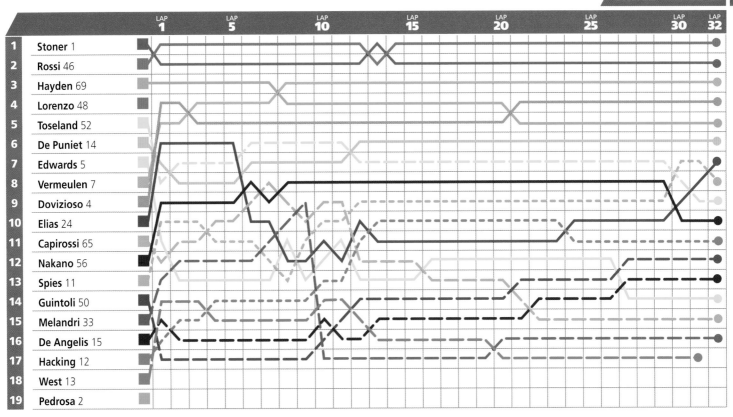

		LAP 1	LAP 5	LAP 10	LAP 15	LAP 20	LAP 25	LAP 30	LAP 32
1	Stoner 1								
2	Rossi 46								
3	Hayden 69								
4	Lorenzo 48								
5	Toseland 52								
6	De Puniet 14								
7	Edwards 5								
8	Vermeulen 7								
9	Dovizioso 4								
10	Elias 24								
11	Capirossi 65								
12	Nakano 56								
13	Spies 11								
14	Guintoli 50								
15	Melandri 33								
16	De Angelis 15								
17	Hacking 12								
18	West 13								
19	Pedrosa 2								

RACE

	Rider	Motorcycle	Race Time	Time +	Fastest Lap	Average Speed
1	Rossi	Yamaha	44m 04.311s		1m 21.713s	97.727mph
2	Stoner	Ducati	44m 17.312s	13.001s	1m 21.488s	97.249mph
3	Vermeulen	Suzuki	44m 30.920s	26.609s	1m 22.499s	96.753mph
4	Dovizioso	Honda	44m 39.212s	34.901s	1m 23.047s	96.454mph
5	Hayden	USA	44m 39.974s	35.663s	1m 22.915s	96.795mph
6	De Puniet	FRA	44m 41.979s	37.668s	1m 23.070s	96.354mph
7	Elias	Ducati	44m 45.940s	41.629s	1m 22.795s	96.212mph
8	Spies	Suzuki	44m 46.238s	41.927s	1m 22.966s	96.202mph
9	Toseland	GBR	44m 47.330s	43.019s	1m 23.216s	96.162mph
10	Nakano	Honda	44m 48.702s	44.391s	1m 23.014s	96.113mph
11	Hacking	Kawasaki	44m 50.569s	46.258s	1m 23.063s	96.047mph
12	Guintoli	Ducati	44m 59.584s	55.273s	1m 23.332s	95.726mph
13	De Angelis	Honda	44m 59.832s	55.521s	1m 23.107s	95.717mph
14	Edwards	Yamaha	45m 06.691s	1m 02.380s	1m 23.394s	95.475mph
15	Capirossi	Suzuki	45m 12.518s	1m 08.207s	1m 23.378s	95.269mph
16	Melandri	Ducati	45m 15.273s	1m 10.962s	1m 23.142s	95.173mph
17	West	Kawasaki	44m 34.872s	1 lap	1m 24.226s	93.592mph
	Lorenzo	Yamaha				

CHAMPIONSHIP

	Rider	Team	Points
1	Rossi	Fiat Yamaha Team	212
2	Stoner	Ducati Team	187
3	Pedrosa	Repsol Honda Team	171
4	Lorenzo	Fiat Yamaha Team	114
5	Dovizioso	JiR Team Scot MotoGP	103
6	Edwards	Tech 3 Yamaha	100
7	Vermeulen	Rizla Suzuki MotoGP	89
8	Hayden	Repsol Honda Team	84
9	Toseland	Tech 3 Yamaha	72
10	Nakano	San Carlo Honda Gresini	70
11	Capirossi	Rizla Suzuki MotoGP	61
12	Elias	Alice Team	46
13	De Angelis	San Carlo Honda Gresini	41
14	De Puniet	LCR Honda MotoGP	40
15	Guintoli	Alice Team	38
16	Hopkins	Kawasaki Racing Team	32
17	Melandri	Ducati Team	32
18	West	Kawasaki Racing Team	22
19	Spies	Rizla Suzuki MotoGP	10
20	Hacking	Kawasaki Racing Team	5
21	Okada	Repsol Honda Team	2

8 BEN SPIES Another impressive performance from the double American Superbike Champion, this time as a wild-card entry. Thought he had a lap left when Elias came past him last time round. Unwell after the race, he was taken to hospital for an appendectomy.

9 JAMES TOSELAND Disappointed with the result but realistic about what he could have achieved with the package available. Got a great start but couldn't get any heat in the front tyre. Had to defend for most of the race due to lack of grip from the rear, but lost two places in the last three laps.

10 SHINYA NAKANO Handicapped by lowly qualifying thanks to a crash in practice, then lost a lot of ground when he ran wide trying to pass Toseland for seventh. Disappointed given the good pace he showed in free practice.

11 JAMIE HACKING Became the oldest GP debutant as he replaced the injured Hopkins. Started slowly from the back of the grid and worked his way up to tenth. Put pressure on Spies, who set his fastest laps holding off his AMA Championship rival. Only Elias's late charge kept the Hacker out of the top ten.

12 SYLVAIN GUINTOLI Lack of feeling from the left side of his rear tyre, so lapping half a second slower than in practice. An off-track excursion didn't help either. 'I should have finished seventh,' said a disgruntled Sylvain.

13 ALEX DE ANGELIS Broke a finger on one of the track markers that denote the pit exit, then broke the thumb on the same hand in qualifying. Not surprisingly, the race was difficult. Complained of being held up by West for a big chunk of the second half of the race.

14 COLIN EDWARDS Michelin didn't bring the front tyre he usually races so had to use harder rubber: 'I just didn't have any confidence in the front end. Everybody knows I'm a front-end guy.' Also, the neck injury from Germany handicapped him more than expected. Not how he wanted to celebrate re-signing with the Tech 3 team.

15 LORIS CAPIROSSI The arm injury from Assen made itself felt in changes of direction after a couple of laps, and on a track with as many corners as Laguna that made for a painful race.

16 MARCO MELANDRI It looked to be going well on a track Marco likes. He was up to ninth on lap nine when a course marker knocked his left hand off the handlebar, causing him to crash. He got back on but took a while to get up to speed again as he assessed the injury.

17 ANTHONY WEST Another weekend ruined by lack of confidence in the front. Temporary team-mate Hacking's form drew a stinging comment from Kawasaki's competition manager, Michael Bartholemy: 'He needs to work hard now to justify his place in MotoGP.'

NON-FINISHERS

JORGE LORENZO His confidence looked to be back after he qualified fourth but a massive highside off a cold rear tyre at the second corner of the first lap put him out. Suffered three fractures in his right foot.

NON-STARTERS

DANI PEDROSA Tried to ride on Friday but the injuries to his left hand from the crash less than week previously proved too much.

JOHN HOPKINS Still out following the crash at Assen. John was at Laguna, but on crutches.

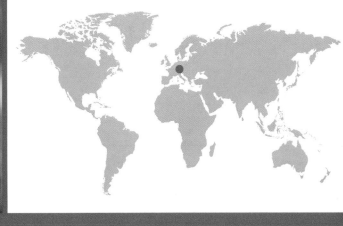

STRIKE TWO

Stoner fell, Rossi won by a distance and Michelin had their third disastrous race in a row

The lesson of Laguna, according to Valentino Rossi, was that if he and his team worked at 100 per cent it was possible to beat Stoner and the Ducati. As the American GP had come after three races in which the Aussie rider disappeared 'like a UFO' it was a timely reminder – and a lesson – which Valentino put to good effect. Here at Brno Casey was only just faster than the rest in free practice, but he demolished the field in wet qualifying to start from pole for the sixth time in a row, a record for the four-stroke MotoGP formula. Rossi was next fastest, while third man was the returning John Hopkins, on the front row for the first time as a Kawasaki rider.

Practice and qualifying had already uncovered yet another disaster for Michelin and their customers. None of their tyres worked on the resurfaced Brno track, with the top six riders in both dry free practice and wet qualifying on Bridgestones. Unlike the previous two races this wasn't a management miscalculation; it was a failure of the product. After a test in June Michelin knew they'd have to design a completely new front tyre for Brno, but they had insufficient data to come up with a new profile, new construction and a new compound. Effectively, their teams got the old tyres with new tread compounds. They didn't work. There were no safety issues: the tyres simply weren't competitive. Not that that stopped Dani Pedrosa's personal manager, Alberto Puig, from agitating for the Michelin teams to pull out of the race. HRC management did tell Pedrosa that if he felt it was unsafe to continue, due to his injuries, the tyres, or both, then he should pull in.

The boycott suggestion came from Puig, no-one else, and it was not given serious consideration by any

Above Casey Stoner slides out of the lead and across the tarmac of Turn 1

Opposite Shinya Nakano got a works-specification Honda RCV and immediately put it to good use

Below Ant West's career-best fifth place was the highlight of a dispiriting season

other team. Dani got off the line well but then slid back through the field, nearly suffering the indignity of being caught by Randy de Puniet, who had fallen and remounted.

Andrea Dovizioso in ninth was the first Michelin/Honda user home, nearly a minute in front of Pedrosa. The young Italian rode a beautifully controlled race, but still finished 38 seconds behind the winner. He was, though, only a couple of seconds behind another Honda, this time de Angelis's Bridgestone-shod V4. And Michelin didn't have the monopoly on tyre trouble, for several of the Japanese company's customers struggled with front-end grip, notably Chris Vermeulen who had qualified on the front of the second row.

To no-one's surprise it was Stoner who hit the first

corner in front, with Rossi pushed back to third by Hopkins. Valentino reckoned he lost half a second to Stoner in getting past the Kawasaki, and he finished the first lap 1.14s behind the Ducati. For the next four laps the pair matched lap times, then on lap six Rossi closed the gap by a third of a second. Stoner slid off three corners after he saw his pit board. Casey wasn't really sure why he'd crashed – Valentino thought he might simply have leant over too far and ridden off the tyre – and, in any case, Brno also has a goodly collection of bumps that might have had a say in proceedings. There was also the matter of the Aussie's health. He had only got back to Europe a few days before the race and was suffering from a bug picked up on the plane. On Friday he 'got tired putting my gloves on' and only went on track for a few laps at a time, although he did start feeling better as the weekend continued.

Rossi maintained that he would have caught Stoner, and he was equally sure that a hard fight would have ensued. Instead he had an easy afternoon, marching on to the biggest dry-weather winning margin yet seen in MotoGP, and leaving the Czech Republic with a handy 50-point lead in the championship table.

Stoner's demise, along with the misfortunes of the Michelin brigade, opened the door for season's best performances from Elias, Capirossi, Nakano and West. Toni Elias stormed through from 13th on the grid to take second before half-distance, demonstrating just how much team morale had improved since Bologna took a more hands-on role with their satellite team. Loris Capirossi indulged in a paint-swapping dice with his team-mate Chris Vermeulen before finishing third. He also had to deal with both Kawasakis, which looked much better motorcycles thanks to engine and chassis

Above Loris Capirossi took third place after a frantic battle with his team-mate Chris Vermeulen

Below The damage from Dani Pedrosa's Sachsenring crash was clearly still a major handicap

Opposite Like most of the Michelin runners, race pace was severely compromised for Pedrosa and Toseland

updates. Ant West had been in his now accustomed last place in practice early on but rocketed up to the end of the second row thanks to the rain in qualifying. Getting away with the leaders seemed to restore his confidence, and he was only edged out of fourth place late in the race.

The man who did take fourth, Shinya Nakano, was also on a new bike. He had a factory-spec Honda chassis but with a conventional, not pneumatic-valve, motor. According to HRC this was a purely pragmatic step to assist with the development of the 2009 customer team bike, a matter of rider and engineers having a common language. Of course it also gave HRC their first data from an RC212V on Bridgestone tyres, leading to more speculation that the Repsol team would change brands for the 2009 season. Whatever the motives, Shinya rode a superb second half of the race after a first-lap collision shunted him back into 12th place.

Casey Stoner's spill immediately had the paddock wondering aloud if the experiences of Laguna Seca had damaged the Ducati rider's confidence, or even shattered it. Before the meeting started Stoner had sought Rossi out to clarify, if not apologise for, his post-Laguna remarks. Casey's view was that all riders can over-react in the aftermath of a tough race, and he mentioned Rossi's fit of pique with Toni Elias after the 2007 Turkish GP. Of course he had a point, but it was difficult not to draw the conclusion that Valentino Rossi already had one hand on his sixth top-class championship – and that the Doctor had now done to Stoner what he had done to previous rivals Gibernau and Biaggi.

PRESSURE DROP

With hindsight, it is posible to see that Michelin's lamentable failure to give their riders rubber on which they could be competitive was a significant step on the road to the one-tyre-supplier rule that came in at the end of the season.

The attitude of HRC was critical. Having been thoroughly exasperated by Michelin's performance in 2007, they stayed loyal over winter, mainly ,one suspected, because of the companies' history together going back to Freddie Spencer's first 500cc title.

However, three consecutive races in which tyre performance totally compromised the factory Honda team's efforts was just too much even for the Japanese managers whose default response to any crisis is to say little or nothing. This time there was pointed and public criticism. The implication was clear, 25 years of mutual success notwithstanding, it would take a massive turnaround in performance to keep Honda on Michelin tyres in 2009.

As Honda's was the only factory team to use Michelins exclusively in 2008, the prospect of them moving to Bridgestone had serious implications. No tyre manufacturer would contemplate the expense of competing in MotoGP if they didn't have a factory team to work with.

The irony of the situation was that it was impossible to find anyone who actively wanted a single-tyre rule but equally difficult to find anyone who didn't want to be on Bridgestones the following season.

Above The relationship between Michelin and the Repsol Honda team reached a new low in Brno

CZECH REPUBLIC GP
AUTOMOTODROM BRNO

ROUND 12
August 17

RACE RESULTS

CIRCUIT LENGTH 3.357 miles
NO. OF LAPS 22
RACE DISTANCE 73.854 miles
WEATHER Dry, 20°C
TRACK TEMPERATURE 29°C
WINNER Valentino Rossi
FASTEST LAP 1m 57.199s,
103.129mph, Casey Stoner (record)
PREVIOUS LAP RECORD 1m 58.157s,
102.294mph, Loris Capirossi, 2006

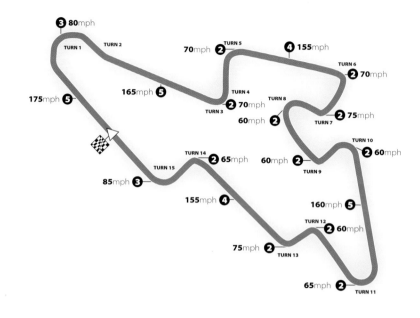

QUALIFYING

	Rider	Nationality	Team	Qualifying	Pole +	Gap
1	Stoner	AUS	Ducati Marlboro Team	2m 11.657s		
2	Rossi	ITA	Fiat Yamaha Team	2m 12.846s	1.189s	1.189s
3	Hopkins	USA	Kawasaki Racing Team	2m 12.959s	1.302s	0.113s
4	Vermeulen	AUS	Rizla Suzuki MotoGP	2m 13.002s	1.345s	0.043s
5	De Angelis	RSM	San Carlo Honda Gresini	2m 13.352s	1.695s	0.350s
6	West	AUS	Kawasaki Racing Team	2m 14.064s	2.407s	0.712s
7	De Puniet	FRA	LCR Honda MotoGP	2m 14.535s	2.878s	0.471s
8	Nakano	JPN	San Carlo Honda Gresini	2m 14.718s	3.061s	0.183s
9	Capirossi	ITA	Rizla Suzuki MotoGP	2m 14.805s	3.148s	0.087s
10	Guintoli	FRA	Alice Team	2m 14.861s	3.204s	0.056s
11	Melandri	ITA	Ducati Marlboro Team	2m 15.880s	4.223s	1.019s
12	Pedrosa	SPA	Repsol Honda Team	2m 16.032s	4.375s	0.152s
13	Elias	SPA	Alice Team	2m 16.510s	4.853s	0.478s
14	Dovizioso	ITA	JiR Team Scot MotoGP	2m 17.632s	5.975s	1.122s
15	Edwards	USA	Tech 3 Yamaha	2m 20.074s	8.417s	2.442s
	Toseland	GBR	Tech 3 Yamaha	2m 23.303s	11.646s	3.229s
	Lorenzo	SPA	Fiat Yamaha Team	2m 23.701s	12.044s	0.398s

FINISHERS

1 VALENTINO ROSSI Lost time to Stoner on the first lap but applied pressure as soon as he got to second place. Confident he would have caught Casey if he hadn't crashed. Greatest-ever margin of victory in a dry-weather MotoGP race – and stretched his lead to 50 points.

2 TONI ELIAS Qualified down in 13th but rode like a devil (as described by Rossi at Estoril in '06), overtaking both Suzukis and Hopkins on the same lap. Got to second place at half-distance and then maintained his concentration to the flag. And just when we thought he might be off to World Superbike…

3 LORIS CAPIROSSI First rostrum in Suzuki colours and a clear indication he was over his injuries, describing third place as 'more like a win because it means so much'. Involved in an entertaining fight with his team-mate early on. And all in his 277th GP, equalling Alex Barros's record number of starts.

4 SHINYA NAKANO A great ride in his first outing on the factory bike. Might have been on the rostrum if he hadn't had a coming-together with another bike off the start and got pushed back to 12th. Overtook people for the first time this year, for his best result since leaving Kawasaki.

5 ANTHONY WEST A career-best result, his highest qualifying of the season so far

and a good start. Might have been expected to do well in wet qualifying but, despite dropping a couple of places early on, reported increasing confidence as the race went on – the first time he'd been able to say that all year!

6 CHRIS VERMEULEN It wasn't just the Michelin users who had tyre problems. Went up to second place when Stoner crashed but as early as lap seven found some difficulty with front-tyre grip – from then on it was a matter of survival. Under the circumstances, sixth was a great result.

7 MARCO MELANDRI Lost something like ten seconds in the opening laps but got quicker as the race went on and gained four places in the last three laps. A better result

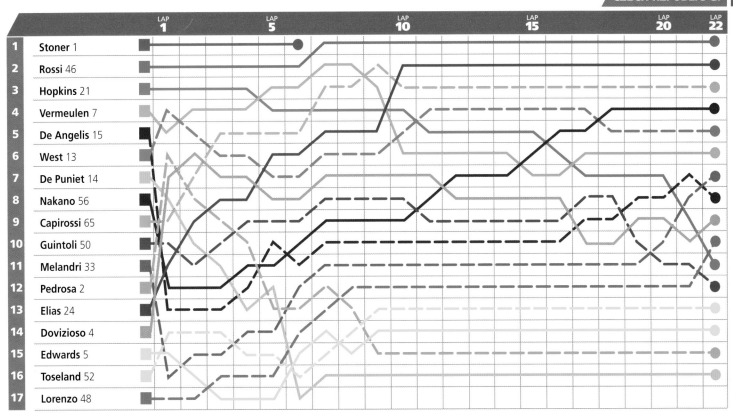

		LAP 1	LAP 5	LAP 10	LAP 15	LAP 20	LAP 22
1	Stoner 1						
2	Rossi 46						
3	Hopkins 21						
4	Vermeulen 7						
5	De Angelis 15						
6	West 13						
7	De Puniet 14						
8	Nakano 56						
9	Capirossi 65						
10	Guintoli 50						
11	Melandri 33						
12	Pedrosa 2						
13	Elias 24						
14	Dovizioso 4						
15	Edwards 5						
16	Toseland 52						
17	Lorenzo 48						

RACE

	Rider	Motorcycle	Race Time	Time +	Fastest Lap	Average Speed
1	Rossi	Yamaha	43m 28.841s		1m 57.228s	101.925mph
2	Elias	Ducati	43m 43.845s	15.004s	1m 58.414s	101.342mph
3	Capirossi	Suzuki	43m 50.530s	21.689s	1m 58.497s	101.085mph
4	Nakano	Honda	43m 54.700s	25.859s	1m 58.174s	100.925mph
5	West	Kawasaki	43m 58.306s	29.465s	1m 59.136s	100.787mph
6	Vermeulen	Suzuki	43m 59.449s	30.608s	1m 58.757s	100.743mph
7	Melandri	Ducati	44m 05.294s	36.453s	1m 58.441s	100.520mph
8	De Angelis	Honda	44m 05.591s	36.750s	1m 59.336s	100.509mph
9	Dovizioso	Honda	44m 07.663s	38.822s	1m 59.368s	100.430mph
10	Lorenzo	Yamaha	44m 08.414s	39.573s	1m 58.995s	100.402mph
11	Hopkins	Kawasaki	44m 08.451s	39.610s	1m 59.230s	100.400mph
12	Guintoli	Ducati	44m 09.733s	40.892s	1m 59.306s	100.352mph
13	Toseland	Yamaha	44m 40.331s	1m 11.490s	2m 00.953s	99.206mph
14	Edwards	Yamaha	44m 49.974s	1m 21.133s	2m 00.801s	98.851mph
15	Pedrosa	Honda	45m 05.879s	1m 37.038s	2m 00.320s	98.270mph
16	De Puniet	Honda	45m 07.248s	1m 38.407s	1m 59.855s	98.220mph
	Stoner	Ducati	11m 49.228s	16 laps	1m 57.199s	102.251mph

CHAMPIONSHIP

	Rider	Team	Points
1	Rossi	Fiat Yamaha Team	237
2	Stoner	Ducati Marlboro Team	187
3	Pedrosa	Repsol Honda Team	172
4	Lorenzo	Fiat Yamaha Team	120
5	Dovizioso	JiR Team Scot MotoGP	110
6	Edwards	Tech 3 Yamaha	102
7	Vermeulen	Rizla Suzuki MotoGP	99
8	Hayden	Repsol Honda Team	84
9	Nakano	San Carlo Honda Gresini	83
10	Capirossi	Rizla Suzuki MotoGP	77
11	Toseland	Tech 3 Yamaha	75
12	Elias	Alice Team	66
13	De Angelis	San Carlo Honda Gresini	49
14	Guintoli	Alice Team	42
15	Melandri	Ducati Marlboro Team	41
16	De Puniet	LCR Honda MotoGP	40
17	Hopkins	Kawasaki Racing Team	37
18	West	Kawasaki Racing Team	33
19	Spies	Rizla Suzuki MotoGP	10
20	Hacking	Kawasaki Racing Team	5
21	Okada	Repsol Honda Team	2

than usual, but Marco was still well beaten by Elias on the satellite bike.

8 ALEX DE ANGELIS Expected a top-six finish but wasted his best qualifying of the season so far with a bad start, though fought back well.

9 ANDREA DOVIZIOSO The top Michelin user, as he'd been in Germany. An astonishing first lap saw him get up to seventh from his fifth-row start, then it was a matter of losing as little ground as possible. A wonderfully controlled ride in the most difficult of circumstances.

10 JORGE LORENZO Only made the grid at the discretion of Race Direction after horrendous qualifying, but scored points for the first time since Assen, giving his

confidence a much-needed boost: actually managed to enjoy racing again. His rear Michelin improved while the front got worse as the race went on.

11 JOHN HOPKINS Still not quite fit after his Assen injuries but extremely fast in qualifying. Not surprisingly had stamina problems in the race and faded towards the flag. Also suffered with loss of grip on the left side, and of course couldn't hold the bike up on his knee.

12 SYLVAIN GUINTOLI Never as fast in the race as he was in practice, qualifying or warm-up (when he was always quicker than his team-mate) because his front tyre lost grip on the right side, leaving him a second a lap slower. Was expecting a top-five position.

13 JAMES TOSELAND Tried to push and nearly crashed several times. Found the pace his tyres would allow 'and that happened to be good enough for 13th place'.

14 COLIN EDWARDS Probably the man who relies more than any other on his front tyre. Rode round in tandem with his team-mate looking totally de-motivated.

15 DANI PEDROSA The highest profile victim of the Michelin debacle. Never possible to hear his engine, just the sound of the traction control cutting in: 'The worst race of my career … I felt impotent and ashamed.' His hand injury from the German crash was also still troubling him.

16 RANDY DE PUNIET Crashed on lap six when he lost the front. Remounted and

got to within 1.5 seconds of Pedrosa. Yet another Michelin runner who reported no feel from his front tyre.

NON-FINISHERS

CASEY STONER Fell three corners into the seventh lap. Got a great start, pulling an instant gap on Rossi and the rest, but crashed when Valentino started closing the gap. His first race crash since he joined Ducati.

NON-STARTERS

NICKY HAYDEN Cracked his right heel practising for the supermoto event at the X-Games in Los Angeles. Consulted several

surgeons, including the renowned Dr Art Ting, before deciding not to race. The heel bone is like a honeycomb, with no way to pin or plate it for a quick fix, so any further damage would have put him out for the rest of the season.

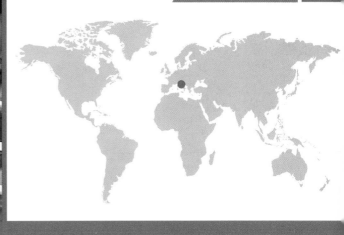

DOUBLE JEOPARDY

Stoner fell again, Rossi won again, Lorenzo returned to the rostrum and Pedrosa defected from Michelin to Bridgestone

This was a race that Valentino Rossi wasn't sure he could win – and it had been pointed out to him before the event started that, with a 50-point advantage, he could afford to think of the title and ride conservatively. He wasn't keen on that idea, though, because he always goes out to win every race. After Stoner had fallen while leading, for the second race in a row, Valentino was eager to lecture the media on the subject. He, Yamaha, and especially his crew, he said, do not think of anything else but winning. The way Jerry Burgess and his mechanics worked through the weekend to try to reel in the speed advantage of Casey Stoner and Ducati certainly backed up Rossi's assertions, although as the Doctor was seven-tenths of a second off the World Champion's pace in final practice it did look a forlorn hope on the short Misano lap.

When Stoner opened up a three-second lead in just two laps it seemed as if the race was going to follow the form book. Instead it was a replay of the previous GP, at Brno, with the Aussie sliding off on lap seven, although this time he wasn't being closed down and his lead had only just dipped a fraction under those three seconds. So why did Casey fall? After Brno he'd reported that his front tyre had been 'destroyed', but here he had used a front that had been scrubbed in for one lap. However, the heating, cooling and heating cycle may have had an adverse effect on the right side and, before he crashed, he had been having trouble with the front in right-handers.

Another problem had made its presence uncomfortably felt: an old scaphoid injury from 2003. Stoner was adjusting his back protector on Friday

'I WASN'T AS CONFIDENT AS I WAS IN BRNO THAT I COULD WIN'
VALENTINO ROSSI

morning when he felt something give in his left wrist, and it became more painful as the session went on. A visit to the Clinica Mobile showed that the old break, which had been stapled, had probably never fully mended and the bone was now in more than one piece. With the wrist well strapped up he was able to qualify on pole, but he later revealed he'd been worried that if he got into a dice he wouldn't be able to ride as he wanted. Here was another reason for Casey to try and open up a gap from the start. The question now was would he need, or would he be best advised, to have surgery before the end of the season.

Despite a near-highside coming on to the back straight for the first time Rossi was up into second before Stoner crashed, but he couldn't repeat the runaway victory of Brno as he was being chased by a trio of Spaniards. Pedrosa got his usual lightning start and held second for a lap and a half before Valentino got past. Dani was then rapidly overhauled, first by Jorge Lorenzo and then by Toni Elias, who broke the habit of a lifetime by both qualifying and racing well on the same weekend. The front four then held

station, although Lorenzo did close in a little on Rossi at one point, and he was in turn harassed by Elias.

Lorenzo's performance in particular deserves praise. It was his first rostrum since he finished second behind Rossi in France, back in May, after which he had suffered a debilitating series of big crashes and a consequent drop in confidence. Jorge was painfully and publicly honest about his problems, and most people were surprised to find themselves happy about his return to form. His second place also marked Michelin's renewed competitiveness – in fact, the top ten finishers alternated between Bridgestone and Michelin users – and much to the relief of everyone the control-tyre debate went quiet, if only for a while.

Despite the top placings being decided after fewer than ten laps there was plenty of action to keep the mainly yellow-clad crowd happy, especially as their local hero was on his way to equalling Giacomo Agostini's record of 68 wins in the top class. Chris Vermeulen had had an even bigger moment than Rossi's at the second turn, putting him back to 13th place. He then rode through the midfield with Rizla Suzuki team-mate Loris Capirossi not far behind. Both were using the new Suzuki chassis designed to let them use the same front tyre as Stoner and Rossi, although Loris couldn't get going properly until late in the race. Chris, though, was able to ride through the hectic set-to between Dovizioso and Toseland into a safe fifth place. The Englishman's sixth position also marked a return to James's early MotoGP form, while his last-lap duel with Capirossi was reminiscent of the confidence and aggression he'd displayed in the first couple of races of the year.

Off track there was drama both before and after the

race. On Friday John Hopkins didn't put in an appearance, thus condemning Kawasaki to another depressing weekend. The team insisted he couldn't ride because of the rib injury that had prevented him testing after Brno, but the paddock was well aware of some public drowning of personal problems earlier in the week. There were those in positions of power within Kawasaki who wanted to sack Hopper on the spot, but calmer counsel prevailed. It is doubtful if he escaped without losing a large chunk of his wages, and the factory's attitude to him in the near future would be worth examining carefully, but Kawasaki's problems were forgotten immediately after the race as rumours circulated that Dani Pedrosa would test on Bridgestone tyres on Monday. A hastily convened press conference soon confirmed that one half of the Repsol Honda team would indeed be switching from Michelin to Bridgestone, and with immediate effect. The sponsor tried to take responsibility but only succeeded in reinforcing the impression that HRC were no longer running their factory team.

None of this impinged on Valentino Rossi and the celebrations of his fans for what was his maiden victory at the circuit on which he had first ridden a racing motorcycle. The most eye-catching aspect of all this was a meeting of the Tavullia town council in full regalia in the Misano grandstands, and the only item on their agenda was the election of one V. Rossi as mayor for a day. Valentino will fulfil his civic duty some time after the end of the season when, after the weekend's events at his local track, he will doubtless also be able to celebrate yet another world title.

Left Casey Stoner was as aggressive as ever, but for the second race in a row he crashed out

Opposite below John Hopkins missed free practice on Friday due to personal problems but was able to qualify on Saturday and race on Sunday

Below Loris Capirossi celebrated his record-breaking 277th GP with seventh place – this pass on Shinya Nakano would have done credit to a teenage 125 racer

CAPIREX

The Grand Prix of San Marino & The Riviera of Rimini was Loris Capirossi's 277th World Championship race, a new record surpassing Alex Barros's mark of 276 races. The Misano race was the 738th GP event to be run in the 60-year history of the motorcycle World Championship, which means that Loris has taken part in an astonishing 37.5% of all the GP events ever run – that's events, not individual races.

The distinction is worth making as riders like Mike Hailwood, the most succesful rider of the 1960s, only rode at 85 events – there were as few as seven races in a championship year. But as he rode in more than one class at each event, Mike the Bike rode in 195 GP races.

The other active riders who have competed in over 200 events are Valentino Rossi with 205 and Roby Locatelli with 204 as of the San Marino GP.

Loris's third place at the Czech Grand Prix two weeks before the Misano race was his 99th rostrum finish in GPs. One more rostrum for Capirossi would make it his 100th, and he would then join Ago, Rossi, Angel Nieto, Phil Read, Mike Hailwood and Max Biaggi in the elite group of multiple World Champions who have passed that mark. He fully intends to score a century of rostrums and compete in 300 GPs before he retires. A few weeks

after Misano, Loris finished tenth in the Australian GP to take his career points tally over the 3000 mark. The only other rider with more career points is Valentino Rossi. Hands up those cynics who said he'd only joined Suzuki to boost his pension plan.

OFFICIAL TIMEKEEPER

SAN MARINO GP
MISANO WORLD CIRCUIT

ROUND 13
August 31

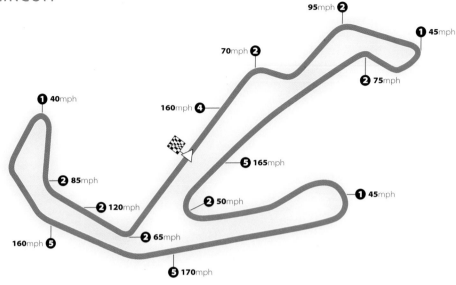

RACE RESULTS

CIRCUIT LENGTH 2.626 miles
NO. OF LAPS 28
RACE DISTANCE 73.529 miles
WEATHER Dry, 35°C
TRACK TEMPERATURE 48°C
WINNER Valentino Rossi
FASTEST LAP 1m 34.904s, 99.614mph, Valentino Rossi (record)
PREVIOUS LAP RECORD (new circuit)

QUALIFYING

	Rider	Nationality	Team	Qualifying	Pole +	Gap
1	Stoner	AUS	Ducati Marlboro Team	1m 33.378s		
2	Rossi	ITA	Fiat Yamaha Team	1m 33.888s	0.510s	0.510s
3	Lorenzo	SPA	Fiat Yamaha Team	1m 33.964s	0.586s	0.076s
4	De Puniet	FRA	LCR Honda MotoGP	1m 34.236s	0.858s	0.272s
5	Elias	SPA	Alice Team	1m 34.322s	0.944s	0.086s
6	Pedrosa	SPA	Repsol Honda Team	1m 34.398s	1.020s	0.076s
7	Vermeulen	AUS	Rizla Suzuki MotoGP	1m 34.461s	1.083s	0.063s
8	Nakano	JPN	San Carlo Honda Gresini	1m 34.494s	1.116s	0.033s
9	Toseland	GBR	Tech 3 Yamaha	1m 34.652s	1.274s	0.158s
10	Edwards	USA	Tech 3 Yamaha	1m 34.795s	1.417s	0.143s
11	Capirossi	ITA	Rizla Suzuki MotoGP	1m 34.926s	1.548s	0.131s
12	Guintoli	FRA	Alice Team	1m 34.961s	1.583s	0.035s
13	De Angelis	RSM	San Carlo Honda Gresini	1m 35.153s	1.775s	0.192s
14	Dovizioso	ITA	JiR Team Scot MotoGP	1m 35.381s	2.003s	0.228s
15	Melandri	ITA	Ducati Marlboro Team	1m 35.418s	2.040s	0.037s
16	Hayden	USA	Repsol Honda Team	1m 35.584s	2.206s	0.166s
17	Hopkins	USA	Kawasaki Racing Team	1m 35.980s	2.602s	0.396s
18	West	AUS	Kawasaki Racing Team	1m 37.047s	3.669s	1.067s

FINISHERS

1 VALENTINO ROSSI Looked like a carbon copy of Brno, but this time Rossi wasn't sure he'd have won without Stoner's crash. Win number 68 in the top class brought him level with Agostini, it all happened just five miles from his home town and Vale now has a 75-point lead in the championship.

2 JORGE LORENZO Not just a welcome return to form – he pushed team-mate Rossi all the way and put Michelin on the rostrum for the first time since Assen. Credited the test after Brno and tyre improvements for restoring his confidence, and consolidated his fourth place in the table and status as top rookie.

3 TONI ELIAS Back-to-back rostrums for the first time in his MotoGP career. Got past fast starter Pedrosa early on, tried to catch Lorenzo, then found himself making mistakes so concentrated on holding off the Repsol Honda. Fourth Ducati rider to achieve consecutive podiums after Capirossi, Gibernau and Bayliss.

4 DANI PEDROSA Back from his German GP injuries for his last race on Michelins. Chose soft tyres on the grid and got the early advantage he'd hoped for but suffered later in the race. Declared himself happy with the result, especially in view of the stifling conditions.

5 CHRIS VERMEULEN Suffered from a near-highside early on that put him way down the field – it was violent enough for Chris to smash part of the fairing with his knee. Rode superbly in his 50th GP to catch the Toseland–Dovizioso dice and go past both. Used Suzuki's new chassis.

6 JAMES TOSELAND His fifth top-six finish of the year and another welcome return to form after a run of disappointing races. Fought with Nakano and Dovizioso early on, but could do nothing when Vermeulen came through. Rode the 'widest Yamaha in history' to hold Capirossi off in the closing stages.

7 LORIS CAPIROSSI Not the result he wanted in his 278th start. Got a bit lost trying to find a set-up for the new chassis, then had to change his front tyre on the grid. Picked up the pace once the tyre came in, involved in a

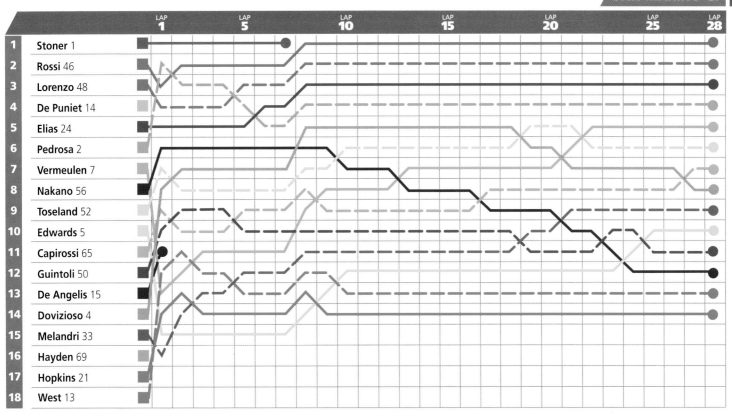

		LAP 1	LAP 5	LAP 10	LAP 15	LAP 20	LAP 25	LAP 28
1	Stoner 1							
2	Rossi 46							
3	Lorenzo 48							
4	De Puniet 14							
5	Elias 24							
6	Pedrosa 2							
7	Vermeulen 7							
8	Nakano 56							
9	Toseland 52							
10	Edwards 5							
11	Capirossi 65							
12	Guintoli 50							
13	De Angelis 15							
14	Dovizioso 4							
15	Melandri 33							
16	Hayden 69							
17	Hopkins 21							
18	West 13							

RACE

	Rider	Motorcycle	Race Time	Time +	Fastest Lap	Average Speed
1	Rossi	Yamaha	44m 41.884s		1m 34.904s	98.700mph
2	Lorenzo	Yamaha	44m 45.047s	3.163s	1m 35.167s	98.584mph
3	Elias	Ducati	44m 53.589s	11.705s	1m 35.221s	98.271mph
4	Pedrosa	Honda	44m 59.354s	17.470s	1m 35.479s	98.061mph
5	Vermeulen	Suzuki	45m 05.293s	23.409s	1m 35.741s	97.846mph
6	Toseland	Yamaha	45m 08.092s	26.208s	1m 35.972s	97.745mph
7	Capirossi	Suzuki	45m 08.708s	26.824s	1m 35.832s	97.723mph
8	Dovizioso	Honda	45m 09.475s	27.591s	1m 35.911s	97.695mph
9	Melandri	Ducati	45m 15.053s	33.169s	1m 35.681s	97.494mph
10	Edwards	Yamaha	45m 18.413s	36.529s	1m 35.766s	97.374mph
11	Guintoli	Ducati	45m 23.965s	42.081s	1m 36.175s	97.175mph
12	Nakano	Honda	45m 25.692s	43.808s	1m 36.351s	97.114mph
13	West	Kawasaki	45m 36.758s	54.874s	1m 36.862s	96.721mph
14	Hopkins	Kawasaki	45m 37.038s	55.154s	1m 36.710s	96.711mph
	Stoner	Ducati	11m 11.968s	21 laps	1m 34.988s	98.480mph
	De Angelis	Honda	1m 46.395s	27 laps	1m 46.395s	88.854mph

CHAMPIONSHIP

	Rider	Team	Points
1	Rossi	Fiat Yamaha Team	262
2	Stoner	Ducati Marlboro Team	187
3	Pedrosa	Repsol Honda Team	185
4	Lorenzo	Fiat Yamaha Team	140
5	Dovizioso	JiR Team Scot MotoGP	118
6	Vermeulen	Rizla Suzuki MotoGP	110
7	Edwards	Tech 3 Yamaha	108
8	Nakano	San Carlo Honda Gresini	87
9	Capirossi	Rizla Suzuki MotoGP	86
10	Toseland	Tech 3 Yamaha	85
11	Hayden	Repsol Honda Team	84
12	Elias	Alice Team	82
13	De Angelis	San Carlo Honda Gresini	49
14	Melandri	Ducati Marlboro Team	48
15	Guintoli	Alice Team	47
16	De Puniet	LCR Honda MotoGP	40
17	Hopkins	Kawasaki Racing Team	39
18	West	Kawasaki Racing Team	36
19	Spies	Rizla Suzuki MotoGP	10
20	Hacking	Kawasaki Racing Team	5
21	Okada	Repsol Honda Team	2

few entertaining fights and passed Toseland on the last lap only to run wide.

8 ANDREA DOVIZIOSO Made a great start from an unusually lowly 14th grid position to get as high as fifth place. Had problems with the right side of his front tyre which compromised corner entry.

9 MARCO MELANDRI Held up first by Vermeulen's big moment on the first lap, then by de Angelis's crash on the second lap. Made up six places on his qualifying position for his second top-ten finish in a row.

10 COLIN EDWARDS Spent three laps trying to get some heat into his rear tyre, but by then had lost too much ground on the short Misano track. His pace in the rest of the race was good enough for a much

higher placing, but the opening few laps had decided his fate.

11 SYLVAIN GUINTOLI A disappointing race, as he wasn't able to match the pace he'd set in practice and qualifying: 'The more I pushed, the more tired I felt, the slower I went.'

12 SHINYA NAKANO Started well but soon felt front-end chatter in a few corners. By the closing stages he was 3s a lap slower than in practice – proof that a factory Honda on Bridgestones isn't a guarantee of success. Doubly disappointing as this was the team's real home race.

13 ANT WEST The new chassis changed Ant's problem from lack of rear-tyre traction to lack of confidence in the front tyre. Spent

the whole weekend dicing with his team-mate at the back of the field.

14 JOHN HOPKINS A weekend worthy of a soap opera. Started by missing Friday practice, officially because he aggravated a Brno rib injury but in reality because of personal problems. Not surprisingly, was then playing catch-up – and all at a track where he'd finished on the rostrum a year ago.

NON-FINISHERS

CASEY STONER A second consecutive crash while well in the lead. Pointed to unusual wear on the right side of his front tyre as a possible cause. Worried by what appears to be an old break to his left scaphoid opening up again.

ALEX DE ANGELIS Tangled with Melandri on the second lap after the Ducati came past in a straight line. Got on the gas early and was pinged out of the seat, tried to hang on but grabbed the brake and went down.

RANDY DE PUNIET Achieved the distinction of not completing a racing lap of Misano by crashing in the last corner of the first lap when he got off line and lost the back. Hurt his right arm. A real disappointment after qualifying fourth.

NON-STARTER

NICKY HAYDEN Had a big crash in practice but went out on Saturday and qualified in 16th. However, his injured right heel was

preventing him using the rear brake and weighting the footpeg as he needs to ('No way it'll go in a boot') so decided not to race and save himself for Indianapolis in two weeks' time.

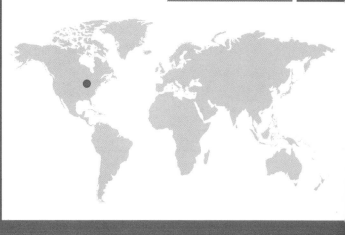

HURRICANE ROSSI

Valentino Rossi overtook Giacomo Agostini's record of 68 wins to become the most successful racer ever in the 500cc/MotoGP class. The weather had the final word, though

The Indianapolis Motor Speedway is not a pretty track. No architect or designer ever got near this place: it is all concrete, steel girders and flaking grey paint. It is blue collar, middle America and differs from Laguna Seca in the way that a workingmen's club in Wigan differs from a gentleman's club in Mayfair. The giant grandstands squat well within the city next to shops and residential streets, and the stadium can seat over a quarter of a million spectators. Historically, the track has only hosted two races a year, the fabled Indy 500 itself and a Nascar event, the Brickyard 400. Formula One did run here for a few years but the inaugural (a word Americans are inordinately fond of) MotoGP event formed the centrepiece of the IMS's celebrations of a century of racing. The very first race on the banking took place on 13 August 1909 and it was a motorcycle race.

As would be expected from a facility that regularly attracts a crowd of something approaching half a million, the Speedway knows how to look after its fans. Promotional activity was everywhere as the organisers did their damnedest to attract and then explain MotoGP to punters more used to watching cars turn left. A four-page brochure handed out on Sunday morning told spectators everything they needed to know about subjects like flags and qualifying as well as providing a full-page illustration of the grid. And, this being America, you were never far from a nourishing snack.

The efforts of the IMS and sponsor Red Bull pulled in a reported 91,000 fans on race day, but unfortunately they had to contend with the fallout from Hurricane Ike. On Friday and on race day

'I WAS THINKING, THIS ONLY HAPPENS IN THE MOVIES!'
NICKY HAYDEN

horizontal rain was driven by winds of over 60mph; Indianapolis Airport actually recorded one gust of 64mph during the MotoGP race.

The track itself is what the locals call a roval because it uses the front straight of the fabled oval plus some of the road course built for F1. There was also a brand-new section, Turns 1 to 4, laid on especially for the bikes. That meant several changes of surface with wildly varying levels of grip, but most riders declared themselves pleasantly surprised by the track and its safety features. As when MotoGP first went to Laguna Seca there were a couple of places where action is needed, but as long as they are sorted out for 2009 everyone will be happy.

Indianapolis is about three hours' drive from Owensboro, Kentucky, home of the Hayden family. This GP was the closest to home Nicky had ever road raced. The local link was emphasised by the Indianapolis Colts gridiron football team's logo atop his Arai. Nicky was still wearing a splint and walking with a stick to keep weight off the injured heel which had kept him out of the previous two races, but that didn't stop him enjoying himself both on and off the

track. At the pre-race press conference he joked pointedly about some people in his team not noticing if he bothered to turn up for the remaining races. Come Sunday he persuaded Michelin to let him have a softer tyre than recommended and promptly led the first 13 laps before Rossi came past. Up to that point he'd been thinking 'This only happens in the movies', then the conditions got slightly better mid-race and the drying track took a toll on Nicky's tyre. And when the rain returned with a vengeance he lost seconds a lap to the charging Jorge Lorenzo.

Casey Stoner could only manage fourth, without ever threatening the leaders. To his obvious annoyance most of the attention directed at him concerned his wrist, and the possibility of him having surgery before the end of the season. In the race he took time to get his hard tyres up to temperature, like most Bridgestone runners, then got the better of a good fight with Andrea Dovizioso and Ben Spies. The now triple American Superbike Champion, riding as a wild card, was by far the best of the Suzuki riders and his progress in the race was only stopped by a fogged-up visor. Ben thought fourth place was there for the taking, but in the end all he could do was follow the men directly in front of him. Unfortunately, on a weekend where many new contracts were announced, it looked as if Spies would be unable to find a MotoGP ride for 2009.

It wasn't actually the rain that caused the red flag to be shown on the 21st of the scheduled 28 laps, but the effects of the wind. Advertising hoardings, Astroturf and sections of air fence were coming away from their moorings while riders reported seeing branches, bottles

Opposite The Indianapolis Motor Speedway is a big place. Here the MotoGP field turns off the oval onto the new section of track

Below Nicky Hayden and his race engineer Pete Benson hard at work persuading Michelin to let them run the softer wet tyre

and all sort of other debris. Rossi could not remember having ridden in worse conditions. Everyone assumed that was the end of proceedings, but since the introduction of flag-to-flag races the rulebook has stated that MotoGP should always run its full quota of laps. This usually means that, if weather conditions change, riders come into pit lane and swap bikes, but at Indy conditions were so severe that the race had to be halted on safety grounds. By the letter of the law there should have been an eight-lap 'race' for the points, as still happens in the smaller classes. As the riders forcibly made their feelings known, however, and then Race Direction inspected the course, they thankfully announced that there was no possibility of a restart, so the result stood.

The local fans enjoyed watching Rossi in action for the first time, and seeing Hayden on the rostrum for the first time this year. Nicky celebrated his Ducati contract for '09 and beating his current 'team-mate' Dani Pedrosa, who was largely anonymous for his first race on Bridgestones, by appearing at Ducati's North American dealers' convention on the Monday after the race. Honda must really have upset him.

As usual, Valentino Rossi was aware of his place in the history books. He announced himself happy to have overtaken Giacomo Agostini's 33-year-old wins record but acknowledged that some of Ago's other marks – his 15 titles, for instance – were probably out of reach. Being 'the first one in a hundred years' to win on two wheels at the Brickyard also pleased him: 'I hear that Indianapolis have only the top class of all motorsport. So, from Indy to Nascar and now MotoGP it's important, something right on the history.'

Above Casey Stoner reflects on the severe weather conditions caused by Hurricane Ike

Below Nicky Hayden wore the badge of the local team, the Colts, and got his first rostrum of the year

Opposite That's why they put the red flag out: Yamaha's exhibition centre collapsed

NUMBERS GAME

Valentino Rossi's win at Indianapolis gve him a full house – he has now won a premier-class race at every track in the MotoGP calendar. It was also his 69th victory in the top class and gave him one of the more significant and coveted records in the sport – the most wins in the top class of racing. The man whose record Vale broke is Giacomo Agostini, the most successful racer of all time with 122 wins in all classes and 15 world titles including the 500cc crown from 1966–72 inclusive. That record at least is out of Valentino's reach. Ago's record total of 159 podiums in all classes must be in danger, though, as the Indy win marked the 147th time Rossi has stood on a Grand Prix rostrum.

The wins record had stood since the final race of the 1976 season when Ago won the West German race at the old Nürburgring on an MV Agusta. It was the last win by a four-stroke in the top class before the advent of the 990cc MotoGP formula in 2002. Like Rossi, Ago had left the most successful manufacturer of the era to move to Yamaha and won the 1975 world title, the first 500cc championship won on a two-stroke.

Ago won 68 500cc races from 119 starts, a strike rate of 57.1%. Valentino's 69 from 146 equates to a strike rate of 47.2%. If you look at rostrum finishes, Valentino comes out just ahead with 76% versus 74%.

There is one more astonishing statistic about Ago's career: he never finished third in a 500cc GP. He won 68 races and finished second 20 times – usually beaten by Hailwood at the begining of his career and Phil Read at the end. The fallibility of machines of the era probably accounts for the other races.

INDIANAPOLIS GP
INDIANAPOLIS MOTOR SPEEDWAY

ROUND 14
September 14

RACE RESULTS

CIRCUIT LENGTH 2.620 miles
NO. OF LAPS 20
RACE DISTANCE 52.396 miles
WEATHER Wet, 21°C
TRACK TEMPERATURE 20°C
WINNER Valentino Rossi
FASTEST LAP 1m 49.668s, 85.999mph, Valentino Rossi (record)
PREVIOUS LAP RECORD (new circuit)

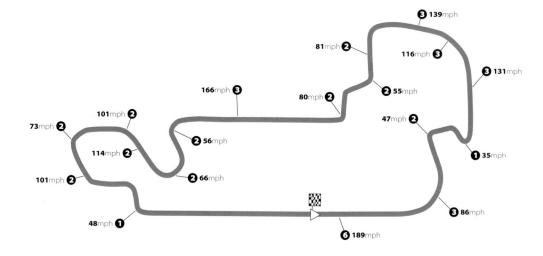

QUALIFYING

	Rider	Nationality	Team	Qualifying	Pole +	Gap
1	Rossi	ITA	Fiat Yamaha Team	1m 40.776s		
2	Stoner	AUS	Ducati Team	1m 40.860s	0.084s	0.084s
3	Lorenzo	SPA	Fiat Yamaha Team	1m 41.177s	0.401s	0.317s
4	Hayden	USA	Repsol Honda Team	1m 41.271s	0.495s	0.094s
5	Spies	USA	Rizla Suzuki MotoGP	1m 41.464s	0.688s	0.193s
6	De Puniet	FRA	LCR Honda MotoGP	1m 41.492s	0.716s	0.028s
7	Dovizioso	ITA	JiR Team Scot MotoGP	1m 41.744s	0.968s	0.252s
8	Pedrosa	SPA	Repsol Honda Team	1m 41.754s	0.978s	0.010s
9	Elias	SPA	Alice Team	1m 41.886s	1.110s	0.132s
10	Toseland	GBR	Tech 3 Yamaha	1m 41.897s	1.121s	0.011s
11	Edwards	USA	Tech 3 Yamaha	1m 41.934s	1.158s	0.037s
12	De Angelis	RSM	San Carlo Honda Gresini	1m 41.969s	1.193s	0.035s
13	Capirossi	ITA	Rizla Suzuki MotoGP	1m 42.305s	1.529s	0.336s
14	Guintoli	FRA	Alice Team	1m 42.405s	1.629s	0.100s
15	Vermeulen	AUS	Rizla Suzuki MotoGP	1m 42.551s	1.775s	0.146s
16	Hopkins	USA	Kawasaki Racing Team	1m 42.673s	1.897s	0.122s
17	Nakano	JPN	San Carlo Honda Gresini	1m 42.732s	1.956s	0.059s
18	Melandri	ITA	Ducati Team	1m 43.807s	3.031s	1.075s
19	West	AUS	Kawasaki Racing Team	1m 43.931s	3.155s	0.124s

FINISHERS

1 VALENTINO ROSSI Victory no. 69 made him the most successful rider ever in the 500cc/MotoGP class, surpassing Agostini's 33-year-old record. He had to work for it. Fifth early on, he broke away from the group to chase Hayden for eight laps before taking the lead and never being headed.

2 NICKY HAYDEN The perfect homecoming – nearly. Top Honda qualifier, led a GP again, and his first rostrum in over a year. Also had the satisfaction of soundly beating Pedrosa. Used a soft rear tyre that worked well early on but wore when the track dried, so lacked grip when the rain returned.

3 JORGE LORENZO First wet-weather rostrum at any level – including the Balearic championships. Qualified on the front row for the fifth time: each time he's finished on the podium. A good start, grew in confidence as he passed people and was easily catching Hayden when the red flag went out.

4 CASEY STONER Off pole for the first time in eight races, then suffered from a rear tyre that tore up earlier than expected. Like Hayden, he was struggling to maintain his lap times when the race was red-flagged, but was able to repass Dovizioso for fourth.

5 ANDREA DOVIZIOSO Led a MotoGP race for the first time thanks to one of his customary bullet starts from the third row. Satisfied he'd got the maximum from his equipment but hinted at a conservative tyre choice: thought he could have fought for a rostrum if the weather had been kinder.

6 BEN SPIES Best showing by a wild card this season, best Suzuki rider all weekend and might've challenged for fourth but for a misting visor. Also best wild-card/replacement rider performance since Bayliss won at Valencia in '06. Rode the old chassis, managed by Suzuki's highly motivated test team.

7 SYLVAIN GUINTOLI Another impressive ride in foul conditions, doubly so since he got a bad start and dropped back to 14th. Took time to gain confidence in his tyres but then gained seven places in a race from which there were no retirements.

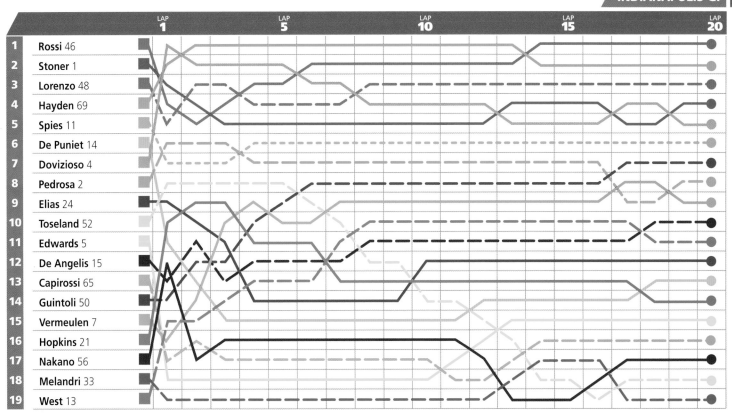

		LAP 1	LAP 5	LAP 10	LAP 15	LAP 20
1	Rossi 46					
2	Stoner 1					
3	Lorenzo 48					
4	Hayden 69					
5	Spies 11					
6	De Puniet 14					
7	Dovizioso 4					
8	Pedrosa 2					
9	Elias 24					
10	Toseland 52					
11	Edwards 5					
12	De Angelis 15					
13	Capirossi 65					
14	Guintoli 50					
15	Vermeulen 7					
16	Hopkins 21					
17	Nakano 56					
18	Melandri 33					
19	West 13					

RACE

	Rider	Motorcycle	Race Time	Time +	Fastest Lap	Average Speed
1	Rossi	Yamaha	37m 20.095s		1m 49.668s	84.204mph
2	Hayden	Honda	37m 26.067s	5.972s	1m 50.057s	83.980mph
3	Lorenzo	Yamaha	37m 27.953s	7.858s	1m 50.418s	83.910mph
4	Stoner	Ducati	37m 48.257s	28.162s	1m 50.989s	83.159mph
5	Dovizioso	Honda	37m 48.919s	28.824s	1m 50.926s	83.135mph
6	Spies	Suzuki	37m 49.740s	29.645s	1m 51.219s	83.104mph
7	Guintoli	Ducati	37m 56.318s	36.223s	1m 51.265s	82.864mph
8	Pedrosa	Honda	37m 57.353s	37.258s	1m 51.789s	82.827mph
9	Vermeulen	Suzuki	37m 58.537s	38.442s	1m 51.761s	82.784mph
10	De Angelis	Honda	38m 02.532s	42.437s	1m 51.040s	82.639mph
11	West	Kawasaki	38m 07.274s	47.179s	1m 51.524s	82.467mph
12	Elias	Ducati	38m 16.057s	55.962s	1m 51.962s	82.152mph
13	De Puniet	Honda	38m 17.461s	57.366s	1m 51.945s	82.101mph
14	Hopkins	Kawasaki	38m 18.448s	58.353s	1m 52.075s	82.067mph
15	Edwards	Yamaha	38m 20.708s	1m 00.613s	1m 52.070s	81.986mph
16	Capirossi	Suzuki	38m 25.715s	1m 05.620s	1m 52.905s	81.808mph
17	Nakano	Honda	38m 25.949s	1m 05.854s	1m 52.830s	81.799mph
18	Toseland	Yamaha	38m 28.063s	1m 07.968s	1m 53.385s	81.725mph
19	Melandri	Ducati	38m 41.118s	1m 21.023s	1m 52.451s	81.265mph

CHAMPIONSHIP

	Rider	Team	Points
1	Rossi	Fiat Yamaha Team	287
2	Stoner	Ducati Team	200
3	Pedrosa	Repsol Honda Team	193
4	Lorenzo	Fiat Yamaha Team	156
5	Dovizioso	JiR Team Scot MotoGP	129
6	Vermeulen	Rizla Suzuki MotoGP	117
7	Edwards	Tech 3 Yamaha	109
8	Hayden	Repsol Honda Team	104
9	Nakano	San Carlo Honda Gresini	87
10	Elias	Alice Team	86
11	Capirossi	Rizla Suzuki MotoGP	86
12	Toseland	Tech 3 Yamaha	85
13	Guintoli	Alice Team	56
14	De Angelis	San Carlo Honda Gresini	55
15	Melandri	Ducati Team	48
16	De Puniet	LCR Honda MotoGP	43
17	Hopkins	Kawasaki Racing Team	41
18	West	Kawasaki Racing Team	41
19	Spies	Rizla Suzuki MotoGP	20
20	Hacking	Kawasaki Racing Team	5
21	Okada	Repsol Honda Team	2

8 DANI PEDROSA A new track in howling rain is not the easiest place to race on new tyres. Qualified a respectable eighth for his first outing on Bridgestones but had to suffer as 'team-mate' Hayden ran away at the front on Michelins, as well as being headed by four other Bridgestone runners.

9 CHRIS VERMEULEN Suzuki's rainmaster was again handicapped by his grid position – a lowly 15th. Quickly made up places early on, but once the drier line had formed he found moving off-line to overtake impossible.

10 ALEX DE ANGELIS Hoped for better after being fast in wet practice. In the race his rear tyre went off quickly – later thought a softer choice might have been a good idea. Took a lot of time to get up to pace and had just caught the group in front when the race was stopped.

11 ANTHONY WEST An impressive ride from dead last on the grid. Made up places early on but used a lot of his tyre in getting up to tenth by lap eight. Couldn't hold off de Angelis's late charge.

12 TONI ELIAS Not happy, but consoled himself with the fact that the four points he earned put him in the top ten of the world championship. Confident he could have fought for another rostrum if the weather had stayed dry.

13 RANDY DE PUNIET Disappointed in what he called 'one of the most hard GPs for me'. Never happy with his set-up, never got the hard Michelins to work properly – and, crucially, didn't realise he was riding with a broken arm from his Misano crash.

14 JOHN HOPKINS Another rider who used the harder rear Bridgestone hoping for a drying track. Got a good start, then dropped back waiting for his tyre to come in. Hamstrung once the rain returned in earnest. Reported that he could deal with the rain but the wind was 'unbelievable'.

15 COLIN EDWARDS Worked on a new set-up for so long in practice he felt he had to use it in the race. That turned out to be a bad decision, as he couldn't get the bike turned. Made the point that there was nothing wrong with his tyres.

16 LORIS CAPIROSSI A weekend he is keen to forget. Never got on the pace in the wet or dry, and when he was pushed wide at the first corner found himself in last position. Described the conditions as the worst he has ever raced in.

17 SHINYA NAKANO Was fourth fastest in Sunday morning warm-up but couldn't deal with the race conditions.

18 JAMES TOSELAND Didn't get a great start but an aggressive first corner gained a few places. However, after half a dozen laps started to drop back through the field as he couldn't speed up when the track started drying. Had the same tyre as Dovizioso, so the blame lies with too soft chassis settings.

19 MARCO MELANDRI Looked good in the wet on Friday but couldn't replicate the feeling on Sunday, especially with the engine braking. Also complained of lack of grip from both front and rear tyres: 'I couldn't ride it from the first lap.'

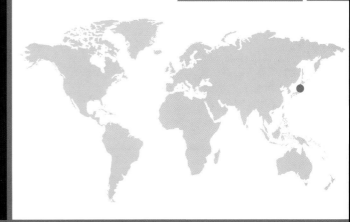

SORRY FOR THE DELAY

Valentino Rossi regained his crown after a two-year gap and helped Yamaha clinch both the Constructors' and Team Championships

Valentino Rossi had never won on a four-stroke at Motegi, nor had he clinched any of his previous seven world titles in Japan. He put all that right with a masterful display which also happened to be his fifth victory in a row and – just to rub it in, at the Honda-owned circuit – the win secured the Team Championship for Fiat Yamaha and the Constructors' title for the Yamaha factory. Valentino declared that this had been the hardest of his titles, requiring levels of concentration and effort 'the highest of any year'. He celebrated with an elaborate stunt featuring a suited lawyer who endorsed his eighth crown with a rubber stamp on a special AGV crash helmet. It's probably very funny if you are Italian. Slightly lame celebration notwithstanding, it's difficult to argue with his assessment. Only Giacomo Agostini had previously regained the premier class title after a two-year gap. Those two years, said Rossi, taught him 'how to lose' and also not to make assumptions: 'In 2006, when I didn't win early, I thought we had time to fix.' Valentino does not make the same mistake twice.

The only trophy Yamaha didn't get their hands on during the Motegi weekend was the Rookie of the Year title, but Jorge Lorenzo continued the return to his early season form by taking pole for the first time since Portugal and beating the absolute lap record of Loris Capirossi and the 990cc Ducati. Nicky Hayden, another rider who'd spent some time in the doldrums, put a second Michelin-shod bike on the front row on a weekend where tyres and the politics of tyre suppliers took up far too much attention. Motegi is a track where Bridgestone have dominated in recent years – the last Michelin winner was Max Biaggi in 2003 – which isn't really surprising given that Bridgestone is a Japanese company. However, this

'THIS YEAR THE LEVEL OF CONCENTRATION AND EFFORT WAS THE HIGHEST'
VALENTINO ROSSI

year there was no major difference in tyre performance until race day, when lower temperatures slightly affected the Michelin users. Nevertheless, the best action came in the closing laps when Lorenzo on Michelins attacked Dani Pedrosa on Bridgestones in a hectic fight for fourth place.

The opening bout saw Casey Stoner and Dani Pedrosa at the front while Valentino Rossi reverted to his old habit of making an average start and having to get past Lorenzo and Hayden before reaching the leading duo. Stoner, who had led the first lap, retook the lead from Pedrosa at the end of the back straight on lap six. It was a tough move. Casey felt moved to wave an apology and later described it as 'not a friendly pass'. Rossi immediately took advantage, moving through into second, with Pedrosa instantly dropping away from the new leading duo. Rossi then shadowed Stoner for eight laps before hitting the front.

It is a characteristic of the Motegi track, with its short, constant-radius bends, that riders can stay in close company but find it almost impossible to overtake unless the man in front makes a mistake. And that's what happened. The gap between Rossi and Stoner increased slowly, while the distance between Stoner and Pedrosa expanded rather more quickly. Casey's wrist didn't appear to affect him too much, a surprise given the number of heavy braking efforts at Motegi, but the injury had prevented him from training properly so he faded a little mid-race before rallying in the last five laps. After the chequered flag confirmed Rossi as champion Stoner was quick to congratulate him, and was again generous with his praise during the post-race press conference. Whatever animosity was generated

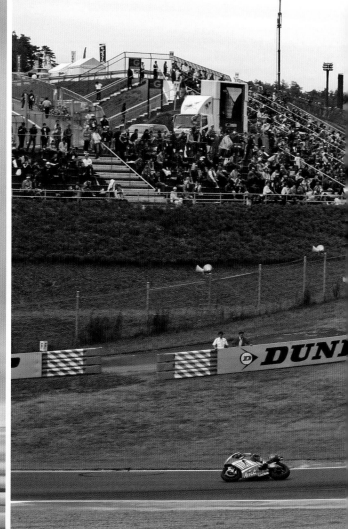

Opposite Dani Pedrosa heads for the rostrum in his first dry-weather race on Bridgestone tyres

Left Unlike some years, everyone got through the first corner

Below The corner at the end of the downhill back straight is the best place at Motegi for overtaking

after Laguna Seca seems to have resolved itself into mutual respect.

It would be easy to dismiss Pedrosa's third place as an under-achievement, but he too was only just recovering from injury and a rostrum finish in his first dry-weather race on new tyres is a not insignificant feat. It looked even better after Dani fended off a spirited attack from Jorge Lorenzo that included a bit of fairing bashing at the hairpin on the last lap.

The coronation of Valentino Rossi took place to a background hum of discussion over tyres – again. There was much politicking, in an effort to maintain competition among the tyre manufacturers into 2009, and with Honda preparing to abandon Michelin and move works and satellite teams to Bridgestone the search was on to find teams who would move the other way. A gentlemen's agreement between the

Above Nicky Hayden qualified well at Motegi but 'didn't have the pace' on race day

Below 'Sorry for the delay' says the T-shirt celebrating Rossi regaining the title after a two-year hiatus

Opposite Yuki Takahashi was announced as Scot Racing's MotoGP rider for 2009

companies specified that they must share teams at least 60/40. To general surprise it was Ducati who animated the debate, offering to put all five of the bikes they are thought to be fielding in '09 on the French rubber. Kawasaki were also interested. Their motive? Ducati were the first big team to move to Bridgestone, and it had been a gamble, but they reasoned they weren't going to beat Rossi on the same equipment and that going with the other tyre company might give them a significant advantage at one or two tracks. The gamble paid off. Now they applied the same logic in reverse. Kawasaki were thinking along similar lines, wondering if they'd be better off with Michelin than at the bottom of Bridgestone's list of priorities. However, the Ducati team's plan didn't meet with the approval of their main sponsors, Philip Morris and Shell, who have relationships with Bridgestone in F1 as well as in MotoGP. Top management at Kawasaki Heavy Industries was similarly unenthusiastic. Michelin therefore couldn't muster the necessary 40 per cent of the grid and so a single tyre supplier for 2009 became inevitable. As the '09 season starts on 27 October, the day after the Valencia GP, there wasn't the luxury of time. Tyre companies were given just five days to submit their proposals to the FIM and Dorna.

Valentino Rossi was also looking forward to 2009. He was due to test what he called the 2008-5 Yamaha on the Monday after the Japanese race. Improving response out of slow corners was supposed to be the first priority. However, a messy night in a Korean restaurant meant the rain put in an appearance before Valentino did. Nice to know that even his new stratospheric levels of concentration don't prohibit the occasional party.

GRAND PRIX OF JAPAN
Motegi 2008

RECORD-BREAKER

Valentino Rossi's sixth title in the premier class took him one clear of Mick Doohan's total, leaving only Giacomo Agostini, winner of eight top-class titles, ahead of him. Add in Valentino's 125 and 250 titles and he has a total of eight World Championship crowns. Mike Hailwood and Carlo Ubbiali each won nine titles, with Angel Nieto (13) and Agostini (15) still leading the field. Rossi's first title came in 1997, eleven years ago. Only Nieto's championship career was longer: he won the 50cc title in 1969 and his final title, the 125, in 1984.

By winning his first title under the 800cc formula, Valentino became the first man to take the premier-class title on four different types of motorcycle, the others being the 990cc Yamaha M1, the V5 Honda RC211V and the 500cc V4 Honda NSR500 two-stroke.

One aspect of the latest title of which Valentino is well aware, and will be content with, is that it means he will be remembered as a Yamaha rider. He has now won 37 races with them, more than with any other factory. He is also Yamaha's most successful rider of all time, with 13 more victories than Kenny Roberts notched up.

As a student of the sport's history, Valentino is well aware of these numbers – and they will undoubtedly form part of his motivation for the next two years.

Above Valentino Rossi presents his eighth world title for validation to the well-known Italian public notary, Dottore Ottaviani Ottavio – whose name, by a strange coincidence, translates to 'Eighth Eight'

JAPANESE GP
TWIN-RING MOTEGI

ROUND 15
September 28

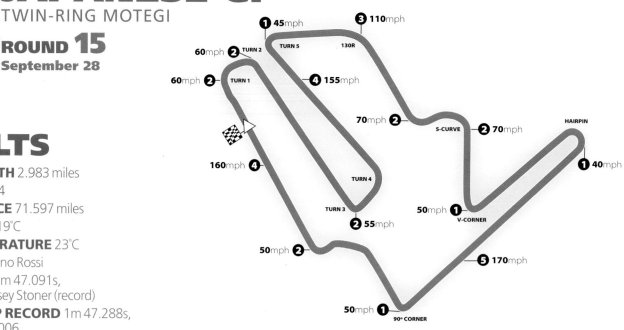

RACE RESULTS

CIRCUIT LENGTH 2.983 miles
NO. OF LAPS 24
RACE DISTANCE 71.597 miles
WEATHER Dry, 19°C
TRACK TEMPERATURE 23°C
WINNER Valentino Rossi
FASTEST LAP 1m 47.091s, 100.288mph, Casey Stoner (record)
PREVIOUS LAP RECORD 1m 47.288s, Valentino Rossi, 2006

QUALIFYING

	Rider	Nationality	Team	Qualifying	Pole +	Gap
1	Lorenzo	SPA	Fiat Yamaha Team	1m 45.543s		
2	Stoner	AUS	Ducati Marlboro Team	1m 45.831s	0.288s	0.288s
3	Hayden	USA	Repsol Honda Team	1m 45.971s	0.428s	0.140s
4	Rossi	ITA	Fiat Yamaha Team	1m 46.060s	0.517s	0.089s
5	Pedrosa	SPA	Repsol Honda Team	1m 46.303s	0.760s	0243s
6	Capirossi	ITA	Rizla Suzuki MotoGP	1m 46.450s	0.907s	0.147s
7	Edwards	USA	Tech 3 Yamaha	1m 46.496s	0.953s	0.046s
8	De Puniet	FRA	LCR Honda MotoGP	1m 46.554s	1.011s	0.058s
9	Nakano	JPN	San Carlo Honda Gresini	1m 46.616s	1.073s	0.062s
10	Toseland	GBR	Tech 3 Yamaha	1m 46.863s	1.320s	0.247s
11	Hopkins	USA	Kawasaki Racing Team	1m 46.888s	1.345s	0.025s
12	Vermeulen	AUS	Rizla Suzuki MotoGP	1m 46.904s	1.361s	0.016s
13	Dovizioso	ITA	JiR Team Scot MotoGP	1m 46.907s	1.364s	0.003s
14	Elias	SPA	Alice Team	1m 46.958s	1.415s	0.051s
15	Guintoli	FRA	Alice Team	1m 47.400s	1.857s	0.442s
16	Melandri	ITA	Ducati Marlboro Team	1m 47.475s	1.932s	0.075s
17	West	AUS	Kawasaki Racing Team	1m 47.669s	2.126s	0.194s
18	De Angelis	RSM	San Carlo Honda Gresini	1m 47.680s	2.137s	0.011s
19	Akiyoshi	JPN	Rizla Suzuki MotoGP	1m 48.671s	3.128s	0.991s

FINISHERS

1 VALENTINO ROSSI His first MotoGP win at Motegi secured that eighth world title, and in style. Qualifying didn't go according to plan – he was off the front row for the first time since Germany – so had to fight past Lorenzo, Hayden, Pedrosa and Stoner to take the lead just after half-distance. Once at the front, Valentino was untouchable.

2 CASEY STONER Didn't relinquish his title without a fight, but the injured wrist had an effect mid-race, not due to the pain but because it hampered his training regime so he wasn't fully fit. Charged again with five laps left but a small mistake at the end of the back straight ended his challenge.

3 DANI PEDROSA On the podium in his first dry race on Bridgestones, ending his longest run of finishes outside the top three since 2001, but well beaten by the front two and couldn't fight back after they went past him. In the closing stages had to hold off a spirited attack from Lorenzo.

4 JORGE LORENZO On pole for the first time since Portugal, and Michelin's first pole since Le Mans. Lower temperatures on race day put the Michelin men at a slight disadvantage but Jorge had enough in hand to attack Pedrosa in the final laps. Made a mistake on the last lap and had to settle for fourth.

5 NICKY HAYDEN Made a qualifier last two laps after being baulked at his first attempt to get on the front row. Started well but couldn't make his tyres last on the cold track. Caught by the four-man group but managed to hold them off to the flag.

6 LORIS CAPIROSSI One of his best races of the season at a track where he'd won the previous three GPs. Lost touch with Hayden at mid-distance when a mistake cost him over 3s. Fought to get on terms again but a rear-wheel slide on the last lap meant he couldn't press home his attack.

7 COLIN EDWARDS Struggled with a spinning rear tyre for the whole race but managed to press Capirossi almost

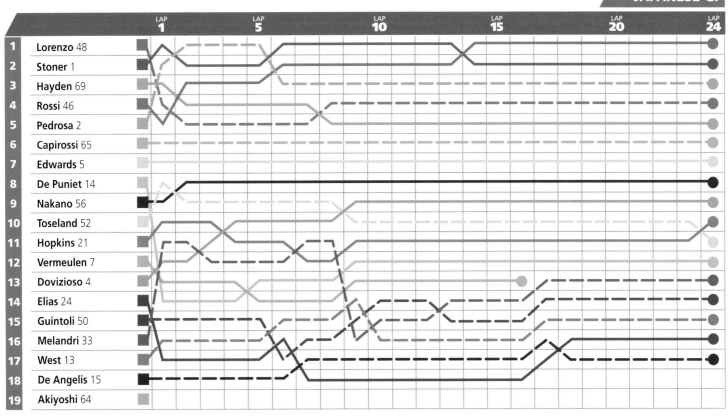

		LAP 1	LAP 5	LAP 10	LAP 15	LAP 20	LAP 24
1	Lorenzo 48						
2	Stoner 1						
3	Hayden 69						
4	Rossi 46						
5	Pedrosa 2						
6	Capirossi 65						
7	Edwards 5						
8	De Puniet 14						
9	Nakano 56						
10	Toseland 52						
11	Hopkins 21						
12	Vermeulen 7						
13	Dovizioso 4						
14	Elias 24						
15	Guintoli 50						
16	Melandri 33						
17	West 13						
18	De Angelis 15						
19	Akiyoshi 64						

RACE

	Rider	Motorcycle	Race Time	Time +	Fastest Lap	Average Speed
1	Rossi	Yamaha	43m 09.599s		1m 47.215s	99.536mph
2	Stoner	Ducati	43m 11.542s	1.943s	1m 47.091s	99.461mph
3	Pedrosa	Honda	43m 14.465s	4.866s	1m 47.354s	99.350mph
4	Lorenzo	Yamaha	43m 15.764s	6.165s	1m 47.418s	99.300mph
5	Hayden	Honda	43m 34.192s	24.593s	1m 47.823s	98.600mph
6	Capirossi	Suzuki	43m 35.284s	25.685s	1m 47.800s	98.559mph
7	Edwards	Yamaha	43m 35.517s	25.918s	1m 48.174s	98.550mph
8	Nakano	Honda	43m 35.602s	26.003s	1m 48.197s	98.547mph
9	Dovizioso	Honda	43m 35.818s	26.219s	1m 48.208s	98.539mph
10	Hopkins	Kawasaki	43m 46.730s	37.131s	1m 48.421s	98.129mph
11	Toseland	Yamaha	43m 47.173s	37.574s	1m 48.404s	98.112mph
12	De Puniet	Honda	43m 47.619s	38.020s	1m 48.503s	98.096mph
13	Melandri	Ducati	43m 49.367s	39.768s	1m 48.293s	98.031mph
14	Guintoli	Ducati	43m 55.445s	45.846s	1m 48.600s	97.805mph
15	West	Kawasaki	44m 05.347s	55.748s	1m 48.441s	97.439mph
16	Elias	Ducati	44m 08.919s	59.320s	1m 48.301s	97.307mph
17	De Angelis	Honda	44m 21.997s	1m 12.398s	1m 49.011s	96.829mph
	Vermeulen	Suzuki	29m 15.247s	8 laps	1m 48.567s	97.900mph

CHAMPIONSHIP

	Rider	Team	Points
1	Rossi	Fiat Yamaha Team	312
2	Stoner	Ducati Marlboro Team	220
3	Pedrosa	Repsol Honda Team	209
4	Lorenzo	Fiat Yamaha Team	169
5	Dovizioso	JiR Team Scot MotoGP	136
6	Edwards	Tech 3 Yamaha	118
7	Vermeulen	Rizla Suzuki MotoGP	117
8	Hayden	Repsol Honda Team	115
9	Capirossi	Rizla Suzuki MotoGP	96
10	Nakano	San Carlo Honda Gresini	95
11	Toseland	Tech 3 Yamaha	90
12	Elias	Alice Team	86
13	Guintoli	Alice Team	58
14	De Angelis	San Carlo Honda Gresini	55
15	Melandri	Ducati Marlboro Team	51
16	Hopkins	Kawasaki Racing Team	47
17	De Puniet	LCR Honda MotoGP	47
18	West	Kawasaki Racing Team	42
19	Spies	Rizla Suzuki MotoGP	20
20	Hacking	Kawasaki Racing Team	5
21	Okada	Repsol Honda Team	2

continuously after nearly being collected by Dovizioso in the first corner. Felt he had a 'solid race under my belt' for the first time in ages.

8 SHINYA NAKANO After an eventful first lap, when he gained and then lost a few places, spent the first part of the race trying to work out how to pass the Yamaha in front of him and the last part concentrating on stopping the Honda behind him overtaking.

9 ANDREA DOVIZIOSO Got past a few riders in the first third of the race, then stuck in the group. Reckoned he had good enough race pace for fifth place but the barging match in the first corner put paid to that.

10 JOHN HOPKINS A better result than it seems on the surface. Felt his pace was good enough to take fifth place and encouraged by some radical set-up changes that also renewed his confidence. Spent the race dicing with Toseland.

11 JAMES TOSELAND Once again a wet Friday meant James couldn't do as much set-up work as he wanted at a track he'd never seen before. Banged fairings with Hopkins for the whole race, only losing out to the Kawasaki rider on the last lap.

12 RANDY DE PUNIET Another victim of the Turn 1 scrum. Got back past Vermeulen and Melandri, then lost grip in

his rear tyre. Not helped on a stop-start track by the cracked bone in his right forearm.

13 MARCO MELANDRI Things looked better on Friday in the wet, but all the old problems came back on Saturday. Started the race well but ran off track and lost five places. Opening the throttle out of corners was, as usual, the big problem.

14 SYLVAIN GUINTOLI Another rider who couldn't reproduce his free practice times in qualifying or the race. Lack of confidence in the front end was the main problem.

15 ANTHONY WEST Like his team-mate made some progress in set-up

which wasn't reflected in the result. A front brake lever that kept coming back to the handlebar caused an off-track excursion, losing him the two places he'd gained in the early laps. After that it was a lonely race.

16 TONI ELIAS Ran off track on lap seven and went to the back of the field. Took another ten laps to hunt down de Angelis, but never got within range of West.

17 ALEX DE ANGELIS Three crashes and his worst result of the year made it a weekend to forget. 'I kept running wide and never found my rhythm' was his simple explanation.

NON-FINISHERS

CHRIS VERMEULEN Going well when he started having problems with the brakes. Ran off track on lap 17 without falling, rejoined the race but had to pull in immediately and retire.

KOUSUKE AKIYOSHI Suzuki's tester had the briefest of wild-card appearances. Wrecked his number one bike in warm-up and started from the back of the grid, blasting past a few riders in the first two corners only to have a huge slide at Turn 3 and crash out.

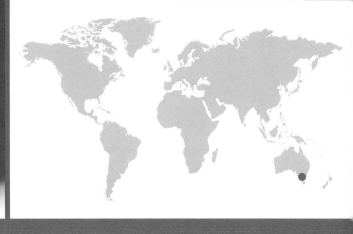

ISLAND LIFE

Yet again the fastest track on the calendar produced some superb racing, although most of it was behind the dominant Casey Stoner

In pure racing terms Phillip Island is, by common consent, the best track that MotoGP visits. The circuit is hard on tyres, tough on bikes and requires a rare combination of skill and bravery from the riders. It can be no coincidence that the three men who stood on the rostrum have shared every MotoGP championship between them. Having seen his title slip away in Japan, Casey Stoner reminded everyone just how good he'd been in 2007 with a stunning qualifying time followed by a race in which he led every lap. This was the Casey who destroyed the opposition last year, and put together that stunning run in the middle of this season. Apart from a few seconds on the front straight, the Ducati's wheels never seemed to be in line – and this on a circuit where big lean angles combined with lots of throttle are the norm. Some tracks never look fast no matter what times the riders are doing. Watching any good racer at Phillip Island is an awe-inspiring experience; watching the MotoGP men is almost overwhelming.

However, there were a worrying number of crashes in which riders from all three classes had lucky escapes from close encounters with the scenery. Valentino Rossi was one of them. He left the track at Turn 3 – the one that Stoner says 'really gets your heart racing' – was flicked off the bike when it hit the gravel trap and ended up against the tyre barrier. The accident happened towards the end of qualifying, which meant the new World Champion would start from twelfth on the grid, lucky to escape with a bit of whiplash and a serious headache.

As Valentino has been saying since Germany, if he doesn't start on the front row he won't be

able to race Casey for the win. That task was left to Nicky Hayden. The American reverted to his favoured medium-compound Michelin after the sighting lap, causing his tyre technician to age ten years. It enabled him to harass Stoner for the first half of the race but in the final few laps he was 'down to the cords' and could do nothing to defend second place. Almost inevitably, the man who emerged from a spectacular fight for third place to catch Hayden was Rossi. Obviously regaining the title seven days previously had done nothing to dampen his enthusiasm for racing.

It only took four laps for Rossi to move up from twelfth to fourth, but that pitched him into a ferocious battle with the Yamahas of Jorge Lorenzo and James Toseland, the Honda of Shinya Nakano and, after a few laps, the satellite team Honda of Andrea Dovizioso, who came back from a fraught first lap. Rossi can be expected to ghost through any group when he catches them, even one with riders of this quality. It didn't happen this time, though, thanks to James Toseland, who surprised the Doctor by repassing him, then holding him off for another six laps before the decisive break was made. There were another two pass/repass moves in those laps, not to mention the close attentions of the rest of the group. Watching three MotoGP machines hammer into the first corner side by side after the long, downhill Gardner Straight is a sight no race fan could ever forget. When he finally shook off Toseland, Rossi went in pursuit of Hayden, leaving the rest of the group to fight over fourth.

Lorenzo was slightly disappointed that he didn't have the pace to race with his Fiat Yamaha team-mate,

'SOMETIMES YOU CAN HAVE THE BEST PACE BUT STILL GET DRAGGED INTO A BATTLE, BUT I WAS ABLE TO GET AWAY'
CASEY STONER

Above Valentino Rossi loves Phillip Island, but it didn't prevent him from crashing in qualifying

Left Casey Stoner was more relaxed at home than he's been all season

Opposite John Hopkins hustling the recalcitrant Kawasaki round the Island; you could never accuse him of not trying

Above Jorge Lorenzo gets the thumbs-up from 1987 World Champion Wayne Gardner

Opposite Nicky Hayden always goes well at Phillip Island, and left with a new lap record

Below The fight for fourth: Toseland leads Lorenzo, Dovizioso and Nakano

but he did manage to break away from the group on the penultimate lap. There was plenty of action at Honda Corner, the only really hard braking effort of the entire lap, and that's where Jorge grabbed a vital few bike lengths as the rest got tangled up. Inevitably, the same corner was the venue for the last-lap sort-out as well. Toseland went in hard and ran Dovizioso wide enough for Nakano take advantage and pass them both. James was consigned to his sixth sixth place of the year, when he probably deserved a career-best finish, and Andrea was seriously displeased with Toseland's move. He wasn't too happy after the pair came together in Jerez either, so that's a

relationship which will bear watching in the future.

The rider who doesn't figure in all this action is Dani Pedrosa, because he crashed on the first lap after getting on the grass when he ran wide out of the Southern Loop. It looked as if Toseland, who was on the inside of Pedrosa, might have had something to do with the incident but the Spaniard reported that they hadn't touched and that it was his own error, for which he apologised to the Repsol team. On the other side of the divided garage Nicky Hayden allowed himself a touch of *Schadenfreude*, admitting that Dani was more than just another opponent. The always well-mannered American's displeasure with Honda can be measured by his willingness to talk about Ducati while he is still under contract to HRC. This time Nicky reported that, while he was following Casey, he was asking himself what he'd be able to do with the red bike he'll be on in 2009.

Away from the track the subject of tyres refused to go away. The deadline for offers to become sole supplier for MotoGP in 2009 was the Friday of the Grand Prix. Bridgestone had already made it known that they would be tendering; Michelin waited until the time limit was up in Europe – not Australia – before announcing that they would not, which means that in 2009 the Japanese company will become the sole tyre supplier to MotoGP. The next step would be making public the technical details of the new regulations. After all, they would effectively come into force on the Monday after the Valencia GP, only 23 days away. The paddock was told to expect a complete rundown of the new rules to be made public at the Malaysian GP in two weeks' time.

FLYING THE FLAG

James Toseland's sixth place in Australia took him past the 100-point milestone, an achievement in itself for the class rookie but also a long-awaited feat for British racing in general. The last Brit to score a century in the top class was Niall Mackenzie back in 1993, the penultimate year of his distinguished Grand Prix career. Niall passed the 100 mark four times, 1988, '89, '90 and '93. He finished fourth overall in 1990, and stood on the rostrum seven times.

The Scot's 1993 season was on a private ROC Yamaha run by the WCM team (later Red Bull Yamaha), an almost analogous situation to Toseland riding for the Tech 3 satellite Yamaha team. However, Niall had a much happier home GP than James, he got on the rostrum when Carl Fogarty's factory Cagiva stuttered coming into Goddards for the final time. It was Niall's last rostrum finish in GPs, he returned to the British Superbike Championship and won a hat-trick of titles between 1996 and '98, again on Yamahas.

Toseland's points tally was even more reassuring for British fans as the 2007 season was the first in the whole history of the motorcycle Grands Prix that a British rider failed to score a single point in the top class.

Above James Toseland may have finished sixth again but Phillip Island was by far his best race of the season

AUSTRALIAN GP

PHILLIP ISLAND

ROUND 16
October 5

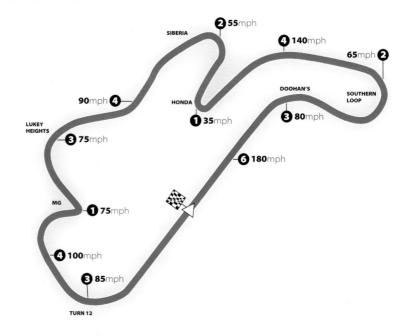

RACE RESULTS

CIRCUIT LENGTH 2.760 miles
NO. OF LAPS 27
RACE DISTANCE 74.620 miles
WEATHER Dry, 17°C
TRACK TEMPERATURE 27°C
WINNER Casey Stoner
FASTEST LAP 1m 30.059s, 110.487mph, Nicky Hayden (record)
PREVIOUS LAP RECORD 1m 30.332s, 110.153mph, Marco Melandri, 2005

QUALIFYING

	Rider	Nationality	Team	Qualifying	Pole +	Gap
1	Stoner	AUS	Ducati Marlboro Team	1m 28.665s		
2	Lorenzo	SPA	Fiat Yamaha Team	1m 28.734s	0.069s	0.069s
3	Hayden	USA	Repsol Honda Team	1m 28.756s	0.091s	0.022s
4	De Puniet	FRA	LCR Honda MotoGP	1m 28.808s	0.143s	0.052s
5	Toseland	GBR	Tech 3 Yamaha	1m 29.031s	0.366s	0.223s
6	Pedrosa	SPA	Repsol Honda Team	1m 29.277	0.612s	0.246s
7	Edwards	USA	Tech 3 Yamaha	1m 29.513s	0.848s	0.236s
8	Dovizioso	ITA	JiR Team Scot MotoGP	1m 29.558	0.893s	0.045s
9	Nakano	JPN	San Carlo Honda Gresini	1m 29.710s	1.045s	0.152s
10	De Angelis	RSM	San Carlo Honda Gresini	1m 29.925s	1.260s	0.215s
11	Capirossi	ITA	Rizla Suzuki MotoGP	1m 29.942s	1.277s	0.017s
12	Rossi	ITA	Fiat Yamaha Team	1m 30.014s	1.349s	0.072s
13	Elias	SPA	Alice Team	1m 30.202s	1.537s	0.188s
14	Guintoli	FRA	Alice Team	1m 30.297s	1.632s	0.095s
15	Vermeulen	AUS	Rizla Suzuki MotoGP	1m 30.545s	1.880s	0.248
16	Hopkins	USA	Kawasaki Racing Team	1m 31.157s	2.492s	0.612s
17	Melandri	ITA	Ducati Marlboro Team	1m 31.939s	3.274s	0.782s
18	West	AUS	Kawasaki Racing Team	1m 31.995s	3.330s	0.056s

FINISHERS

1 CASEY STONER Pole position and victory at his home race despite a nasty crash in practice. It was Casey at his best, forcing the Desmosedici to shimmy, slide and shake as he used way more lean angle and track than anyone else. Not a bad way to celebrate Ducati's 100th MotoGP race.

2 VALENTINO ROSSI Started from the fourth row after a big crash in qualifying which left him with a stiff neck and a serious headache. Narrowly missed de Angelis's crash on the first lap, then fought with Lorenzo and Toseland before jumping across a 6s gap to pass Hayden on the last lap.

3 NICKY HAYDEN Always fast at Phillip Island. Started from the front row on softer tyres than his Michelin engineer suggested and set the fastest lap of the race, pressuring Stoner. The tyres did fade late on, helping Rossi to catch him, but Nicky was happy with his race.

4 JORGE LORENZO Only Stoner was faster in qualifying but Jorge never quite had the same pace on race day and was disappointed with his result, conceding that any chance of taking third in the championship had gone. Too much weight transfer under braking was his main problem.

5 SHINYA NAKANO Shadowed the dice for third for much of the race and took advantage on the final lap. Chose

a medium rear Bridgestone which gave the bike really good balance and enabled him to push hard over the last five laps. 'It has been a long time since I enjoyed a race like this.'

6 JAMES TOSELAND Sixth place for the sixth time this year, but by far his best race and on his 28th birthday ... not many people repass Rossi and then hold the Doctor off for five laps. Managed to annoy Dovizioso again but Rossi had no complaints about James's riding – quite the reverse.

7 ANDREA DOVIZIOSO Another splendid ride on the satellite Honda despite being pushed off track on lap one. Came back to join the fight for third but lost out on the final lap after going wide

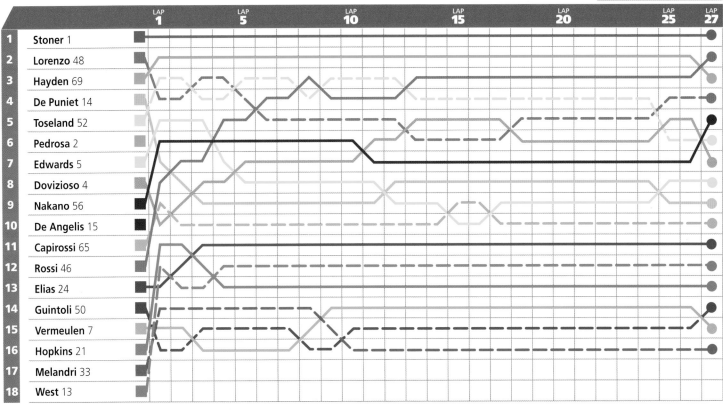

		LAP 1	LAP 5	LAP 10	LAP 15	LAP 20	LAP 25	LAP 27
1	Stoner 1							
2	Lorenzo 48							
3	Hayden 69							
4	De Puniet 14							
5	Toseland 52							
6	Pedrosa 2							
7	Edwards 5							
8	Dovizioso 4							
9	Nakano 56							
10	De Angelis 15							
11	Capirossi 65							
12	Rossi 46							
13	Elias 24							
14	Guintoli 50							
15	Vermeulen 7							
16	Hopkins 21							
17	Melandri 33							
18	West 13							

RACE

	Rider	Motorcycle	Race Time	Time +	Fastest Lap	Average Speed
1	Stoner	Ducati	40m 56.643s		1m 30.067s	109.360mph
2	Rossi	Yamaha	41m 03.147s	6.504s	1m 30.284s	109.071mph
3	Hayden	Honda	41m 03.848s	7.205s	1m 30.059s	109.040mph
4	Lorenzo	Yamaha	41m 08.143s	11.500s	1m 30.702s	108.850mph
5	Nakano	Honda	41m 08.557s	11.914s	1m 30.595s	108.832mph
6	Toseland	Yamaha	41m 08.886s	12.243s	1m 30.802s	108.817mph
7	Dovizioso	Honda	41m 09.423s	12.780s	1m 30.585s	108.794mph
8	Edwards	Yamaha	41m 22.563s	25.920s	1m 31.083s	108.218mph
9	De Puniet	Honda	41m 22.680s	26.037s	1m 30.873s	108.213mph
10	Capirossi	Sukuki	41m 23.442s	26.799s	1m 30.971s	108.180mph
11	Elias	Ducati	41m 23.670s	27.027s	1m 31.201s	108.170mph
12	West	Kawasaki	41m 44.451s	47.808s	1m 31.915s	107.272mph
13	Hopkins	Kawasaki	41m 44.976s	48.333s	1m 32.010s	107.249mph
14	Guintoli	Ducati	41m 45.542s	48.899s	1m 31.528s	107.225mph
15	Vermeulen	Suzuki	41m 45.578s	48.935s	1m 31.313s	107.224mph
16	Melandri	Ducati	42m 08.410s	1m 11.767s	1m 32.519s	106.256mph

CHAMPIONSHIP

	Rider	Team	Points
1	Rossi	Fiat Yamaha Team	332
2	Stoner	Ducati Marlboro Team	245
3	Pedrosa	Repsol Honda Team	209
4	Lorenzo	Fiat Yamaha Team	182
5	Dovizioso	JiR Team Scot MotoGP	145
6	Hayden	Repsol Honda Team	131
7	Edwards	Tech 3 Yamaha	126
8	Vermeulen	Rizla Suzuki MotoGP	118
9	Nakano	San Carlo Honda Gresini	106
10	Capirossi	Rizla Suzuki MotoGP	102
11	Toseland	Tech 3 Yamaha	100
12	Elias	Alice Team	91
13	Guintoli	Alice Team	60
14	De Angelis	San Carlo Honda Gresini	55
15	De Puniet	LCR Honda MotoGP	54
16	Melandri	Ducati Marlboro Team	51
17	Hopkins	Kawasaki Racing Team	50
18	West	Kawasaki Racing Team	46
19	Spies	Rizla Suzuki MotoGP	20
20	Hacking	Kawasaki Racing Team	5
21	Okada	Repsol Honda Team	2

while under attack from Toseland. Nakano then took them both; Andrea was not happy.

8 COLIN EDWARDS A big front-end moment early on disconcerted him severely – there had been no warning all weekend and it limited him to mid-1m 31s laps. That was fast enough for him to catch de Puniet at the end, but it wasn't the way he wanted to celebrate his 100th GP.

9 RANDY DE PUNIET Stunningly fast in practice and qualifying but 'missed the train' on Sunday – instead of joining in the fight for third he ended up dicing with Edwards. Took a while to get by the Yamaha, then had to watch the American come

back past on the straight a few laps from home.

10 LORIS CAPIROSSI Given that the Suzuki GSV-R has never worked well round Phillip Island, this was a far from disappointing race. Lap times were much improved but it was obvious that Loris was severely outgunned on the straight: a hard-fought tenth place.

11 TONI ELIAS His race was seriously compromised by his tyre selection: took his tyre technician's advice but never made any of his allocation work. Grateful to have scored points under the circumstances.

12 ANTHONY WEST Sideways out of corners for most of the race thanks to

the usual traction problems, but steered the bike by letting it spin the rear and moving his body weight around. Found enough drive out of the corners to keep his team-mate behind him.

13 JOHN HOPKINS Suffered even more than his team-mate with grip, especially with the left side of the rear tyre. Also caught up in Pedrosa's crash and then had a big moment when he lost the front at Honda Corner. After that it was a matter of racing with West.

14 SYLVAIN GUINTOLI Raced in some pain after a big crash in practice that hurt his shoulder. Went off track when he made a mistake in the aftermath of Pedrosa's crash, then joined forces with Vermeulen to hunt down the Kawasakis.

Used the Ducati's pace to out-drag the Suzuki on the last lap.

15 CHRIS VERMEULEN A victim of the domino effect of Pedrosa's crash. Sent off track with Guintoli, then had to work hard to stay with the Alice Ducati which was considerably faster and used its tyres better.

16 MARCO MELANDRI Two crashes, including one in warm-up which hurt him, demoralised Marco before the race had even begun. It's difficult to believe that he won this race as recently as 2006.

DANI PEDROSA Crashed at the third corner of the first lap after getting off line and running onto the grass. Gave his left knee a severe jolt but fortunately there was no damage to any bone or ligament.

ALEX DE ANGELIS Crashed on the first lap after nearly tailgating de Puniet. Seriously disappointed because he'd gone well in practice and, for once, had got a good start. Luckily didn't take de Puniet down with him, or the following Rossi.

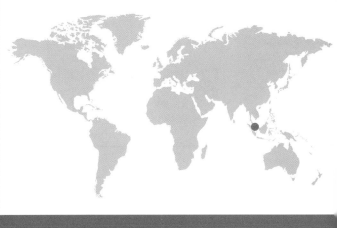

TOTALLY TROPICAL

Rossi beat Pedrosa, Dovizioso beat Hayden and the weather nearly beat them all

According to the man himself, this race was won at the winter tests on the Sepang circuit where the Fiat Yamaha team put a lot of effort into running race simulations. That would have been the first time that Valentino Rossi rode race distances at race speeds on Bridgestone tyres. The times were so impressive that Vale told his tyre engineer he'd win the Grand Prix. He was as good as his word.

Rossi had to overcome two major obstacles – first, the most extreme weather conditions anyone could remember, and second, a very fast Dani Pedrosa who showed he was adapting to Bridgestone tyres faster than most of the paddock thought possible. Ambient temperatures were more than 40° Centigrade (well over 100° Fahrenheit) and there was oppressive tropical humidity as the regular afternoon thunderstorms built up. The MotoGP riders were lucky because they had the benefit of the burgeoning cloud cover. The 250s were less fortunate, because their race took place under clear skies, with one top rider forced out of the contest by heat exhaustion and new champion Marco Simoncelli unable to string a coherent sentence together for the TV interviewers.

Such extreme conditions hinder anyone carrying an injury, usually because it will have prevented him from training properly. Casey Stoner mentioned this after the Motegi race, and in Malaysia things got really serious, with his injured left hand starting to go numb. He then had to over-compensate, which of course resulted in his right hand becoming stressed and starting to give him trouble too. Casey confirmed that the urgently required bone-graft operation

'I AM HAPPY THAT WE ARE
MAKING PROGRESS WITH
OUR NEW BIKE AND TYRES'
DANI PEDROSA

would take place the week after the Valencia race and he would need around ten weeks of recuperation before he could get on a motorcycle again. For the first time Stoner's wrist kept him out of contention for a rostrum position, but how he'd managed even to compete with a scaphoid in several pieces remained a mystery to most people.

There were also questions over Pedrosa's fitness. His crash at Phillip Island had hurt his left knee and left him limping badly. Dani started the weekend slowly, as he did when he first moved up from the 250 class, but just when everyone thought Rossi had pole position sewn up the Repsol Honda rider went four-tenths of a second quicker. It would have been an astonishing enough achievement under normal circumstances, but in only his fourth race on Bridgestone tyres it was completely breathtaking. He carried that speed through to the race, getting the rocket start everyone has come to expect.

Sepang is a track which repays a good start more than most; overtaking is notably difficult unless the leading rider makes a mistake. Sixth-placed qualifier Andrea Dovizioso was the main beneficiary of this effect. He got into Turn 1 in second place and the only man who got past him all race was Valentino Rossi. Dovi had been quietly impressive all year on a very stock customer Honda, taking three fourth-place finishes. This time he hung on for that final rostrum spot, although he had to deal with a sustained and spirited attack from Nicky Hayden. With Lorenzo crashing out immediately after an overtaking move, third place in the race gave Dovizioso a slim chance

Opposite It was hot in Sepang, seriously hot. Dani Pedrosa gets some assistance to cool down on the grid

Above Suzuki's wild card Nobu Aoki dicing with de Angelis and Melandri – note big-bore exhaust pipe

Below Andrea Dovizioso just held off Nicky Hayden and the factory Honda for his first rostrum in MotoGP

of catching the Spaniard for third place in the championship, and with it taking the Rookie of the Year title. More tangibly, it was a deserved reward for both the rider and his team. The Scot team have bought Andrea on since he came to GPs as a Mugello wild card in 2001. They won the 125 title together in 2004 and gave Jorge Lorenzo an unfeasibly hard time in 250s before coming to MotoGP this season. For 2009 Dovi will move to the factory team. HRC preferred to allocate the last available '09 Honda to the Scot team rather than the JiR operation who had joined forces with Scot after their Minolta sponsorship dried up. They divorced towards the end of the season and JiR boss Luca Montiron left the paddock aiming some acerbic comments at Honda.

Andrea was happy he had managed to give the team a rostrum before he left them, while everyone watching was happy that his fight with Hayden provided some on-track action. The young Italian only sighted Nicky once, when the American briefly got ahead four laps from home, but he knew he was there and was 'very afraid' for the last three laps. As we've come to expect, Rossi spent half the race shadowing Pedrosa before passing and pulling away. He made it look easy, but even the Doctor suffered in the dreadful conditions. Valentino stopped looking at the lap indicator, had some trouble with his vision and needed 20 minutes after the race to regain his composure. Beforehand, Rossi and the riders' safety commission had rejected the idea of the Sepang race being run under floodlights. It wouldn't be surprising if a few of them had a rather different opinion after this race.

Above A happy, smiling Andrea Dovizioso before the race – he was even happier afterwards

Below If there were an architectural prize for MotoGP tracks, Sepang would win it

MONOGOMMO IS GO

As expected, the formal announcement of Bridgestone as the single tyre supplier for MotoGP was made on the Saturday of the Sepang race. The Japanese company was the only one to submit a proposal and was duly confirmed with a three-year contract. Details of the regulations weren't officially released but the riders' safety commission were told that, as with their F1 system, Bridgestone will make their tyre in up to seven compounds and bring two to each race. Riders would get 20 tyres per weekend – four front and six rear – in both of the two compounds. The riders' first reaction was far from favourable.

Further meetings with Hiroshi Yamada of Bridgestone calmed things down a little. He assured the riders that Bridgestone knew what they were doing: their products worked over a broad spectrum of conditions, and if the allocation of 20 tyres proved inadequate then the company would increase it. Most seemed reassured. Concerns were still voiced, but now they were about matters other than the central issue of the number of tyres. Jorge Lorenzo wondered who would do the development work. Andrea Dovizioso wasn't worried about the number of tyres for a race weekend but was concerned about the suggestion that the tyres available for testing would be strictly limited. Another issue in the draft regulations was the very small number – four sets – of wet-weather tyres in only a medium compound.

The riders' prime concern was that, with only two choices, if one tyre didn't work because of significantly different track temperatures morning and afternoon, for instance, then they wouldn't waste tyres by going out in the morning session. For similar reasons, it's easy to envisage a pretty empty track on Friday.

The allocation is very unlikely to be increased, so riders will have to learn to cope with the reality of a single tyre supplier.

Above It'll be Bridgestones all round in 2009: the single tyre supplier was confirmed on the Saturday of the Malaysian race

MALAYSIAN GP
SEPANG INTERNATIONAL CIRCUIT

ROUND 17
October 19

RACE RESULTS

CIRCUIT LENGTH 3.447 miles
NO. OF LAPS 21
RACE DISTANCE 72.394 miles
WEATHER Dry, 39°C
TRACK TEMPERATURE 42°C
WINNER Valentino Rossi
FASTEST LAP 2m 02.249s, 101.523mph, Valentino Rossi
PREVIOUS LAP RECORD 2m 02.108s, 101.640mph, Casey Stoner, 2007

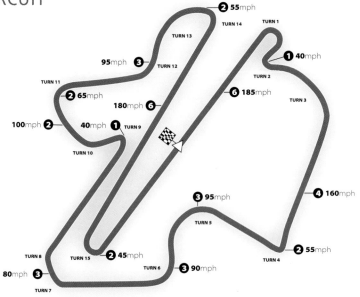

QUALIFYING

	Rider	Nationality	Team	Qualifying	Pole +	Gap
1	Pedrosa	SPA	Repsol Honda Team	2m 01.548s		
2	Rossi	ITA	Fiat Yamaha Team	2m 01.957s	0.409s	0.409s
3	Lorenzo	SPA	Fiat Yamaha Team	2m 02.171s	0.623s	0.214s
4	Hayden	USA	Repsol Honda Team	2m 02.192s	0.644s	0.021s
5	Edwards	USA	Tech 3 Yamaha	2m 02.245s	0.697	0.053s
6	Dovizioso	ITA	JiR Team Scot MotoGP	2m 02.836s	1.288s	0.591s
7	Stoner	AUS	Ducati Marlboro Team	2m 02.953s	1.405s	0.117s
8	Capirossi	ITA	Rizla Suzuki MotoGP	2m 03.078s	1.530s	0.125s
9	De Puniet	FRA	LCR Honda MotoGP	2m 03.110s	1.562s	0.032s
10	Hopkins	USA	Kawasaki Racing Team	2m 03.184s	1.636s	0.074s
11	Vermeulen	AUS	Rizla Suzuki MotoGP	2m 03.271s	1.723s	0.087s
12	Toseland	GBR	Tech 3 Yamaha	2m 03.282s	1.734s	0.011s
13	West	AUS	Kawasaki Racing Team	2m 03.392s	1.844s	0.110s
14	Melandri	ITA	Ducati Marlboro Team	2m 03.835s	2.287s	0.443s
15	Nakano	JPN	San Carlo Honda Gresini	2m 04.001s	2.453s	0.166s
16	Guintoli	FRA	Alice Team	2m 04.378s	2.830s	0.377s
17	De Angelis	RSM	San Carlo Honda Gresini	2m 04.679s	3.131s	0.301s
18	Aoki	JPN	Rizla Suzuki MotoGP	2m 04.835s	3.287s	0.156s
19	Elias	SPA	Alice Team	2m 05.120s	3.572s	0.285s

FINISHERS

1 VALENTINO ROSSI A last-minute swap to a harder front tyre proved decisive in the fight with Pedrosa, but once past the Honda he pulled away to notch up the 150th rostrum of his career in all classes. The only thing that could've beaten him was the weather.

2 DANI PEDROSA Couldn't respond when Rossi came past, unsurprisingly given their relative experience on Bridgestones. But a rostrum in his fourth race on new rubber, in these conditions, was really impressive, especially considering the knee problem.

3 ANDREA DOVIZIOSO First MotoGP rostrum in his penultimate race for the

Scot team, having ridden for them for seven years and won the 125cc title. Result based on a great start from the second row and then an impressively precise ride to fend off Hayden.

4 NICKY HAYDEN Had a better race than practice suggested he might: pressed Dovizioso hard and even got in front twice for short periods. The second time Dovi passed him back at the next corner and Nicky made a small mistake that was enough to lose the tow.

5 SHINYA NAKANO Another impressive ride on the factory bike, on the weekend his prospective ride for '09 on a third Kawasaki fell through. Stalked Stoner, after another great start, getting past when he noticed the Aussie was having problems, apparently with the front tyre.

6 CASEY STONER Made sure of the runner-up spot but his shattered scaphoid now causing real problems: lost all feeling in his left hand and then overstressed his right; cramps meant he couldn't fully open the throttle on the straight. In the circumstances, sixth was close to heroic.

7 LORIS CAPIROSSI A combative race that was a lot better than it looks on paper. Took a while to get past Edwards, then ran off track twice attacking Stoner. Ended the race in a seven-bike train, all of them in sight of the last rostrum place.

8 COLIN EDWARDS Suffered in the barging at the first corner before recovering, then ran into trouble when the balance of the bike changed as the tyres wore. Disappointed with eighth, but still his best-ever result at Sepang.

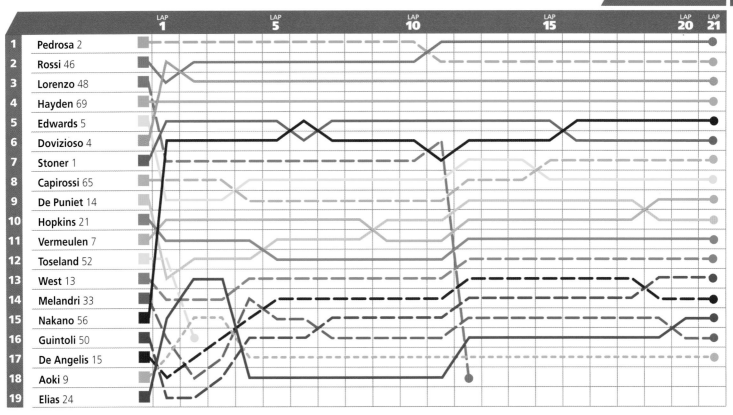

		LAP 1	LAP 5	LAP 10	LAP 15	LAP 20	LAP 21
1	Pedrosa 2						
2	Rossi 46						
3	Lorenzo 48						
4	Hayden 69						
5	Edwards 5						
6	Dovizioso 4						
7	Stoner 1						
8	Capirossi 65						
9	De Puniet 14						
10	Hopkins 21						
11	Vermeulen 7						
12	Toseland 52						
13	West 13						
14	Melandri 33						
15	Nakano 56						
16	Guintoli 50						
17	De Angelis 15						
18	Aoki 9						
19	Elias 24						

RACE

	Rider	Motorcycle	Race Time	Time +	Fastest Lap	Average Speed
1	Rossi	Yamaha	43m 06.007s		2m 02.249s	100.785mph
2	Pedrosa	Honda	43m 10.015s	4.008s	2m 02.379s	100.629mph
3	Dovizioso	Honda	43m 14.543s	8.536s	2m 02.881s	100.454mph
4	Hayden	Honda	43m 14.865s	8.858s	2m 02.758s	100.441mph
5	Nakano	Honda	43m 16.590s	10.583s	2m 02.797s	100.374mph
6	Stoner	Ducati	43m 19.647s	13.640s	2m 02.759s	100.256mph
7	Capirossi	Suzuki	43m 21.943s	15.936s	2m 02.927s	100.168mph
8	Edwards	Yamaha	43m 24.809s	18.802s	2m 02.898s	100.057mph
9	Vermeulen	Suzuki	43m 29.181s	23.174s	2m 03.371s	99.890mph
10	De Puniet	Honda	43m 31.523s	25.516s	2m 03.032s	99.800mph
11	Hopkins	Kawasaki	43m 33.616s	27.609s	2m 03.543s	99.721mph
12	West	Kawasaki	43m 47.406s	41.399s	2m 04.127s	99.197mph
13	Guintoli	Ducati	43m 51.624s	45.617s	2m 04.229s	99.038mph
14	De Angelis	Honda	43m 55.010s	49.003s	2m 04.292s	98.911mph
15	Elias	Ducati	44m 05.146s	59.139s	2m 03.330s	98.532mph
16	Melandri	Ducati	44m 09.335s	1m 03.328s	2m 04.412s	98.376mph
17	Aoki	Suzuki	44m 54.370s	1m 48.363s	2m 05.100s	96.732mph
	Lorenzo	Yamaha	25m 38.557s	9 laps	2m 02.748s	96.800mph
	Toseland	Yamaha	4m 19.122s	19 laps	2m 06.389s	95.793mph

CHAMPIONSHIP

	Rider	Team	Points
1	Rossi	Fiat Yamaha Team	357
2	Stoner	Ducati Marlboro Team	255
3	Pedrosa	Repsol Honda Team	229
4	Lorenzo	Fiat Yamaha Team	182
5	Dovizioso	JiR Team Scot MotoGP	161
6	Hayden	Repsol Honda Team	144
7	Edwards	Tech 3 Yamaha	134
8	Vermeulen	Rizla Suzuki MotoGP	125
9	Nakano	San Carlo Honda Gresini	117
10	Capirossi	Rizla Suzuki MotoGP	111
11	Toseland	Tech 3 Yamaha	100
12	Elias	Alice Team	92
13	Guintoli	Alice Team	63
14	De Puniet	LCR Honda MotoGP	60
15	De Angelis	San Carlo Honda Gresini	57
16	Hopkins	Kawasaki Racing Team	55
17	Melandri	Ducati Marlboro Team	51
18	West	Kawasaki Racing Team	50
19	Spies	Rizla Suzuki MotoGP	20
20	Hacking	Kawasaki Racing Team	5
21	Okada	Repsol Honda Team	2

9 CHRIS VERMEULEN Like all the Suzuki riders suffered from lack of top end on a circuit that needs good top speed. Front-end grip went first in the heat, with rear adhesion problems surfacing eight laps from the end. Still managed to pass de Puniet close to the finish.

10 RANDY DE PUNIET Lost places off the start when he pulled a wheelie, then nearly got mixed up in Toseland's crash. Going well when his injured wrist started to give trouble, making braking and changing direction difficult.

11 JOHN HOPKINS The usual Kawasaki traction problems made life difficult. Not only did it spin on the edge of the tyre, but also when getting the bike upright onto the fat part of the rubber. Rear grip

disappeared with five laps to go, so no chance of catching the dice in front.

12 ANTHONY WEST His grip problems started with the rear tyre breaking away on a closed throttle going into the tight left-hander of Turn 2. Struggled with lack of grip going into and coming out of corners for most of the race.

13 SYLVAIN GUINTOLI Last for the first three laps, then started to develop some confidence in the front of his Ducati and found the pace to pass two riders in the closing laps and score three points.

14 ALEX DE ANGELIS Got a good start but was pushed wide in the first corner, for which he blamed Toseland. Spent a lot of time trying to get past Melandri, after which his tyres were shot. A bad weekend.

15 TONI ELIAS Qualified dead last and then got a ride-through penalty for jumping the start. Getting a point after all that has to be seen as some sort of triumph.

16 MARCO MELANDRI Another fraught race. Started with no feeling from the front but a soft rear tyre at least gave him some grip. After a couple of near-crashes in the fast corners when that grip went away he lost 'any shred of confidence I had left'.

17 NOBUATSU AOKI Suzuki's test rider was a wild card on a GSV-R with a very different set of exhaust pipes from the regular bikes. Contemplating a point or two when the engine started playing up – hoped it'd rain so he could swap bikes, but it didn't – so Nobu nursed it home.

NON-FINISHERS

JORGE LORENZO Nowhere near as comfortable on race day as he had been in practice and qualifying. Another bad start and crashed after getting several warnings. Felt frustrated as he'd considered there was a chance to get on the rostrum.

JAMES TOSELAND Never happy all weekend and fell while pushing to make up places. Chose a harder front tyre to make the race distance and may not have given it time to get up to temperature – or he may simply have been trying too hard.

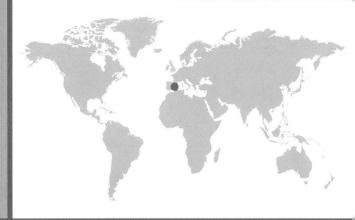

THE END

Casey Stoner won his last race carrying the number-one plate, but yet again the Circuito Ricardo Tormo wasn't kind to Valentino Rossi

The Valencian Grand Prix is always a great event, an end-of-term party for the paddock, followed immediately by the first day of the next season when testing starts. The race never fails to attract an enthusiastic crowd of well over 100,000 to the unique stadium circuit and everyone has a good time. As usual, the 125cc and 250cc races were barn burners, but also as usual the MotoGP race rapidly turned into a high-speed parade. Valencia is a twisty circuit with one long, fast straight and serious overtaking opportunities are limited to the first two corners. The effect is to string the MotoGP bikes out, and it is another characteristic of the circuit that a gap of, say, half a second here is equivalent to one second or more at most of the other tracks on the calendar.

Dani Pedrosa must have been relieved to be at home in front of his uncritical fans although, as ever, he didn't exactly seem to be a seething cauldron of emotion. He qualified on the front row, and when he got the holeshot most people thought they would see the same disappearing act he'd performed 12 months previously. That scenario lasted until the second corner of the first lap, when Casey Stoner, the pole-sitter, went underneath the Honda and inexorably started to draw away. 'He managed the gap very well,' said Pedrosa, with characteristic understatement.

As had become the norm in the 2008 season, the weather played a part. Rain persisted throughout most of practice and qualifying, complicating decisions about when riders would take their qualifying tyres. It was an anti-climactic farewell to the all-out lunacy of the qualifying tyre, which has provided the paddock with some epic moments at the end of the one-hour

Above Colin Edwards on his way to a strong sixth, his best race since Assen

Below Lorenzo decked in the flags of all nations, well the ones that he's won in

Opposite Even on the straight Casey Stoner never has the wheels in line

session. The sight of riders going a second and more quicker than they could achieve with race rubber has gone. At Valencia the best time ever recorded was 1m 31.002s by Rossi, back in qualifying for the 2006 GP, the last race of the 990 era. Stoner's pole time for this race was 1m 31.502s and he set a new lap record in the race (lap records can only be set in competition) of 1m 32.582s. One of the effects of the single-tyre rule coming in for 2009 will be to ensure that some of today's lap records will have a much longer lifetime than has been the case.

With an eye on the threatening clouds, Valentino Rossi rushed through his four qualifiers well before the end of the session. When he was baulked on his last run, the fourth row beckoned. The team didn't seem too upset – 'All the big prizes have gone,' remarked a laconic Jerry Burgess. 'Our target is to give Valentino a good enough bike to enjoy the race, we know that the rest will come from him,' echoed team-manager Davide Brivio. That trust was well placed. It took just six laps for Valentino to get up to third place, but by then he was four seconds behind Stoner and over three behind Pedrosa; even the new World Champion wasn't going to close those sorts of gaps on the second- and third-best riders in the world. In fact, the top six places didn't change once after lap six, although there was some healthy scrapping in the midfield. Colin Edwards had his best ride for half a season, and when James Toseland held onto eleventh spot for the last three very combative laps Tech 3 secured fourth in the teams' championship by just one point from Rizla Suzuki.

Jorge Lorenzo reprised his early-season habit of starting slowly, then getting faster and faster as the race went on, and it even looked as if Marco Melandri was going to say goodbye to Ducati with his best ride of the year. From dead last on the grid he rode through to tenth place, behind Lorenzo; then he found a false neutral instead of first gear and ran off track, losing 20 seconds. And there was no fairytale ending to the season for either Kawasaki or Suzuki. The Valencia track exposed the weaknesses of both their machines, with lack of power still a problem for Suzuki, while Kawasaki's traction problems have been all too evident all year long.

There was some light relief in the shape of a rash of special colour schemes for the race. Repsol celebrated their 40th year in racing by turning out not just Pedrosa and Hayden but also their 125 and 250 teams in a retro all-white livery. Elderly paddock inhabitants recalled seeing the capital 'R' in a circle logo for the first time on the side of Angel Nieto's bike back in the late 1960s. Never one to be outdone, Jorge Lorenzo also wore white. His 'Lorenzo's Land' scheme featured the flags of all the countries where he has won a GP – no flag of Valencia by the way. Like the Austin Powers paint job Valentino sported at Valencia in his last race for Honda at the end of 2003, this was the result of a magazine competition in co-operation with Fiat. The legend 'Free Man Racing' on the back of his helmet had a very different connotation; it referred to the rather messy split with his manager, Dani Amatriain.

The race at the front may have been lacking in action, but there was something right about seeing the men who were unquestionably the three best riders of the year all ending the season on the rostrum.

'WE COULDN'T HAVE ASKED FOR MUCH MORE TODAY'
CASEY STONER

Right It's the first day of the 2009 season – Nicky Hayden gets on the Ducati on the Monday after the GP

Below The Repsol Hondas wore a special retro paint scheme to celebrate the company's 40 years in motorsport

COMING SOON...

There was as much expectation around Valencia about the Monday test as about the race on Sunday. It gave the paddock a first look at new bike-and-rider combinations and a lot of riders their first taste of the new Bridgestone tyres. Only the Tech 3 team was absent as Andrea Dovizioso rode the works Repsol bike and Yuki Takahashi took over his customer bike. Much interest was centred on Nicky Hayden's first ride on a Ducati and the man he replaces, Marco Melandri, who had his first ride on the Kawasaki. Thankfully, both men seemed to get on with their new bikes. Ducati and Kawasaki's lead riders, Stoner and Hopkins, stay.

The satellite Ducati squad, the Alice Team, are changing both riders. Out go Toni Elias – to the Gresini Honda team to partner de Angelis – and Sylvain Guintoli – to the Suzuki team in the British Championship, where he'll be in the right place to take advantage of any misfortune for the MotoGP riders as both teams are run by the Crescent organisation. In come Ducati's test rider Niccolo Canepa and 250 ace Mika Kallio of Finland. The Bologna factory is taking a much more hands-on role with the Alice team than in previous years: think of it as a junior or academy team designed to give young riders a first taste of MotoGP competition without the pressure of a full works ride.

There'll also be a fifth Ducati in 2009. Sete Gibernau, the second most successful rider of the 990cc era, returns after a two-year absence to ride in the colours of Spanish construction company Onde 2000. After much negotiation it appears that the chances of there being a third Kawasaki on the grid in 2009 are very slim indeed.

Four teams remain unchanged for 2009. Both Yamaha squads, the works Fiat and satellite Tech 3 teams keep both riders, as does the factory Suzuki team. The LCR Honda team also keeps Randy de Puniet.

The biggest question that will be answered over winter is how the new single-tyre rule will affect the status quo. In fact we'll probably have to wait until racing starts again to get the answer to that one.

VALENCIAN GP
CIRCUITO RICARDO TORMO

ROUND 18
October 26

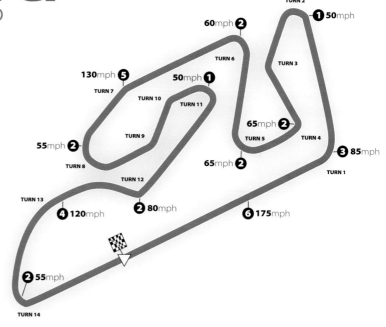

RACE RESULTS

CIRCUIT LENGTH 2.489 miles

NO. OF LAPS 30

RACE DISTANCE 74.657 miles

WEATHER Dry, 26°C

TRACK TEMPERATURE 34°C

WINNER Casey Stoner

FASTEST LAP 1m 32.582s, 96.772mph, Casey Stoner (record)

PREVIOUS LAP RECORD 1m 32.748s, 96.598mph, Dani Pedrosa, 2007

QUALIFYING

	Rider	Nationality	Team	Qualifying	Pole +	Gap
1	Stoner	AUS	Ducati Marlboro Team	1m 31.502s		
2	Pedrosa	SPA	Repsol Honda Team	1m 31.555s	0.053s	0.053s
3	Hayden	USA	Repsol Honda Team	1m 31.703s	0.201s	0.148s
4	Edwards	USA	Tech 3 Yamaha	1m 32.212s	0.710s	0.509s
5	Toseland	GBR	Tech 3 Yamaha	1m 32.518s	1.016s	0.306s
6	De Puniet	FRA	LCR Honda MotoGP	1m 32.572s	1.070s	0.054s
7	Lorenzo	SPA	Fiat Yamaha Team	1m 32.594s	1.092s	0.022s
8	Capirossi	ITA	Rizla Suzuki MotoGP	1m 32.614s	1.112s	0.020s
9	Dovizioso	ITA	JiR Team Scot MotoGP	1m 32.734s	1.232s	0.120s
10	Rossi	ITA	Fiat Yamaha Team	1m 32.962s	1.460s	0.228s
11	Elias	SPA	Alice Team	1m 32.983s	1.481s	0.021s
12	Vermeulen	AUS	Rizla Suzuki MotoGP	1m 33.017s	1.515s	0.034s
13	Guintoli	FRA	Alice Team	1m 33.352s	1.850s	0.335s
14	Hopkins	USA	Kawasaki Racing Team	1m 33.681s	2.179s	0.329s
15	Nakano	JPN	San Carlo Honda Gresini	1m 33.767s	2.265s	0.086s
16	De Angelis	RSM	San Carlo Honda Gresini	1m 33.848s	2.346s	0.081s
17	West	AUS	Kawasaki Racing Team	1m 33.879s	2.377s	0.031s
18	Melandri	ITA	Ducati Marlboro Team	1m 34.174s	2.672s	0.295s

FINISHERS

1 CASEY STONER Once he took the lead from Pedrosa on the second corner there was no doubt what was going to happen: he pulled away steadily, managed the gap and won unchallenged. Heaped praise on his team for getting the bike so right with so little dry track time in practice.

2 DANI PEDROSA Generous in his praise of Stoner and pleased with his progress since changing to Bridgestone tyres for the last five races of the year. Reminded a large crowd that, despite a difficult season, he is still one of the top three riders in the world.

3 VALENTINO ROSSI There's only so much a rider can do from 10th on the grid here, but Vale did it, gaining three places on the first lap and up to third by lap six. For a time seemed he might close on Pedrosa, but it wasn't possible. Still, 16 rostrums from 18 starts isn't a bad season!

4 ANDREA DOVIZIOSO Another who made a good start, found his position early and hung on to it. Got past Hayden and Toseland, but by then the leaders had gone. Arrived back at his pit to symbolically hand his bike over to Yuki Takahashi as he prepared to join the works team the following day.

5 NICKY HAYDEN Fastest in all three practice sessions, third in qualifying but disappointed with his last outing on a Honda. His race was compromised by a big crash in Sunday morning warm-up that meant he had to use his number-two bike for the race.

6 COLIN EDWARDS First top-six finish since his rostrum at Assen. Gambled on set-up and a soft tyre, in third early on but then encountered wheelspin: 'The others disappeared up the road.' Very happy helping Tech 3 to fourth in the teams' championship, ahead of two works squads.

7 SHINYA NAKANO Content with what may prove to be his last MotoGP race. Started well from 15th on the grid, then used his hard tyre sensibly to ensure a strong finish.

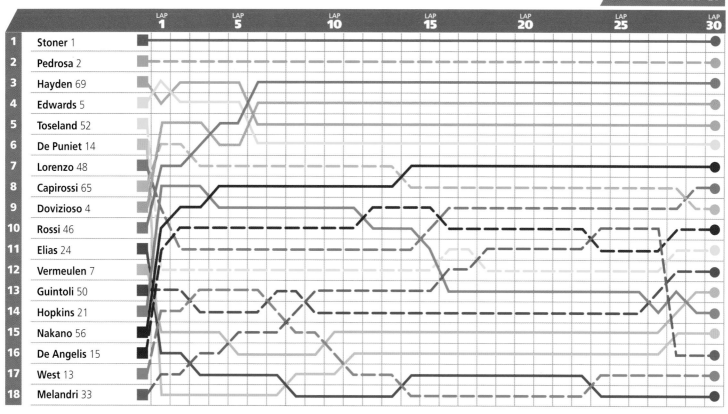

		LAP 1	LAP 5	LAP 10	LAP 15	LAP 20	LAP 25	LAP 30
1	Stoner 1							
2	Pedrosa 2							
3	Hayden 69							
4	Edwards 5							
5	Toseland 52							
6	De Puniet 14							
7	Lorenzo 48							
8	Capirossi 65							
9	Dovizioso 4							
10	Rossi 46							
11	Elias 24							
12	Vermeulen 7							
13	Guintoli 50							
14	Hopkins 21							
15	Nakano 56							
16	De Angelis 15							
17	West 13							
18	Melandri 33							

RACE

	Rider	Motorcycle	Race Time	Time +	Fastest Lap	Average Speed
1	Stoner	Ducati	46m 46.114s		1m 32.582s	95.783mph
2	Pedrosa	Honda	46m 49.504s	3.390s	1m 32.796s	95.668mph
3	Rossi	Yamaha	46m 58.308s	12.194s	1m 33.075s	95.369mph
4	Dovizioso	Honda	47m 10.273s	24.159s	1m 33.313s	94.966mph
5	Hayden	Honda	47m 12.346s	26.232s	1m 33.393s	94.896mph
6	Edwards	Yamaha	47m 18.323s	32.209s	1m 33.399s	94.696mph
7	Nakano	Honda	47m 20.685s	34.571s	1m 33.550s	94.618mph
8	Lorenzo	Yamaha	47m 21.775s	35.661s	1m 33.884s	94.581mph
9	Capirossi	Suzuki	47m 24.342s	38.228s	1m 33.626s	94.496mph
10	De Angelis	Honda	47m 33.697s	47.583s	1m 33.839s	94.186mph
11	Toseland	Yamaha	47m 38.221s	52.107s	1m 34.150s	94.037mph
12	Guintoli	Ducati	47m 38.464s	52.350s	1m 34.462s	94.029mph
13	Vermeulen	Suzuki	47m 38.947s	52.833s	1m 34.595s	94.013mph
14	Hopkins	Kawasaki	47m 39.341s	53.227s	1m 34.035s	94.000mph
15	De Puniet	Honda	47m 39.525s	53.411s	1m 34.225s	93.994mph
16	Melandri	Ducati	47m 54.501s	1m 08.387s	1m 34.117s	93.504mph
17	West	Kawasaki	47m 57.295s	1m 11.181s	1m 34.715s	93.413mph
18	Elias	Ducati	48m 23.169s	1m 37.055s	1m 34.634s	92.581mph

CHAMPIONSHIP

	Rider	Team	Points
1	Rossi	Fiat Yamaha Team	373
2	Stoner	Ducati Marlboro Team	280
3	Pedrosa	Repsol Honda Team	249
4	Lorenzo	Fiat Yamaha Team	190
5	Dovizioso	JiR Team Scot MotoGP	174
6	Hayden	Repsol Honda Team	155
7	Edwards	Tech 3 Yamaha	144
8	Vermeulen	Rizla Suzuki MotoGP	128
9	Nakano	San Carlo Honda Gresini	126
10	Capirossi	Rizla Suzuki MotoGP	118
11	Toseland	Tech 3 Yamaha	105
12	Elias	Alice Team	92
13	Guintoli	Alice Team	67
14	De Angelis	San Carlo Honda Gresini	63
15	De Puniet	LCR Honda MotoGP	61
16	Hopkins	Kawasaki Racing Team	57
17	Melandri	Ducati Marlboro Team	51
18	West	Kawasaki Racing Team	50
19	Spies	Rizla Suzuki MotoGP	20
20	Hacking	Kawasaki Racing Team	5
21	Okada	Repsol Honda Team	2

8 JORGE LORENZO Started cautiously and slipped to 11th before finding his rhythm and setting his fastest lap last time round. Ensured fourth overall in the championship and Rookie of the Year title, the highest a rookie has ever finished since the introduction of the MotoGP formula in 2002.

9 LORIS CAPIROSSI Up to sixth after a good start, then his soft front tyre started to move around and he also lost edge grip on the rear. Couldn't stop Lorenzo coming past on the straight.

10 ALEX DE ANGELIS Felt he'd ended his rookie season on a positive note after having 'lost our way a little in the last races'. Suffered from the lack

of dry weather practice time but put in a typically wholehearted race to thank his crew for their work in a tough year.

11 JAMES TOSELAND Didn't take advantage of his second-row start. A good fight with Lorenzo, then lost touch after raising a hand to apologise for a tough pass and missing his braking marker. Had to fight Guintoli at the end, but that helped Tech 3 take fourth in the teams' championship by one point.

12 SYLVAIN GUINTOLI Found some pace as the race went on and grabbed a couple of places in the final laps. Gave Toseland a very tough time for the last three laps. Leaving MotoGP to ride for Suzuki in the British Superbike Championship, a job that will surely

make him a future replacement rider for the MotoGP team.

13 CHRIS VERMEULEN Gambled on a harder compound rear tyre but it didn't pay off. Struggled for the whole race to get any feeling, although he did get past Hopkins two laps from the flag.

14 JOHN HOPKINS Got a great start but immediately knew that problems in getting the bike turned would exacerbate rear tyre wear and season-long issues with traction. After the first few laps it was a matter of defending as strongly as possible.

15 RANDY DE PUNIET Went wide at Turn 2 on the first lap and lost over 10s to the rest. Not surprisingly, his injured arm started to ache a lot on the tight and

twisty track, so under the circumstances a point has to be considered a decent result.

16 MARCO MELANDRI This was his best ride on the Duke since China: up to tenth a few laps from home after catching and passing a big group, then found a false neutral and ran off track. Got back but lost 20s and any chance of a point.

17 ANTHONY WEST A frustrating end to a frustrating season. Lack of dry practice time and a 'questionable' tyre choice meant the inevitable traction problems arrived even earlier than usual. Ant will be a Honda World Supersport rider in 2009.

18 TONI ELIAS His last race with the Alice Ducati squad before returning to Fausto Gresini's team for '09. No confidence in rear grip levels meant a lack of confidence to push hard on race day.

WORLD CHAMPIONSHIP CLASSIFICATION

MotoGP

	Rider	Nation	Motorcycle	QAT	SPA	POR	CHN	FRA	ITA	CAT	GBR	NED	GER	USA	CZE	RSM	INP	JPN	AUS	MAL	VAL	Points
1	Rossi	ITA	Yamaha	11	20	16	25	25	25	20	20	5	20	25	25	25	25	25	20	25	16	373
2	Stoner	AUS	Ducati	25	5	10	16	–	20	16	25	25	25	20	–	–	13	20	25	10	25	280
3	Pedrosa	SPA	Honda	16	25	20	20	13	16	25	16	20	–	–	1	13	8	16	–	20	20	249
4	Lorenzo	SPA	Yamaha	20	16	25	13	20	–	–	10	10	–	–	6	20	16	13	13	–	8	190
5	Dovizioso	ITA	Honda	13	8	–	5	10	8	13	11	11	11	13	7	8	11	7	9	16	13	174
6	Hayden	USA	Honda	6	13	–	10	8	3	8	9	13	3	11	–	–	20	11	16	13	11	155
7	Edwards	USA	Yamaha	9	–	13	9	16	11	11	13	16	–	2	2	6	1	9	8	8	10	144
8	Vermeulen	AUS	Suzuki	–	6	8	–	11	6	9	8	9	16	16	10	11	7	–	1	7	3	128
9	Nakano	JPN	Honda	3	7	6	6	6	7	7	7	8	7	6	13	4	–	8	11	11	9	126
10	Capirossi	ITA	Suzuki	8	11	7	7	9	9	–	–	–	9	1	16	9	–	10	6	9	7	118
11	Toseland	GBR	Yamaha	10	10	9	4	–	10	10	–	7	5	7	3	10	–	5	10	–	5	105
12	Elias	SPA	Ducati	2	1	4	8	5	4	–	5	4	4	9	20	16	4	–	5	1	–	92
13	Guintoli	FRA	Ducati	1	–	2	1	3	5	3	3	6	10	4	4	5	9	2	2	3	4	67
14	De Angelis	RSM	Honda	–	2	5	–	4	13	–	1	–	13	3	8	–	6	–	–	2	6	63
15	De Puniet	FRA	Honda	7	–	1	3	7	–	–	4	–	8	10	–	–	3	4	7	6	1	61
16	Hopkins	USA	Kawasaki	4	9	11	2	–	–	6	–	–	–	–	5	2	2	6	3	5	2	57
17	Melandri	ITA	Ducati	5	4	3	11	1	–	5	–	3	–	–	9	7	–	3	–	–	–	51
18	West	AUS	Kawasaki	–	3	–	–	2	1	4	6	–	6	–	11	3	5	1	4	4		50
19	Spies	USA	Suzuki	–	–	–	–	–	–	–	2	–	–	8	–	–	10	–	–	–	–	20
20	Hacking	USA	Kawasaki	–	–	–	–	–	–	–	–	–	–	5	–	–	–	–	–	–	–	5
21	Okada	JPN	Honda	–	–	–	–	–	2	–	–	–	–	–	–	–	–	–	–	–	–	2

CONSTRUCTOR

	Motorcycle	QAT	SPA	POR	CHN	FRA	ITA	CAT	GBR	NED	GER	USA	CZE	RSM	INP	JPN	AUS	MAL	VAL	Points
1	Yamaha	20	20	25	25	25	25	20	20	16	20	25	25	25	25	25	20	25	16	402
2	Ducati	25	5	10	16	5	20	16	25	25	25	20	20	16	13	20	25	10	25	321
3	Honda	16	25	20	20	13	16	25	16	20	13	13	13	13	20	16	16	20	20	315
4	Suzuki	8	11	8	7	11	9	9	8	9	16	16	16	11	10	10	6	9	7	181
5	Kawasaki	4	9	11	2	2	1	6	6	–	6	5	11	3	5	6	4	5	2	88

TEAM

	Team	QAT	SPA	POR	CHN	FRA	ITA	CAT	GBR	NED	GER	USA	CZE	RSM	INP	JPN	AUS	MAL	VAL	Points
1	Fiat Yamaha Team	31	36	41	38	45	25	20	30	15	20	25	31	45	41	38	33	25	24	563
2	Repsol Honda Team	22	38	20	30	21	19	33	25	33	3	11	1	13	28	27	16	33	31	404
3	Ducati Marlboro Team	30	9	13	27	1	20	21	25	28	25	20	9	7	13	23	25	10	25	331
4	Tech 3 Yamaha	19	10	22	13	16	21	21	13	23	5	9	5	16	1	14	18	8	15	249
5	Rizla Suzuki MotoGP	8	17	15	7	20	15	9	10	9	25	17	26	20	7	10	7	16	10	248
6	San Carlo Honda Gresini	3	9	11	6	10	20	7	8	8	20	9	21	4	6	8	11	13	15	189
7	JIR Team Scot MotoGP	13	8	–	5	10	8	13	11	11	11	13	7	8	11	7	9	16	13	174
8	Alice Team	3	1	6	9	8	9	3	8	10	14	13	24	21	13	2	7	4	4	159
9	Kawasaki Racing Team	4	12	11	2	2	1	10	6	–	6	5	16	5	7	7	7	9	2	112
10	LCR Honda MotoGP	7	–	1	3	7	–	–	4	–	8	10	–	–	3	4	7	6	1	61

www.shark-helmets.com

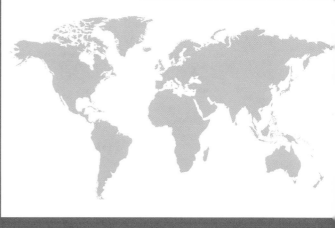

NOT FADE AWAY

Marco Simoncelli doesn't just have great hair, he's fast too. Fast enough to give the historic Gilera marque their first world title in the quarter-litre category

In 2008 it was a case of out with the old, as Lorenzo, Dovizioso and de Angelis moved into the premier class, and in with the new, with Faubel, Pasini and Pesek coming up from 125s. The 250 World Championship title looked as though it was going to be open to all comers, although there were a number of favourites for the punters to argue about. After a year in the saddle the likes of Luthi, Bautista, and Kallio looked good bets, along with old hands Debon, Barbera and even returning champion and enigma Poggiali.

One of the favourites had to be Alvaro Bautista, a brilliant 125 World Champion in 2006, and then a multiple race winner in his first year on a 250. He came close to winning a few more, as well as setting a fastest lap, in his first season on the quarter-litre machinery. Bear in mind, too, that this was during a year when Lorenzo had been almost undisputed master of the class.

Next in the frame was Mika Kallio. The Finn is just about the most consistent rider in the class, and arguably the most consistent rider of recent years in both the 125 and 250 categories. He is, however, to use a quaint English expression, 'always the bridesmaid but never the bride'; he has yet to secure a world title. Also counting against him on this occasion was the KTM 250: the bike is no match for the powerhouse Aprilia at some tracks, although it does have some strengths, and a distinct advantage on the tighter circuits and when the weather turns bad, much like the Hondas in years past.

Maybe this was one of the reasons why Aprilia decided they would field an unusually large number

Top left Manuel Poggiali and Eugene Laverty; neither would finish the season

Top right Tom Luthi got his first two rostrums in the 250 class at Mugello and Assen

Right Bautista leads the field through the slowest corner of the year, the chicane at Estoril

Opposite top Hiro Aoyama on the KTM at Phillip Island

Opposite bottom Karel Abraham proves that you can still crash no matter how much traction control you have

of factory bikes on the grid throughout the season. At the first race in Qatar there were no fewer than five RSA (full factory) Aprilias, with those in favour with the Italian manufacturer and getting the total package comprising a who's who of possible champions. Bautista, Debon, Luthi, Barbera and, somewhat surprisingly, Pasini all had the new shorter-engined and longer-swingarmed bikes that Bautista, Debon and Luthi had developed from the previous season.

KTM fielded a Repsol-sponsored bike for Julian Simon, as well as their own full factory team of Kallio and Japanese rider Hiroshi Aoyama, the latter capable

of extracting exceptional tyre wear from the KTM and consequently always being strong at the end of the full race distance.

There was even an old dog sitting in the wings – not a championship contender, but having Yamaha back on the grid for a full season with Indonesian rider Doni Tata Pradita was a good thing, if only for those who remember the good old days of 250 GPs with Honda, Yamaha and Aprilia all fighting it out.

As the 125s, however, the 250s had their fair share of problems in the first night race at Qatar. Once again the Dunlop technicians found themselves scratching their

1 – QATARI GP

In the dark at Qatar the 250s were having a hard time adjusting to racing in artificial light. The biggest issue was their choice of visor, as some parts of the track were blinding while others had darker patches.

Eventually Alex Debon (arguably one of the championship favourites) took pole position, with Hector Barbera hard on his heels, but it was Thomas Luthi who led off the line. He'd jumped the start, though, and had to complete a pit-lane ride-through that removed him from the battle for the lead. There was then an intense fight, with several riders taking turns to head the pack, but mechanical problems for Bautista and falls by Simoncelli and Pesek left the door open for 250 rookie Mattia Pasini to take the win.

2 – SPANISH GP

Back in Europe and the form started to take shape and follow the pundits' predictions, with home rider Alvaro Bautista taking pole from Kallio and just 0.040s separating them.

Once the flag dropped an intense battle developed between Marco Simoncelli and Bautista, with neither rider giving quarter. It lasted until Bautista's engine failed, resulting in a collision with Simoncelli that took both riders out of the race on the final lap. This gifted the race win to Mika Kallio, with rookie Pasini in second place and still leading the championship. Japanese Honda rider Yuki Takahashi was third, Luthi crashed out of a potential podium placing when battling to overtake Kallio towards the end of the race.

3 – PORTUGUESE GP

Simoncelli continued his good form by taking his maiden pole position for the Portuguese GP, he was joined on the front row by Bautista, Pasini and Kallio. Once the lights went from red to go, however, it was the Spaniard who dominated, leading the race from first corner to chequered flag with a huge gap of more than seven seconds over second-placed Simoncelli.

Marco was almost caught by Kallio on the final lap, and it was only sheer horsepower that allowed the Italian to stay ahead of the Finn and score his first finish of the season. Luthi pushed hard all race and made it from 11th on the first lap to fourth. Debon and Pasini both crashed, allowing Kallio to take the title lead, closely followed by Pasini and Barbera, with Simoncelli in ninth.

4 – CHINESE GP

The changeable weather conditions proved to be a challenge for the 250 boys. Bautista started the race well from pole, but dropped to third on the second lap as Barbera took the lead. By the fifth lap Bautista was in front again until Kallio took over on the ninth lap after Alvaro lowsided; the Spanish rider remounted to finish the race in a lowly 12th position. Kallio then led all the way to the flag, closely followed by his Japanese team-mate Hiroshi Aoyama to make it a KTM one–two, with the Finn extending his championship lead.

Pasini clawed his way to the final podium position after Yuki Takahashi made a mistake on the last lap and dropped to seventh, the Aprilia rider struggling with a wet tyre in drying conditions that made his bike very unstable on the long back straight.

5 – FRENCH GP

The bad weather followed the the MotoGP circus back to Europe. Debon, Baustista, Simoncelli and Luthi formed the front row. At the start of the race conditions were far from stable and a wise tyre choice was the name of the game. Debon went for slicks right from the start, despite the rain, and that proved to be a good decision as conditions started to dry: he led from the very first lap, for every single lap, and took the chequered flag by a comfortable five seconds.

Aprilia announced that Debon had traction control on his bike, along with Bautista, but the younger rider could only manage 14th. In an all-Aprilia podium Debon was joined by Simoncelli (Gilera-badged Aprilia) and Pasini. Kallio finished fifth and retained his title lead, while other usual front runners, Luthi and Barbera, could only manage 11th and 12th respectively. Simoncelli was moving steadily up the championship table and now lay in fifth place.

collective heads when the tyres just did not work as expected in the cooling conditions. Bautista even went off record to say that his tyres started to deteriorate after just four laps, and he was not the only one who had problems, with some riders blaming their crashes on the tyres while others were clearly having problems as their bikes spent most of the time going sideways instead of straight on.

At the second round, in Jerez, the engine became an issue for Bautista as his motor seized and took out Marco Simoncelli, gifting Kallio his first race win of the season. Suddenly Simoncelli was also looking a good bet, even though he did a good impression of a hand grenade about to go off at nearly every turn: people started to take an interest in the Gilera garage.

By the end of the first part of the season Aprilia had begun handing certain advantages to some of their RSA riders. First there was traction control for Bautista and Alex Debon. A few races later all the RSA riders had the seven-stage system. Some of them liked it while others decided that it was better turned off, particularly – and in complete contradiction of what seems logical thinking – in the wet. The reason was that the traction-control system didn't allow some riders to get a good feeling for grip and, if the bike started to slide, they were unsure about their machine's traction and therefore went slower.

The KTM riders reported a slightly different situation, their problems were with feeling rather than traction control. New frames were fitted to Kallio's bike in a bid to improve the feeling. By Mugello in June, Simoncelli and the Gilera could no longer be ignored. In his first ever 250 victory the man with the hair was now getting press coverage for the right things, namely winning rather than his old habit of crashing. Kallio was still the championship leader, thanks to his consistency, but the lanky Italian was making big inroads into Mika's points lead.

The unseen but amazing part of the Simoncelli story was that the bike he was using, the Gilera, was actually a re-badged Aprilia LE (LE standing for Last Edition, meaning that it was a 2007 model and therefore a customer bike, not a full factory machine). Things were to change, however, after a two-day test at Brno in July when the Italian got to ride the full factory RSA bike and Aprilia, pleased with the results, decided that it

6 – ITALIAN GP

Mugello always produces some interesting challenges and a fanatical crowd of fans, so Simoncelli was looking for a home win. He was third in qualifying, with Spaniards Barbera and Bautista first and second on the grid.

Simoncelli battled hard with Bautista and Barbera in the first six laps until Bautista crashed out, leaving Barbera and Simoncelli to fight for the win. In a thrilling dice Barbera clipped the back of Simoncelli's bike as they went down the very fast finishing straight, causing the Spaniard to have a massive high-speed crash. He later blamed his Italian rival for the accident, claiming he could have been killed.

This incident elevated Debon and Luthi to second and third places – they had been fighting hard for the final rostrum spot. Kallio took fourth after crashes by Lukas Pesek, Hector Faubel and Takahashi, which helped Mika to hang onto the title lead. Simoncelli moved him up to fourth in the championship.

7 – CATALAN GP

Local favourite Bautista took pole from fellow Spaniards Debon and Barbera, with Simoncelli fourth.

A massive, race-long battle developed between Simoncelli and Bautista, right from the second lap when Simoncelli managed to take the lead but promptly lost it again. He regained the initiative on lap six, but once again lost it almost immediately. Bautista then headed the race until the final lap when Simoncelli managed to push the Spaniard wide – he was unable to take back the position – and the young Italian won, to move into second place in the title chase, now just three points behind Kallio. The Finn suffered engine failure on lap 20 out of the 23 and failed to finish.

8 – BRITISH GP

The weekend started off with more bad weather, but by race day the circuit was dry but windy. Luthi now had traction control on his RSA Aprilia, with seven settings, but he found he could go faster with it turned off as that gave a better feeling for available grip.

The two KTMs of Kallio and Aoyama led from the start, but the power of the Aprilias put Simoncelli and Pasini in front at the end of the first lap, with Kallio and Aoyama dropping back to seventh and tenth, respectively. Mika then began to slowly fight his way forwards, up to third by the ninth lap and into a massive fight with Simoncelli and Bautista. The Finn took the lead with two laps to go when the other two got tangled up going into the final turn. Kallio held his advantage to the finish as the two Aprilia riders fought over second place. Simoncelli took second, but Kallio extended his championship lead to eight points.

9 – DUTCH TT

The Dutch TT produced yet more bad weather, although the final qualifying session was dry. Bautista, Barbera, Simoncelli and Debon filled the front row, the circuit suiting the more powerful Aprilias. Kallio was down on the third row.

The start was delayed and it was declared a wet race. Luthi made a classic holeshot, leaving Debon and the rest in his wake, but Bautista soon began to move through the field and upto the Swiss rider, the two of them battling each other and the conditions that changed lap by lap. Luthi took advantage of a lull in the weather to retake the lead, but Bautista fought back to retake Luthi on lap 19 of 24 and then led to the finish. Luthi was second, with Simoncelli third and Kallio behind team-mate Aoyama in seventh. Simoncelli had now closed to within one point of Kallio in the title chase.

10 – GERMAN GP

Kallio suffered a leg injury in a test session at Brno between the Dutch and German rounds, dealing a blow to his title aspirations. He still managed fourth slot on the front row but was hurting more because Thai rider Ratthapark Wilairot had taken him out in the last minutes of final qualifying. Simoncelli, on a full works RSA Aprilia for the first time, took pole position.

The weather turned bad yet again, with the heavens opening as racing began. Simoncelli was in excellent wet-weather form and dominated in the difficult conditions to lead right from the first lap and build up a seven-second lead with only a third of the race completed. Behind him a massive scrap for second place involved Barbera, Bautista, Kallio and Simon, who finished in that order. The tricky conditions claimed Pesek, Abraham, Sandi and Debon.

Simoncelli's easy victory meant he had finally taken the championship lead from Kallio.

would now field six factory machines for the rest of the season.

Things were not going so well for all the riders in the quarter-litre class, however, with former 125 and 250 World Champion Manuel Poggiali deciding to call it a day. And that was not the only thing to call it a day: weather conditions at the new US Indy GP were so extreme that a decision was made to cancel the 250 race because the howling winds and rain made it unsafe to run.

It was not all doom and gloom, though. The 2008 season and Simoncelli's race win in Japan gave tyre manufacturer Dunlop their 200th consecutive race win in the quarter-litre category. At the penultimate round, Sepang in Malaysia, Simoncelli could sum up his season with the words, 'I was a nobody and now I am the World Champion.' Certainly no-one could have predicted that outcome at the beginning of the season.

Similarly, it was never expected that KTM would withdraw from the 250 World Championship for 2009, along with several well-established teams like Campetella. This makes the future of the class uncertain, as it looks like there may well be only 14 riders competing for the title next season. The reasons for such low numbers are to be found in the forthcoming rule changes that will make the 250 two-strokes a thing of the past, just like the 500s when the MotoGP superseded them. The problem for the series is that neither Aprilia nor KTM have any intention of making the new 600cc four-strokes that the new rules will allow, or the budgets to do so. It may be that grids will become smaller before they get bigger…

11 – CZECH REPUBLIC GP

Simoncelli took pole position for the second race running in wet qualifying. The race, however, was dry, with the starting pack consisting of Simoncelli, Luthi, Debon, Kallio and Pasini. Once more it looked to be developing into domination by Simoncelli after Luthi crashed out, but Debon had other ideas. Taking Simoncelli on the seventh lap, Alex looked like he had it sewn up, but Marco fought back. By lap 12, though, Debon was back in front. He then lost the lead with two laps to go and Simoncelli started to pull a gap on him, but the Spanish rider made another great comeback to cross the line in front, taking his second career victory. Bautista, meanwhile, had also slipped past Simoncelli and beaten him to the line by a slim tenth of a second.

Kallio looked to be losing his grip on the title as he could only manage a fifth place, while Simoncelli's third moved him further ahead.

12 – SAN MARINO GP

Manuel Poggiali, World Champion in both the 125 and 250 classes, announced his retirement from racing, Barbera beat Simoncelli to pole position, but the racce went to Alvaro Bautistat. The 2006 125 champion worked his way to the front from the third row of the grid with 18 laps of steady progression through the field, then held onto the lead until the flag.

Simoncelli could only manage a disappointing sixth place, but he was in luck because Kallio failed to make the finish. The race saw a number of big crashes and hard overtakes, the reason why nine of the riders did not make it to the finish. Hector Barbera did himself no favours with the local crowd as he was involved in an incident that resulted in Pasini ending up in the gravel. Bautista, Takahashi and Barbera went to the podium but Simoncelli extended his lead in the title race.

13 – INDIANAPOLIS GP

Indy was supposed to be the first time in the MotoGP era that all classes would compete in America (Laguna Seca is only for the premier class), but the weather dominated once more as Hurricane Ike played havoc with the weekend's arrangements.

High winds and rain were interspersed with some sunny spells, and on Friday Czech rider Karel Abraham got on provisional pole when he took full advantage of the weather conditions. On the Saturday it was once again Simoncelli who produced the pole-winning time, but the red flag came out when Luthi crashed. The Swiss rider ended up with concussion and a nasty thumb injury that would preclude him from racing on Sunday as well as in Japan and at Phillip Island. In the event the outcome was not so bad for Luthi as Sunday's race was cancelled due to the hurricane.

14 – JAPANESE GP

With no severe weather warnings the riders could look forward to a weekend of normal race conditions in Japan. Simoncelli was on pole again, but Barbera was taken to hospital after a crash in the morning's free practice session and was unable to race as he had suspected back fractures.

In the race Simoncelli was chased and harassed, first by Simon on the Repsol KTM, and then by Bautista who set a series of new lap records chasing down the Italian. Unfortunately his push was halted when he had to slow to overtake some backmarkers, and although he set the fastest lap in the final lap of the race it was not enough to catch Simoncelli. Debon caught up to Simon by hanging onto Bautista's tail and grabbed third position from the KTM. Kallio was fifth.

Simoncelli now had a lead of 32 points over Bautista; Kallio slipped down to third in the title chase.

15 – AUSTRALIAN GP

Phillip Island always produces good racing and this year was to prove no different, as Simoncelli smashed Sebastian Porto's long-standing 2004 lap record with times good enough for him to qualify for the MotoGP race! With the Island being one of Bautista's favourite and most successful tracks he was sure to give Simoncelli a run for his money. The pair shared the front row of the grid with Kallio and Aoyama, the Italian taking pole yet again.

From halfway through the race Simoncelli and Bautista started to battle it out for the win. It was a hard skirmish and the two riders had a coming-together on the final lap – both managed to stay upright and it was Simoncelli who took the victory. Kallio managed to regain some momentum by taking the third podium slot, but it was not enough to put him back into championship contention. Simoncelli, meanwhile, had increased his lead.

Rider	Nation	Team	Motorcycle	Points
1 Marco Simoncelli	ITA	Metis Gilera	Gilera	281
2 Alvaro Bautista	SPA	Mapfre Aspar Team	Aprilia	244
3 Mika Kallio	FIN	Red Bull KTM 250	KTM	196
4 Alex Debon	SPA	Lotus Aprilia	Aprilia	176
5 Yuki Takahashi	JPN	JiR Team Scot 250	Honda	167
6 Hector Barbera	SPA	Team Toth Aprilia	Aprilia	142
7 Hiroshi Aoyama	JPN	Red Bull KTM 250	KTM	139
8 Mattia Pasini	ITA	Polaris World	Aprilia	132
9 Roberto Locatelli	ITA	Metis Gilera	Gilera	110
10 Julian Simon	SPA	Repsol KTM 250cc	KTM	109
11 Thomas Luthi	SWI	Emmi-Caffe Latte	Aprilia	108
12 Aleix Espargaro	SPA	Lotus Aprilia	Aprilia	92
13 Ratthapark Wilairot	THA	Thai Honda PTT SAG	Honda	73
14 Hector Faubel	SPA	Mapfre Aspar Team	Aprilia	64
15 Lukas Pesek	CZE	Auto - Kelly CP	Aprilia	43
16 Karel Abraham	CZE	Cardion AB Motoracing	Aprilia	40
17 Alex Baldolini	ITA	Matteoni Racing	Aprilia	35
18 Fabrizio Lai	ITA	Campetella Racing	Gilera	33
19 Manuel Poggiali	RSM	Campetella Racing	Gilera	16
20 Imre Toth	HUN	Team Toth Aprilia	Aprilia	9
21 Eugene Laverty	IRL	Blusens Aprilia	Aprilia	8
22 Federico Sandi	ITA	Zongshen AOS Racing	Aprilia	6
23 Manuel Hernandez	SPA	Blusens Aprilia	Aprilia	5
24 Simone Grotzkyj	ITA	Campetella Racing	Gilera	5
25 Daniel Arcas	SPA	Blusens Aprilia	Aprilia	2
26 Shoya Tomizawa	JPN	Project U FRS	Honda	2
27 Toni Wirsing	GER	Racing Team Germany	Honda	2
28 Doni Tata Pradita	INA	Yamaha Pertamina Indonesia	Yamaha	1

16 – MALAYSIAN GP

Luthi returned to the paddock after missing three races and having several operations on his ground-away left thumb, but it was Aoyama's KTM, not that of Kallio, that took pole position in Malaysia. Not many riders improved on their Friday qualifying times, but Simoncelli was one of them.

Bautista needed to win the race if he was to have any chance of taking the world title but the outcome also depended on where and if Simoncelli finished. As it was, Bautista fought his way to the front of the field and even tried to slow the pace to allow other riders to get between himself and Simoncelli. When he realised his plan was not working he pulled out all the stops and ended up winning the race by an wide margin. Aoyama took second, with Simoncelli third – enough for the Italian to take the World Championship title.

17 – VALENCIAN GP

Come the final round of the season and the weather was not going to let anyone forget its influence on racing in 2008. Friday was terrible, with cold and wet conditions, and a lot of riders fell. By Saturday it had improved, but the semi-dry and cold conditions made qualifying difficult. Newly crowned champion Simoncelli took pole position, joined on the front row by Debon, Simon and Kallio. Barbera, unfortunately, did not make it back from his injury for the final race of the season.

The race initially saw Simoncelli back in fifth or sixth as the KTMs of Kallio and Simon led the pack, and it wasn't until the ninth lap that Marco found his way to the front. Kallio pushed the Italian hard, but on the penultimate lap he was trying a little too much and crashed out, leaving Takahashi and the Honda to grab second and gifting Bautista the final podium place.

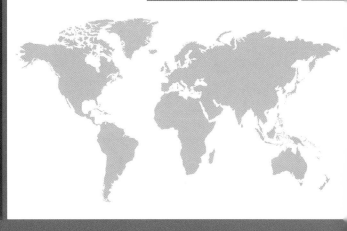

FRENCH RESISTANCE

Mike di Meglio became France's youngest ever World Champion in a season that saw him morph from fast but flawed young charger into a complete racer

At the beginning of the season it was unclear who the main contenders for the 125 title were likely to be. Testing provided no real clues as to who was going to be up there, with best guesses including Gabor Talmacsi managing to make it a double. The trouble with that idea was the curse of the number-one plate – not since Haruchika Aoki on Honda machinery in 1995 and 1996 has the 125 title been retained.

That left a pack of good but as yet largely unproven riders looking to step up to the plate. All the old hands had moved on to the bigger and harder to ride 250s, so the likes of Lukas Pesek and Mattia Pasini were no longer on hand to provide a threat.

Before the first race in Qatar, then, there were a huge number of riders who were in with a shout. Of course Talmacsi could not be ruled out, but what about Bradley Smith, Joan Olive, Sandro Cortese, Stefan Bradl, Esteve Rabat, Nicolas Terol, Simone Corsi, Andrea Iannone, Sergio Gadea, Raffaele de Rosa, Pol Espargaro, Mike di Meglio, Tomoyoshi Koyama and Danny Webb?

You could make an argument for nearly half the grid being in a position to challenge for the top spot. Some riders needed to get used to new bikes and new teams, but most of them had been in the game for more than a season. That said, British hope Bradley Smith's chances seemed to be in the balance as he crashed regularly in the pre-season practice while getting to grips with the Aprilia, which he found harder to ride than the fluffier Honda. Danny Webb, among others, was discovering the same thing.

As far as the manufacturers were concerned, the battle between them was as fierce as the fight between the riders. KTM upped their game and were supplying

Above Talmacsi leads Iannone, Olive, Terol and Bradl in typical 125 action; Brits Redding and Smith are numbers 45 and 38, respectively

bikes to customer teams for the first time, while Aprilia made sure that nearly all their riders were on the same RSA (factory) machinery, their thinking being that if it was not clear exactly who might be a top contender then why not let them all have a bike that could do the job. Honda faded even further away. Only the Swiss rider Thomas Luthi, World Champion in 2005, has really shown what the Japanese bike had been capable of recently. Now the factories of Austria and Italy made sure that the void left by the mighty HRC was filled. Realistically, racing a Honda meant a rider might as well give up before the lights changed from red to go.

How bad the Honda had become was immediately highlighted by the results of Bradley Smith and Danny Webb, neither of whom had done brilliantly in 2007. Now, mounted on Aprilias, they really started to shine, notwithstanding regular crashes.

The riders had their first real test right at the start of the season, with the first ever night race in Qatar. In the event, the nocturnal aspect of the racing was not too much of an issue as the riders quickly adapted to the massive floodlights and all the reflections and shadows caused by the huge light spectacular. Riding in the 'dark' was not the big issue everyone in the

1 – QATARI GP

Bradley Smith set provisional pole in the darkening conditions and managed to hold on to it, to start the race and the season from the top slot. Scott Redding made history as the youngest rider to grace the front row in 125s. He led the first lap but Gabor Talmacsi was hard on his heels. A mistake on the second lap caused the Brit to drop to eighth, allowing Talmacsi to go to the front with a whole pack of riders chasing behind him.

By lap ten Sergio Gadea had taken the lead, although Talmacsi briefly got back to the front until suffering engine problems and slipping back. Gadea took the win, despite being in great pain from a shoulder injury, with Joan Olive second and Stefan Bradl third – a sign of the young German's potential, which had been seen last season before he walked away from the paddock in a childish strop.

2 – SPANISH GP

Smith took pole for the second race in a row. Randy Krummenacher was taken to hospital with a spleen injury from a mountain bike crash. Smith led the first lap again, but Nicolas Terol took over on lap two. Simone Corsi caught up from the second row to take the lead on lap 11 and retained it under heavy pressure from Terol and Smith all the way to the flag. Further down the field Bradl, Pablo Nieto, Stevie Bonsey and Redding all placed well, but World Champion Talmacsi suffered from bike failure. (Was this the curse of the number-one plate striking again?)

3 – PORTUGUESE GP

Corsi continued his confident start to the season, taking the top spot in qualifying, with Bonsey, Terol and young Brit Danny Webb joining him on the front row.

Terol led the first three laps until Olive made a move, the two of them battling back and forth until a small mistake from Terol dropped him down to fifth. Corsi then took up the challenge, keeping in front of Olive to take the chequered flag and the championship lead. Terol was third. Talmacsi took sixth behind American Bonsey and Webb, both scoring their highest-placed finishes of the season. Bradley Smith and Karel Pesek crashed out in spectacular style.

4 – CHINESE GP

Smith was on pole once again, with Terol, Frenchman Mike di Meglio and Talmacsi joining him on the front row. Race conditions were difficult, varying from wet to dry and back on different parts of the track. Andrea Iannone and Talmacsi made the most of the conditions, battling alone until di Meglio joined in on the tenth lap, but Iannone took back the lead on the next lap and held off his two rivals to the flag. Twelve riders didn't make it to the finish line.

5 – FRENCH GP

If the gods were watching then they had a trick up their sleeves for the French round at Le Mans. A cracking race was stopped as the heavens opened and the riders then had a five-lap dash to the finish -- it was like watching a frantic club race in the UK! Attrition was high as seven riders did not make it to the dash, and a further five didn't make the finish, leaving wet-weather specialist di Meglio to win at home, while Smith and Terol came in second and third respectively. The French rider moved into first place in the championship.

paddock and the media thought it might be, with one major exception – Dunlop.

For a normal race weekend teams can, in dry conditions, watch as the track temperature rises and the surface gets hotter and hotter, making tyre choice relatively easy for the riders. Actually, with the 125s, there is not really a massive choice of sizes, compounds and constructions, but when the sun goes in and the track starts to cool instead of getting hotter it's a totally different story. Even come the race no-one was completely sure what would be the right choice. All the testing had been done in daylight, so the information

gathered there could not be relied on. Even the free practice sessions and qualifying sessions were at different times of the evening to the time scheduled for the race, making the job for the teams, tyre manufacturers Dunlop and the riders even harder.

By the start of the race the track temperature was only 28° Centigrade (at most other tracks it is in the mid to high 30s), the air temperature was 20°C and humidity was high at 59%. Partly because of this, and first-race bravado, nine of the 34 riders on the grid did not finish the race.

This could be why Bridgestone decided to get in on

Top Sandro Cortese bites the dust, Olive and Redding hurry by

Above Oxfordshire's Bradley Smith got poles and rostrums but the win didn't come

Above left Bradley Smith at speed past the splendid scenery of Malaysia's Sepang Circuit

---

6 – ITALIAN GP

Italian rider Raffaele de Rosa took pole for the Mugello race on a customer KTM, with Talmacsi, di Meglio and Pol Espargaro joining him on the front row. Terol and di Meglio once again swapped paint and places, but it was Corsi who finally made the decisive move and squeaked the win from Talmacsi and Espargaro. This helped the Italian draw level with di Meglio in the title race, but the likes of Terol, Olive and Bradl were not far behind them.

7 – CATALAN GP

A surprise pole position for Espargaro at his home GPs made the youngest points scorer and podium finisher a favourite for the race, while the other Spanish riders felt the pressure and Terol crashed out. Espargaro made it to the podium, however, with di Meglio taking the win and the title lead, and Talmacsi coming in third. All Corsi could manage was a 'lowly' fifth place. Esteve Rabat had a bad crash on the Friday and had to go to hospital. Local favourite Gadea couldn't rediscover his Qatar form and only managed ninth position.

8 – BRITISH GP

The English weather was as unpredictable as ever, with wet qualifying sessions and high winds. Corsi, not renowned as a wet-weather rider, took pole from Talmacsi and Gadea. Donington again proved the quality of the field, with local boy Scott Redding getting his first ever race win (and setting fastest lap), making him the youngest 125 rider ever to stand on the top step of the podium. Meanwhile, di Meglio built on his lead with a solid second place, now 23 points clear of Corsi and ahead of Bradl by 55 points. The championship was finally taking shape after eight hard-fought races.

9 – DUTCH TT

The wet weather followed the riders from Donington to Holland, but Corsi made sure that he headed the grid before the start of the race. Just as things were looking good for di Meglio, however, the weather turned bad and set up another 'dash for the cash' five-lap race, shunting him back to seventh and, more importantly, allowing Corsi to take third behind Olive, with Talmacsi seizing the win. German Sandro Cortese began to show some form with a fourth, while Smith finished fifth after crashing when leading the first part of the race. The title gap narrowed to a sweet 16 points between di Meglio and Corsi.

10 – GERMAN GP

Talmacsi took pole position holding off a strong challenge from three-times pole-man Bradley Smith. Di Meglio was in a lowly eighth place by the end of the first lap but worked his way slowly through the field, finally taking the win by more than two seconds from Bradl, with Talmacsi third. Corsi finished in sixth spot, opening the points gap at the top of the table up again, while Bradl's second place helped him to gain on reigning World Champion Talmacsi, who had sneaked ahead over the last few races.

the 125 act by supplying tyres to wild-card riders Joey Litjens and Jasper Iwema at Assen. This might well be the start of Bridgestone looking to take away Dunlop's dominance of the junior GP class.

During the season KTM showed that even without the likes of Mika Kallio they could be strong contenders, and they tried out new chassis with their top teams in time for Mugello. Aprilia, too, were making sure that at the start of the season all their riders got the new parts that might help the Italian factory keep hold of the title that Alvaro Bautista had won for them in 2006. In true Italian style, however, it did not take long for the new parts to find their way to the more 'home-based' teams – those with Italian chief mechanics and Italian riders. Unfair? Yes, but that's sometimes how it works in the paddock.

It's undeniable that getting new parts can make a positive difference, as Aprilia-mounted Talmacsi was to discover during the first two races of the season when he had terrible engine problems. And he wasn't the only one.

KTM had problems as well: Esteve Rabat was discovered to be using illegal fuel in the race at the Sachsenring in Germany in mid-July. Was this a sign of the desperation KTM was feeling faced with the Aprilia onslaught? It was certainly bad news for Rabat, who was excluded from the results.

The GP circus went to China for the last time, so it was strange but not unpredictable that a new Chinese-backed team was announced that would be ready for the 2009 season. The Maxtra Racing Project intends to use Haojue machinery produced by the Grand River Group. As the project is to be led by the highly experienced Garry Taylor (who ran the 500GP Suzuki team for many seasons) and Austrian racer Michael Ranseder has been signed as one of their riders, it is sure to give KTM and Aprilia something to think about. And while it might be easy to think they will be a second-rate team, never forget what the Europeans thought when the Japanese started racing. Overall, it can only help the diversity of the 125 grid next season.

11 – CZECH REPUBLIC GP

After the traditional summer break, and the even more traditional return from that break to Brno, it was Bradl who proved himself well rested, taking the victory and moving back into third in the championship table. Di Meglio came in second, though, to consolidate his lead, while Corsi saw his title hopes slipping away as he could only manage tenth. Olive took third spot in the race, once he had managed to push Talmacsi back into fourth. Some riders, including Bonsey, Webb and de Rosa, were unable to complete the race, but Terol and Smith took fourth and fifth, proving themselves to be both ready and able to make it onto the podium.

12 – SAN MARINO GP

Talmacsi took his third consecutive pole position and pretty much led the whole race from the second corner. A mid-race slip saw him let Bradley Smith past, but he soon regained the lead and won by over 5.5 seconds.

The real race was for third, with Olive looking to have it tied up until he slipped on the final corner while under pressure from Corsi.

Misano was a disaster for title leader di Meglio. He and Bradl ended up in the gravel trap in separate incidents nine laps from the finish. The gap between Corsi and di Meglio closed up, and the title was now back in the Italian rider's sights. Talmacsi's win also helped him to gain ground on the other championship-chasing riders.

13 – INDIANAPOLIS GP

The new GP at Indianapolis had its share of problems, mainly due to the hurricane that was raging nearby, but this did not deter Espargaro from taking his second pole position of the season. Bradl took third slot on the front row, his second personal best for qualifying, and Webb again made it onto the first row of the grid. Talmacsi fractured his scaphoid in the Friday practice session and could only manage 14th in the race.

In the end it was Terol who seized control of the race and took the win, with Espargaro second and Bradl third when the race was stopped because of the adverse weather conditions. It was actually Pol who crossed the line first, but the race result was counted back to the previous full lap. Neither Corsi nor di Meglio got on well with the track – seventh and tenth places were definitely less than ideal results – and the gap between them closed a little further.

14 – JAPANESE GP

Amazing as it sounds, it was not until Japan that di Meglio took the first pole position of his career. The race turned out to be a huge battle between the top three riders, di Meglio, Bradl and Talmacsi, the latter recovering from an operation on his scaphoid the day after Indianapolis. Di Meglio got himself into gear by grabbing the second spot, with Bradl taking another win, Talmacsi a brave third and Corsi beginning to flounder in seventh. Not only had Bradl beaten Talmacsi on the track, he was now in front of the 2007 title-holder in the championship race – and with three rounds to go and a 36-point advantage for di Meglio over Corsi, the outcome was starting to look inevitable.

15 – AUSTRALIAN GP

Phillip Island proved – as ever in the 125 class – to be the point of no return for the championship, with di Meglio riding high after his first pole in Japan and managing to take a second one here. He then ran an almost untroubled race after Bradley Smith, who took the holeshot, crashed out of the lead on the first lap. The Frenchman won with an enormous ten-second lead over second-placed rider Bradl at the flag; Talmacsi was third. Corsi could only manage eighth, so di Meglio's lead of 36 points turned into a championship-winning 50 and, as with Bautista in 2006, the title was decided on 'the Island'. At 20 years old di Meglio is the youngest French rider ever to win a Grand Prix championship.

Above Stefan Bradl leads di Meglio and Talmacsi – the young German's form was one of the highlights of the year

Left Mike di Meglio raced a near perfect season, was the dominant character of the class and fully deserved his world title

Opposite top Simone Corsi leads Joan Olive – the Roman led the championship chase after Mugello

Top Scott Redding on top of the rostrum at Donington Park, the youngest ever British winner of a Grand Prix

Opposite Outgoing champion Gabor Talmacsi's season started with engine breakdowns and ended with a broken scaphoid

Above Dominique Aegerter and Esteve Rabat have a disagreement over ownership of a patch of tarmac

	Rider	Nation	Team	Motorcycle	Points
1	Mike Di Meglio	FRA	Ajo Motorsport	Derbi	264
2	Simone Corsi	ITA	Jack & Jones WRB	Aprilia	225
3	Gabor Talmacsi	HUN	Bancaja Aspar Team	Aprilia	206
4	Stefan Bradl	GER	Grizzly Gas Kiefer Racing	Aprilia	187
5	Nicolas Terol	SPA	Jack & Jones WRB	Aprilia	176
6	Bradley Smith	GBR	Polaris World	Aprilia	150
7	Joan Olive	SPA	Belson Derbi	Derbi	142
8	Sandro Cortese	GER	Emmi-Caffe Latte	Aprilia	141
9	Pol Espargaro	SPA	Belson Derbi	Derbi	124
10	Andrea Iannone	ITA	I.C. Team	Aprilia	106
11	Scott Redding	GBR	Blusens Aprilia Junior	Aprilia	105
12	Sergio Gadea	SPA	Bancaja Aspar Team	Aprilia	83
13	Marc Marquez	SPA	Repsol KTM 125cc	KTM	63
14	Esteve Rabat	SPA	Repsol KTM 125cc	KTM	49
15	Stevie Bonsey	USA	Degraaf Grand Prix	Aprilia	46
16	Dominique Aegerter	SWI	Ajo Motorsport	Derbi	45
17	Tomoyoshi Koyama	JPN	Red Bull KTM 125	KTM	41
18	Raffaele De Rosa	ITA	Onde 2000 KTM	KTM	37
19	Danny Webb	GBR	Degraaf Grand Prix	Aprilia	35
20	Efren Vazquez	SPA	Blusens Aprilia Junior	Aprilia	31
21	Pablo Nieto	SPA	Onde 2000 KTM	KTM	25
22	Lorenzo Zanetti	ITA	ISPA KTM Aran	KTM	22
23	Michael Ranseder	AUT	I.C. Team	Aprilia	22
24	Takaaki Nakagami	JPN	I.C. Team	Aprilia	12
25	Randy Krummenacher	SWI	Red Bull KTM 125	KTM	10
26	Pere Tutusaus	SPA	Alpo Atletico de Madrid	Aprilia	9
27	Stefano Bianco	ITA	S3+WTR San Marino Team	Aprilia	8
28	Alexis Masbou	FRA	Loncin Racing	Loncin	4
29	Lorenzo Savadori	ITA	I.C. Team	Aprilia	3
30	Marcel Schrotter	GER	Toni Mang Team	Honda	3
31	Robin Lasser	GER	Grizzly Gas Kiefer Racing	Aprilia	2
32	Enrique Jerez	SPA	ISPA KTM Aran	KTM	1
33	Adrian Martin	SPA	Bancaja Aspar Team	Aprilia	1
34	Jonas Folger	GER	Red Bull KTM 125	KTM	1
35	Hugo Van den berg	NED	Degraaf Grand Prix	Aprilia	1

16 – MALAYSIAN GP

Malaysia saw another rider taking his first ever pole position: Andrea Iannone. No-one could get close to the time he'd set before, once again, the weather came into play. As a good and proven wet-weather rider the Italian was hoping for rain on Sunday too. Unfortunately for him it turned out dry, and Talmacsi pulled the perfect holeshot, moving away from Iannone and the rest on the sixth lap. The Hungarian was chased hard by Smith, who'd made his way up the field to second position and was catching Talmacsi before he ran out of laps. It was Smith's fourth podium of the season; Corsi was third.

Talmacsi's win meant he was now in front of Corsi and Bradl in the fight for second place in the world standings.

17 – VALENCIAN GP

The final race of the year saw Talmacsi once again working hard to set the fastest time in qualifying. Friday's times were a washout, with heavy rain all day, while pole was set in tricky, semi-dry conditions, after a lot of the field ended up in the gravel traps.

Race day was greeted with brilliant Valencian sunshine, however, and once the red light went out the battle started in earnest. The fight for the lead was a five-way affair between Corsi, Terol, di Meglio, Smith and Cortese, after Bradl crashed out and took race favourite Gadea with him. Talmacsi also went out with what looked like gearbox problems. The top five swapped positions and paint until near the end, when Corsi, Terol and di Meglio managed to ease away from the following Smith and Cortese.

Corsi crossed the line first to take the chequered flag, and second in the championship.

RED BULL ROOKIES
PETER CLIFFORD

Above The American Rookies got to race on Grand Prix weekend at Laguna Seca

The best of the world's developing teenage talents faced off against each other twice at the end of the season. The top ten from the Red Bull MotoGP Rookies Cup clashed with the top ten from the sister AMA U.S. series at the GPs in Indianapolis and Valencia.

The two teams fought for the Red Bull Riders Cup and on both occasions the MotoGP Rookies took home the trophy. A sprinkle of rain before the start of the US round prompted a change to treaded tyres and while the track was dry as the race started, by half distance it was soaked. The changing conditions really played to the Europe-based squad and 16-year-old Norwegian Sturla Fagerhaug crossed the line first ahead of 16-year-old South African Mathew Scholtz and 17-year-old Briton Matthew Hoyle.

The race winner might well have been one of the AMA U.S. team though as 13-year-old Hayden Gillim had led at

one point and was fighting for first when the slippery conditions caught him out and he crashed. Gillim was second in the 10-race AMA U.S. Cup that featured the best riders from all over the Americas. Third in the AMA U.S. series was 16-year-old Argentine Leandro Mercado and the Rookies Cup went to 13-year-old Californian Benny Solis, who was ninth at Indianapolis just behind the first of his team members, Jake Gagne, a 15-year-old Californian motocrosser. Gagne was the find of the season in the US as he came to grips with racing on tarmac and finished the Rookies Cup year fourth with two wins and a second in the last three races.

Having won the Riders Cup in Indianapolis by 114 points to 26, the MotoGP Rookies were confident as they faced the rematch in Valencia. It's a holders' trophy so they carried no points advantage to Spain: if the AMA

NEW KIDS ON THE BLOCK

U.S. team won by a single point the Riders Cup would be carried off across the Atlantic. Once again, though, the weather was no friend to the visiting US-based squad.

Rain showers through the three sessions of practice meant that the tarmac was either soaking or patchy and all but three of the 20 Rookies fell at least once. The MotoGP Rookies were almost as accident-prone as the AMA teenagers, though, and if they repeated that in the race the points could well add up either way.

That looked a possibility when Scholtz crashed on lap 2 while chasing Hoyle for the lead, but on a dry track there were no more fallers and Hoyle won the race comfortably, leading the MotoGP team to another clear Riders Cup win. The 17-year-old Spaniard Luis Salom was a good second, pulling through from a poor start and grid position and for a while towing along the impressive

Gagne. The American was on the limit, though, and when he was almost highsided he ran over his own foot as he fought to stay aboard. The broken toe was very painful but he still finished third.

It was Hoyle's first Rookies win and he was thrilled. Salom was a little frustrated with second as he had started the season with four wins from the first five races, but not as frustrated as he was when he crossed the line third at the final MotoGP Cup race only to be told that the Rookies Cup for 2008 had gone to J.D. Beach, the 16-year-old American who had started in the MotoGP Cup in 2007 before there was a series in the US. Beach had no luck in the Riders Cup races: he was sick to be seventh at Indy and in Valencia he was forced off the track and into a run through pitlane that dropped him to 11th place. But his MotoGP team still took the Riders Cup 91 to 49.

Above if you are an American Rookie you get to follow mentor Kevin Schwantz for a lap or two

RIDERS FOR HEALTH

BARRY COLEMAN

riders

Health workers from Vumilia in western Kenya pose with the bikes that have helped them reach over 200% more patients

ANNUAL REPORT

You'd be surprised if on Day of Champions you were standing between Vale's technical truck and his pit box and you saw Bill Gates stepping over the hoses and cables and making his way towards you. Of course behind him would be a retinue.

I imagine a cool adviser or two, or a calm, silent administrator – the hi-tech version of what Randy Newman once called 'a short fat man with a notebook in his hand'. It's an electronic notebook, these days.

Now what would Bill be looking for? A man who has, without any question, transformed the world and in the process become the richest person in it? A man, furthermore, who with his wife Melinda has turned his hand to spending billions on the barriers and mysteries of global health?

Don't step aside. Don't look over your shoulder. Bill and Melinda are looking for you. Because you have made Riders for Health what it is. And you have made this sport what it is – unique, in every way.

Aren't you proud of our sport? How could your chest not swell with pride to be part of a sport that includes such characters as Valentino Rossi, Wayne Rainey or Randy Mamola? Or the divine James, who tirelessly turns his hand to the piano (or the microphone) for Riders? Or Shinya, or Lucio, who faithfully make donations from their own pockets each year? All of them make Andrea and me so proud that at times it's hard not to burst into tears.

None of this stuff is skin deep. Graziano Rossi, for example, has passed on not just his DNA to his son but that of the sport itself. Between practice sessions he would sort of lie in a deck chair and talk about Italian literature. For many years we had a cat named after the father (there was no son when the cat was named). Graziano always asked, always laughed: 'Come il gatto, Rossi?' He hasn't asked recently. Sorry to say, il gatto e well and truly morte. It is no more.

Back to Bill. So, we have a sport with real depth, real character, really serious DNA. And we know stuff that no-one else knows. That's why you see Bill and Melinda coming towards you. The truth is that, some time last year, back at the Gates Foundation in Seattle, B&M were getting a trifle short-tempered. They had spent money on a cosmic scale but the results weren't matching their intentions or their input. To put it bluntly, it wasn't really working, for the simple reason that the miracle drugs (or, for that matter, the $5 mosquito nets) weren't reaching the people who so desperately needed them. And their statistical projections said it wasn't going to work for at least another 27 years, unless they found a solution to the fundamental problem of delivery.

A new look was called for, a renewed effort, with different thinking. There were a lot of answers, but one small voice at the back said 'Er, we know these people called Riders for Health, in England. They know how to deliver health care. That's what they do. They say they can do it anywhere. And save money while they are at it.'

And a tall, slim man with a notebook in his hand flew from Seattle to Daventry to see if it was true.

And it is.

I'm not going to labour the point. Yes, I am. The world needs us to help sort out the appalling problem of access to health care for the poor – especially the rural poor. The world doesn't know how to do it. But we do. So picture Bill and Melinda at Day of Champions, back of the pits, asking you if you can help. 'Yes,' you say, 'our sport started working on this question some time in the mid-'80s. And it was 20 years ago exactly that Andrea sent Barry and Randy (talking of DNA) to Somalia so we could really start sorting it out. Go and see Randy – he's probably down on the infield with Jules and Toby. We have teams all over Africa. Brilliant, African people. We'll sort you out mate, no problem.'

And so it was that the unusual sport of motorcycle racing, unique among sports, brought something to the world that not only no other sport had managed, but no other institution of any kind whatsoever had either. And are we big-headed?

You bet we are. It's been a long time coming. But we'll be nice about it. We always are.

WHAT IS RIDERS FOR HEALTH?

Riders is an international humanitarian organisation – born out of the world of motorcycle racing – which works to improve the delivery of health care in Africa. Our vision is of a world in which no-one will die of an easily preventable or curable disease because barriers of distance, terrain or poverty prevent them from being reached. Our mission is to strengthen health systems by addressing one of the most neglected, yet vital, aspects of development for the health of Africa – transport and logistics.

Riders began work in 1989 when its founders – Barry and Andrea Coleman, and Grand Prix racer Randy Mamola – became determined to find a solution to the problem that they recognised as undermining the development of Africa: the lack of appropriate transportation infrastructure. They realised that vehicles themselves were not the answer – the key is to have sound management systems and regular maintenance to keep the vehicles running day in, day out. Today, Riders employs over 200 local staff in Africa and helps to maintain over 1000 vehicles used by professional health workers and local community organisations. In total, our programmes are helping over 10 million people across Africa to receive regular, reliable health care. ∎

Opposite Sir Elton John at the launch of the Lesotho project funded by his foundation

Below Bill Gates listens intently to Andrea and Barry Coleman, co-founders with Randy Mamola of Riders

'AFRICA'S MEDICAL MIRACLE: WHEELS'

One of Riders' key priorities is to make transport for health care delivery in Africa highly visible, so that it can be fully addressed and ultimately return to its rightful place of invisible predictability. In doing so, we also help to raise the profile of motorcycling and show the general public how fantastic motorcyclists are.

Riders' work gained huge recognition in December 2007, when *The Times* of London selected us – from hundreds of applications – to be the international charity for its annual Christmas fundraising appeal. The newspaper featured a series of twelve articles about Riders throughout December and January, including a cover photograph and headline describing our work as 'Africa's medical miracle'. The appeal was a great success, raising over £200,000 and bringing the vital role of transport to the attention of a whole new audience.

NEW CHALLENGES IN 2008

Thanks to your support this year we have taken several great steps towards our goal of reaching an additional 10 million people by 2010. We have expanded our work with community groups in Kenya, and launched a new nationwide programme in Lesotho, meaning that thousands more families in rural communities are now able to receive the kind of reliable health care we so often take for granted.

KENYA

In Kenya and Tanzania, Riders for Health works closely with organisations dedicated to addressing vital health issues including HIV/AIDS, malnutrition, tuberculosis and malaria. This year, we have begun a new partnership with Vumilia – a grass-roots women's self-help group based in the Kabras district of western Kenya. The women – who are HIV positive themselves – work to overcome HIV/AIDS in their communities through the psychological, social and economic empowerment of women.

Riders trained six of Vumilia's carers to ride and maintain motorcycles. Before Vumilia started working with Riders, they were covering 150 households. Now, they are reaching 500 households with regular support and care.

'Everyone at Vumilia would like to thank our friends Riders for Health for their support at this time,' says Rose Ayuma Moon, founder of Vumilia. 'By providing us with the motorcycles and all the training, technical and managerial support needed to ensure that we can use and care for them well, we have been able to extend our home-based care programme, to reach very many more bedridden patients in our community, and greatly improve our medical care and referral service. This is such good news.'

LESOTHO

And it is good news, too, in Lesotho, where Riders has begun a new programme in partnership with the Elton John AIDS Foundation. Having previously worked in Lesotho in the early 1990s, Riders' return to the country was prompted by the rapid and alarming decline of the country's public health status. Over the last 10 years HIV/AIDS has had a devastating impact and it is estimated that 23 per cent of 18–49 year olds are HIV positive.

Average life expectancy is just 42 years. Lesotho has also been hugely affected by diseases such multi-drug-resistant tuberculosis, which target weakened immune systems.

Working with the Elton John AIDS Foundation, the Ministry of Health and other health-focused partners, Riders is mobilising 120 health workers who are in the front line in the fight against AIDS and TB.

'My new motorcycle has changed my life and the life of my patients', says Nthabieng Metsing, a health worker from the capital, Maseru. 'Thanks to my motorcycle, I can now reach hundreds of patients I could not have reached before, even those in the most rural communities.'

Throughout 2008 the money raised in MotoGP has also helped to support the work of our dedicated African teams in the Gambia, Zimbabwe and Nigeria, who continue to work tirelessly to keep health workers 'on the road'.

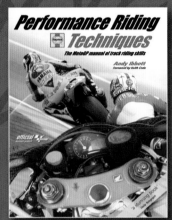
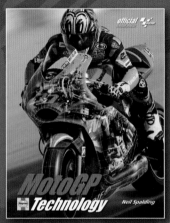
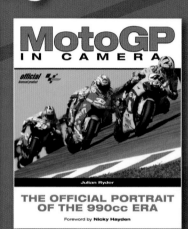
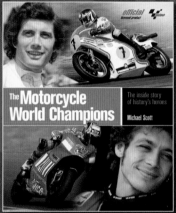

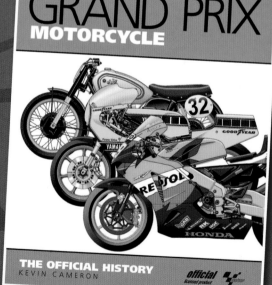
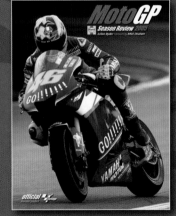